LOVE,
Finkelstein

Adrian

Marilyn Monroe
RETURNS

Also by Adrian Finkelstein

Your Past Lives and the Healing Process: A Psychiatrist Looks at Reincarnation (1985)

A Psychiatrist's Search for God: Back to God, Finding Joy in Divine Union (1996)

To God

To fans of Marilyn Monroe known now as
Sherrie Lea Laird

To my family and to the world as a family

Edited by John Nelson
Cover design by Marjoram Productions
Cover photo © Hulton Archive/Getty Images

Hampton Roads Publishing Company, Inc.
1125 Stoney Ridge Road
Charlottesville, VA 22902

434-296-2772
fax: 434-296-5096
e-mail: hrpc@hrpub.com
www.hrpub.com

If you are unable to order this book from your local
bookseller, you may order directly from the publisher.
Call 800-766-8009, toll free.

Library of Congress Cataloging-in-Publication Data

Finkelstein, Adrian.
  Marilyn Monroe returns : the healing of a soul / Adrian Finkelstein.
    p. cm.
  Summary: "A psychiatrist reveals evidence that one of his patients is the reincarnation
of Marilyn Monroe. Sherrie Lea, a Canadian singer, shares similarities with the leg-
endary icon: facial bone structure, handwriting, voice pattern, personality quirks, and
more. Dr. Finkelstein discusses his extensive videotaped past-life regressions with
Sherrie Lea, solving Marilyn Monroe mysteries that have gone unanswered for decades"
--Provided by publisher.
  ISBN 1-57174-484-3 (6 x 9 tc : alk. paper)
  1. Reincarnation therapy. 2. Psychiatry--Miscellanea. 3. Parapsychology. 4.
Occultism. I. Title.
  RC489.R43F56 2006
  616.89'14--dc22
                          2006008704

ISBN 1-57174-484-3
10 9 8 7 6 5 4 3 2 1
Printed on acid-free paper in Canada

Marilyn Monroe RETURNS

The Healing of a Soul
Adrian Finkelstein, M.D.

HAMPTON ROADS
PUBLISHING COMPANY, INC.
for the evolving human spirit

TABLE OF CONTENTS

ACKNOWLEDGMENTS

I am deeply grateful to sweet and beautiful from the inside out, world-class singer Sherrie Lea Laird, the reincarnation of Marilyn Monroe; all my patients; my Masters; and above all to the Higher Power that sustained and inspired me to write this book.

I commend Kezia Laird for her involvement and support of this project as well as Sherrie's other family members who indirectly supported this work, especially her parents Margaret and Claude Laird. I thank Chris Papp, Sherrie's boyfriend for his hardship, patience, and cooperation in bearing with his beloved being very busy in the process of creating this book.

I am indebted to those others who made this book possible, in particular to Dr. Walter Semkiw for his friendship, support, and practical advice, as well as his passion and awesome research work in the subject matter of reincarnation reflected in his book, *Return of the Revolutionaries.* Special thanks go to Kevin Ryerson, world-famous channeler and friend.

I take this opportunity to thank The Founding Mystics, a group of highly distinguished scientists, artists, government leaders, scientists, and intuitives, founded by Dr. Walter Semkiw, and to which I am honored to belong as a member. The Founding Mystics favorably received my presentation of the reincarnation of Marilyn Monroe on July 4, 2005, and encouraged me to write this book as a contribution to humanity.

Special thanks go to Joe Bruggeman, who encouraged me to pursue my discovery of PPL-IRCT (Past/Present Life-Iris

Recognition Comparison Test) and other similar comparisons of fingerprint and voice recognition.

Certainly, our family friends Emily Lodmer and Trisha Horton, who edited the manuscript and offered valuable recommendations, need to be praised for their help.

I must thank Bob Friedman, president of Hampton Roads Publishing for his open-mindedness and the trust he put in me to write this book.

My heart goes to my grandchildren, Joshua, Daniel, Gabriella, Rachel, Rivkah-Baila, and Yehezkiel-Shalom, as well as my dear daughters and sons-in-law Drorit, Sarah, Barry, and Shimon; I love you all.

And to Parvaneh-Shula, my dear wife, life companion, and my soul-mate over lifetimes, I thank you for your understanding and patience which enabled me to write this book. You occupy the center of my heart; you are my best friend, you are my love, you are my bridge to heaven.

INTRODUCTION

It was in October of 1998 that, after practicing past-life regression therapy as a psychiatrist for more than 20 years, I was contacted by Sherrie Lea Laird, a professional singer in Canada who was having repeated flashbacks and dreams of a past life as Marilyn Monroe.

After a series of e-mail exchanges, I contacted her and listened with an open mind to her very sad story. She had been having frightening nightmares as well as dreadful flashbacks of Marilyn Monroe since childhood. And since the age of 14 she has claimed that her life, including her effect on men and her ambitions for herself, was set in motion by this other "grown-up woman" imposing her will on her. It was an extreme reaction to a fairly typical scenario involving past-life memories, a kind of possession by the other persona. There were other indications, together with her extreme emotional distress, that this woman's assertion was legitimate, a claim from a troubled psyche seeking relief, not notoriety. In my experience, despite what the general public may infer about past-life regression, I had never had at the time such a "famous" patient.

I proceeded with my inquiry, taking down her medical history through e-mail correspondence and phone conversations since she couldn't travel from Toronto to Los Angeles for treatment due to passport problems. Since I wasn't licensed to treat patients in Canada, I would have to consider our work a research endeavor, which would also have therapeutic benefits for Sherrie—especially if I could conduct past-life regressions on her as part of my research. Another indication of legitimacy, probably less credible for some, was a series of "coincidences" that began to crop up. Sherrie had first contacted me when she was 35 years old going on 36, the age Marilyn Monroe had died, indicating psychological pressure to resolve her dilemma before a similar fate ensued. (She told me of two previous suicide attempts.) Sherrie was also concerned that close friends from Marilyn's life were getting older and may die before she could contact them. (Joe DiMaggio passed away on March 8, 1999, within weeks of Sherrie breaking off contact with me.)

However, the biggest coincidence was when I ran into Ted Jordan at a social gathering during the holiday season of 1998–1999. We met at the Christmas party of Cedars-Sinai Medical Center, Department of Psychiatry. He was there with a lady friend who was a nurse on the psychiatric staff. Without knowing his "Marilyn" connection, I struck up a friendship with him. As it turned out, Ted was a retired Hollywood actor who had written a controversial book about his longtime relationship with Marilyn Monroe entitled *Norma Jean: My Secret Life with Marilyn Monroe.* During a lunch several weeks later, I mentioned, since he was an actor of that era, Sherrie's claim to be the reincarnation of Marilyn Monroe. He was excited, and with their mutual consent, I put the two of them in touch with each other.

They conducted almost daily phone conversations and reported in gushing terms to me their mutual recognition. The way Sherrie came across to Ted—her voice, vocal mannerisms, and little girl giggling, along with sharing intimate details of their romantic affair and later friendship—was very convincing. When I showed him a music video of Sherrie, her great physical resemblance to Marilyn, her postures and movements, and her singing style unequivocally convinced Ted Jordan that Sherrie Lea Laird was indeed the reincarnation of his former lover and friend, Norma Jean Baker, or Marilyn Monroe. Ted made plans to fly to Toronto and meet up with Sherrie, but a recurring back injury landed him in the hospital and quashed those plans. As fate would have it, due to increasing psychological pressure and fears that public knowledge of her claim could ruin her budding singing career, Sherrie broke off contact with me and Ted in March of 1999.

Reviewing my six-month contact and investigation of Sherrie's case, I was convinced that only past-life regression therapy could purge her demons, after repeated drug therapy and hospitalization in Canada had failed over the years. I came to that conclusion after having been classically trained as a psychoanalytic therapist and having discovered that some patients suffered from psychological or spiritual trauma in which their personal histories revealed few causative factors from either their childhoods or adult lives. This conclusion, and my pursuit and later practice of regression therapy, had brought me into conflict with the medical establishment and its emphasis on "organic" therapies, or drug treatments aligned with the standard medical practices and procedures of pharmaceutical companies.

I had always been interested in the "big" questions, an interest few of my colleagues in psychiatry shared. They wanted to "fix" the mind like we mend a broken leg. As a child in war-torn Romania, what had most bothered me were the existential questions of life and death. From an early age, I had witnessed so much pain, suffering, death, and destruction during World War II. It had a very profound emotional impact on me as my heart ached for the wounded, the infirm, and the old who would eventually become weak, ill, and die. I decided to become a doctor to alleviate human suffering and prolong people's lives, beginning with my own parents. I was so sure there must be a way to conquer death.

In medical school, I switched from internal medicine to psychiatry after witnessing the incredible therapeutic effects of hypnosis on selected cases, then a very little regarded and rarely used technique. My goal now is to relieve emotional trauma and its effects on the body. I trained in medicine at the Hebrew University, Hadassah Medical School in Jerusalem, Israel, from 1961–1968. I began my training in hypnosis during my medical school curriculum as an elective, and I've been practicing it ever since. I've held various positions, first serving as a medical officer in the Israeli Army in 1967. Then I passed a concourse and was accepted to specialize in psychiatry at the prestigious Menninger School of Psychiatry & Mental Health Services in Topeka, Kansas. There I had some of the most illustrious psychoanalysts in the country as my teachers. I was infatuated with psychoanalysis. After all, it was developed by the greatest psychoanalyst ever, Sigmund Freud. Upon graduation I was given two distinguished awards for the best research of 1972: dealing with mind over matter by the Menninger School of Psychiatry & Mental Health Services and a national forum from the U.S. Central Neuropsychiatric Association.

During 1972–1975, I was assistant professor of psychiatry at the Chicago Medical School, University of Health Sciences, and chief of outpatient psychiatry at Mount Sinai Medical Center in Chicago. From 1975–1990, I was assistant professor of psychiatry at Rush Medical School and University in Chicago. I maintained offices and a private practice in both Illinois and California. In the early 1970s I was analyzed by a training psychoanalyst for more than seven hundred hours. It helped me to better understand myself and to sensitize me to my patients and their difficulties. In 1979 I passed the American Board of Psychiatry and Neurology and became a board-certified psychiatrist.

Unfortunately, even armed with such a powerful therapeutic tool as psychoanalysis, I didn't see substantial psychological relief for many of my patients. Too, the investment of time and money in this form of therapy is immense. I wasn't satisfied, as one of my colleagues had said, in "just helping patients adapt to their neurosis." As I grew frustrated with psychoanalysis, one early morning I had an overwhelming personal experience, a spontaneous recall of one of my past lives. It was extremely emotional, moving me to tears of joy as I realized the therapeutic value of such a recall. My official research into past-life regression therapy began in 1977, when I conducted a project regressing some seven hundred volunteers from all walks of life. The results, at least in my mind, not only scientifically validated reincarnation, but also showed the tremendous therapeutic value of regression therapy. Eventually, I was forced to take my therapy into private practice where I've experienced day in and day out the therapeutic results of past-life regression therapy on countless patients. Over the course of three decades, I've conducted literally thousands of regressions and have seen that the traumas from past lives sometimes carry over into our current lives, just as much as childhood abuse.

In 1990 I moved to Los Angeles, where I became an assistant clinical professor of psychiatry at UCLA and an attending psychiatrist on the medical staff of Cedars-Sinai Medical Center. Due to my intense research and practice as a past-life therapist, I took a hiatus from teaching for several years, but then resumed teaching in 2002. Currently, I'm on the medical teaching staff at Cedars-Sinai Medical Center, where I teach UCLA psychiatric residents, medical students, psychologists, and social workers complementary and alternative medicine, and holistic therapeutic hypnosis including orientation/introduction to past-life therapy and spiritual healing concepts and practices.

In April 2005, after a six-year absence, Sherrie Lea Laird contacted me again. She related how her nightmares and flashbacks of Marilyn Monroe had intensified and worsened. It had come to the point where she was less concerned about jeopardizing her singing career and more about reclaiming her own life and protecting her daughter, family, and friends from her Marilyn demons. She had attempted suicide twice since our last contact and begged me for help. I could sense that she was at a critical juncture; I immediately made plans to fly to Toronto to conduct a series of past-life regression sessions with Sherrie, which I felt was the only hope at this stage to relieve the pressure.

I flew to Toronto with my wife, Shulah, in early May of 2005 to meet with Sherrie and her daughter, Kezia. (As it turned out there was "coincidental" proof that Kezia was the reincarnation of Marilyn's mother, Gladys Baker—later substantiated by her own past-life regression.) I conducted an initial regression with Sherrie on May 3, 2005, which was more of an exploration and to familiarize Sherrie with the process.

On May 4, 2005, I conducted a second and more extensive past-life regression on Sherrie, which included more than one hundred carefully researched questions about Marilyn Monroe's life that, from a deep somnambulistic hypnotic trance, Sherrie answered in a very convincing manner: not only being factually correct but also "emotionally" correct as well in many responses. I must admit that one of the major problems of this research and subsequent therapy, as well as its presentation to a doubting public, is that Marilyn Monroe's life has been so thoroughly dissected and the details are so readily available to all. I must emphasize, as cited in repeated journal articles in the book and from 30 years of experience, the absolute prohibition of selective amnesia about the use of conscious-mind information during a somnambulistic state of hypnosis. And Sherrie reached such a state, as evidenced by clinical signs of amnesia. So, I can unequivocally state that in such a hypnotic trance, which is tantamount to "truth serum," Sherrie was unable to "act out." She was compelled by my suggestions to tell the truth after erasing from her mind all acquired knowledge about Marilyn Monroe from books, magazines, films, the Internet, and any other source of information.

The first round of regressions came to an end. We all felt a great sense of accomplishment. I had no doubt that Sherrie Lea Laird was indeed the reincarnation of Marilyn Monroe. More important, she began to experience a relief of the psychological symptoms of anger, depression, and fear that were associated with her Marilyn memories for so long. In fact, after this session Sherrie and Kezia cried in each other's arms for some time. Now came the more daunting task, once we were both convinced of the authenticity of her past-life recall: to heal the soul of Marilyn/Sherrie and free Sherrie to pursue her own designs in this life.

Given the travel constraints on Sherrie and my inability to practice in Canada, our work would remain a research project. However, it would have therapeutic benefits as Sherrie helped me in my comparative research, giving her a focus and a gentle way to confront her memories and integrate them at each stage of our inquiry. This research would consist of comparing personality traits, physical and emotional problems, linguistics, writing and singing styles, graphology, and biometrics (such as facial bone architecture; body, hands, and feet constructs; voice comparisons; and iris similarities). There is considerable evidence, including the work of famed researcher Ian Stevenson, suggesting that biometric traits are passed on from one lifetime to the next.

This first round of regressions would only begin the healing of the soul. In November of 2005 I returned to Toronto for an even more extensive series of past-life regressions on Sherrie, which also served as mainly cathartic healing sessions. Here I probed such areas as Marilyn's death, her drug addictions, her relationship with the Kennedy brothers, and other significant relationships and traumatic events in her life. I also regressed Kezia and, if she were the reincarnation of Gladys Baker, released some of the guilt associated with her abandonment of Marilyn and her compulsion to "mother" Sherrie in this life.

I can only hope that the effect of this sensational case history will convince readers and medical professionals to take the subject of reincarnation and past lives more seriously and to consider the karmic and traumatic effects of those lives on our present health and well-being. But, as a physician, what was and is foremost in my mind is the therapeutic healing of my research subject. Today, seeing her more adjusted and healthy and pursuing her singing career are the main fruits of this inquiry.

Part I

THE MAKING OF A
REGRESSION THERAPIST

It was early in the morning. The sun was still hidden from view. It was the fateful day of our arrival in Israel. I could hear in the distance the sirens of ships going through a port. They were very faraway sounds. The sky started to redden on the horizon. It was about six o'clock in the morning. It was still dark for the most part. My family was sleeping. I was watching from the deck of the ship with nostalgia and great expectations. It seemed like time itself was thick, tangible. I wanted to stretch it, stretch it as far as I could so that in no time I would see the shores of the Promised Land. Suddenly, as if my prayers were being answered, I could see land. It could not be any other land but the land of Israel. I started shouting with enthusiasm, as Israel symbolized so many things for all of us: that we had gone through suffering and pain, through anguish, through suppression and persecution and, finally, here was that land. In retrospect, I realize that it was not a nationalistic enthusiasm and discharge of feelings on my part; it was a release of all the deep-seated pain and negativity that, throughout the years, had burdened me. In that moment I was making use of that moment, using that land, using our destination as an opportunity for an outpouring of endless joy. I immediately awakened my parents. They came stumbling toward the deck very happy, especially my father, who was as enthusiastic as I. So was my mother, but she was more preoccupied with the practical details of our arrival.

We were supposed to choose where to go, whether to the ocean or the mountains, to Nahariah, or to Natsrat Elit (Nazareth Elit). We chose Natsrat Elit. The government provided us with a free apartment in Shikun that overlooked the highway and was almost on the top of the mountain. It was a beautiful town. Once my parents got jobs we were supposed to pay minimal rent for our apartment. It consisted mainly of two rooms, a living room and a bath. We were given provisions of sardines and other foodstuffs that would not spoil, and an icebox. Also, we had a small primus stove heated with kerosene on which to do our cooking. A small heating lamp was provided, too. It was February 4, 1961. I was 22 years old.

Shortly thereafter, I applied to the Hebrew University Hadassah Medical School in Jerusalem, for concourse. The competition was fierce. I prepared myself very intensely, studying many hours a day without interruption. I was determined to succeed. I was forced, though I succeeded in the concourse, to start medicine from my second year. Although I had completed nearly three years in Romania, because the subjects were quite different they were not credited in Israel. Still, I was very happy that I was accepted. It was difficult to understand the lectures in anatomy and physiology or any other subject in Hebrew, but little by little I was able to grasp more, and my colleagues helped me understand the Hebrew and English languages. I was very grateful to them.

In the last year, 1965–1966, just before my graduation from the medical school, I had an elective in hypnosis at Tel Hashomer Hospital in Tel Aviv with Dr. Dan Medina, psychologist and head of the unit for memory research. I embarked on that elective because I was very impressed by the cure of an 18-year-old female university student who had to interrupt her studies due to asthma attacks. She would end up in the hospital at Hadassah Hospital with status asthmaticus four or five times a year, requiring the administration of large amounts of steroids—which produced bad side effects—in order to be brought back to life. One day, Dr. Dan Medina arrived and demonstrated how, with hypnosis, he could help this girl. Eventually, she recovered. This made a tremendous impression on me as I could see that with mind over matter, illnesses that otherwise cannot be cured or improved through medical means could be treated effectively. I had been thinking of becoming a surgeon or an internist, but after witnessing this miracle, I decided that mind over matter would be my direction from then on.

I got a diploma about one year after finishing the medical course and practicing as a physician with a temporary license in the army, and later in what is called "kupat cholim," a public clinic that treats patients on an outpatient basis. I obtained an official diploma with my M.D. degree in August of 1968. I undertook a second year of internship, this time in Denver, Colorado, at St. Anthony's Hospital. The internships at Ichilov Hospital, as well as the one in Denver, were rotating. In other words, I had to go through the main branches of medicine and have exposure to them in my training.

When I was in my third year of medical school, I found Parvaneh-Shulah, my future wife in this lifetime. She was studying medicine in Jerusalem, in her second year, a year behind me. We met at Bible class but I got acquainted with her shortly before that through a friend of mine. We fell in love, but we waited to get married because we were studying. She is Persian-Jewish and I am Romanian-Jewish. Like others, we got into the melting pot of "Kibbutz Galuiot," which means literally bringing back together the diasporas. Our two daughters, Drorith, born in Jerusalem, and Segalith, born in Topeka, came seven years apart—like my siblings and me. Our family life has been typically middle class.

My specialization benefited me in the United States, where I was accepted at the Menninger School of Psychiatry in Topeka after completing two years of internship: one in Tel Aviv and one in Denver. My psychiatric residency training and fellowship took place initially at McGill University in Montreal, Canada, and continued at the Menninger School of Psychiatry. I was attracted to that training center mainly because of its reputation as the foremost psychiatric center in the nation, and I wanted to learn as much as I could.

My graduation paper was entitled "The Relationship between Dreams and Symptoms under Hypnotic, Posthypnotic, and Natural Conditions." I wanted to prove that mind over matter is important in psychopathology as well as in our everyday lives. And indeed, through multi-analysis of various factors, it could be demonstrated that dreams precede a physical symptom whether these dreams are natural or induced through hypnosis. Furthermore, I wanted to demonstrate that even if a dream is not remembered, its impact is felt through the manifestation of the same physical symptom(s). In other words, whether the subject remembers or not, the dream is traumatic enough to precipitate the physical symptom(s) which still occur as severely as before.

This paper is a continuation of my previous work at McGill University, entitled "Dreams That Precede a Psychosomatic Illness." I was amazed by the results and especially the practical implication of dreams. If dreams can be such traumatic experiences in our lives that they can trigger physical and emotional symptoms, then it stands to reason that stopping such dreams, or changing them into more benevolent ones, would be a promising direction to pursue in order to prevent the occurrence of life-threatening symptoms such as heart attack, stroke, and the like.

I was surprised when my work was honored, not only for a distinguished award in 1972 for my research study at the Menninger School of Psychiatry, but also by the Central Neuropsychiatric Association, which granted me its first distinguished A. E. Bennett award in 1972 for the same study. It seems as if a higher power directed and guided my study and I am thankful for the positive results. What fascinated me was that I could prove that traumatic dreams occurred first in sequence, followed by the occurrence of physical and emotional symptoms. This sequence was also proven in a very convincing way by Nolan and Andrissani, who demonstrated that changes in the electroencephalogram during a dream precede the changes in the electrocardiogram at a time when a person experiences a heart attack.

Among the many cases in my study, I remember vividly one that made a significant impression on me. It was one of the volunteers in my research project at the Menninger School who happened to be one of my teachers, a psychoanalyst who had been suffering from severe migraine headaches for many years. He was involved in the biofeedback treatment program given by Elmer Green at the Menninger Foundation for two years prior to his volunteering for my research project. He happened to be a very good hypnotic subject. During one of our sessions, he entered into a very deep hypnotic trance, and I asked him to tell me the order of the occurrence—a symptom followed by a dream or a dream followed by a symptom (in this case, the symptom was his migraine headache). He indicated that a dream occurred first, which was very interesting. He described a dream wherein he was running along the top of a train pulled by an old black engine. He was running in the opposite direction from the engine. Looking to his left, he could see a very deep chasm and gradually but relentlessly his left eye started to hurt, after which the pain expanded to the left side of his head and gave him a full-blown migraine headache.

I asked him to forget about the dream at the count of ten and to come out of his hypnotic trance. When I would tap on the desk three times, he would be able to recall the dream and stop the migraine headache. So he did. However, upon coming out of his trance, he continued to suffer from a migraine headache. I asked him if he knew what had happened, to which he replied, "No, but all I know is that I have a terrible migraine headache." At that point, I tapped on the desk three times as I instructed him in the posthypnotic suggestion, and he recalled the entire dream (hypnotically induced). The migraine headache stopped. We had several more sessions, in which he discovered a childhood conflict he experienced with his mother. He associated the old, black engine of the train in the dream with his mother who had black hair. His running away from her was associated with his discomfort when he used to be forced by his mother to sleep in the early afternoon, after lunch, by her side (and by the way, she was sleeping on his left side). He could not help but see her through transparent clothing. As a ten-year-old boy, he felt a mixture of excitement and disgust. At the same time, he felt very guilty about his feelings. This resulted later in life in his left-sided migraine headache, which was his subconscious way not only of punishing himself for the forbidden urge, but also of distracting him from an intolerable experience.

Four years later, after I left the Menninger School and was engaged in my private practice, I received a letter from this subject. In the letter he stated that after I worked with him he never experienced another migraine headache. He asked me to write a scientific paper with him, which I regret to say I did not get a chance to do. But my purpose in conducting that particular research project was not to show that I could cure someone, or even that I had helped a particular person, but to prove that symptoms are preceded by a traumatic dream. The fact that he was helped was an unplanned bonus, but I was glad he benefited from it.

After my graduation from the Menninger School of Psychiatry, I became director of the outpatient psychiatry division at Mount Sinai Hospital in Chicago. I accepted the position in addition to my full-time work as assistant professor of psychiatry at Chicago Medical School, University of Health Sciences. Then, after two-and-a-half years, I decided to move my private office to Palatine, a northwest suburb of Chicago. I also moved to another medical school and became an assistant professor of psychiatry at Rush University, Rush Presbyterian St. Luke's Medical Center. But, despite the academic positions that I held, I was soon to realize that my training was insufficient to help a large number of my patients. What was really required, I thought, was an empathic humanitarian approach. I decided to go into private practice.

As I still was infatuated with psychoanalytic theory, I undertook personal analysis for about seven hundred hours with a training analyst at the Psychoanalytic Institute in Chicago. This training, perhaps more than any other, helped me to become more sensitive to my patients' problems. The experience also made me keenly aware of facts connected with a genetic explanation of a patient's psychological conflicts in this lifetime. It was years before I finally decided to acknowledge that, even backed by such a powerful approach as psychoanalysis, I could not accomplish what I wanted: to help a great number of people. It always seemed I would fall short of my expectations in helping many of my patients despite empathizing profoundly with them. Indeed, many times I did not know how to help them to become self-sufficient and able to solve their own problems. Though there were many patients who improved and did well under treatment, there were always a significant number who did not.

Despite my best efforts, it was apparent to me that there was more to the human psyche that standard techniques were not uncovering or, to quote the lyrics from a song in the movie, *On a Clear Day You Can See Forever*, "There is more to us than surgeons can remove." Besides the body-mind connection, there is the unfathomable mystery of Spirit. At the time, I recalled another song from that movie, "On a clear day, rise and look around you and you'll see who you are . . . On a clear day, how it will astound you that the glow of your being outshines every star . . . On a clear day, you can see forever and ever more . . . ." The movie is about reincarnation and it reminded me of the bedtime story my mother read to me about youth without aging and life without death. It posited perfection as an ideal, which is an absolute, as opposed to disease or health, both of which are relative. If I could only penetrate the mystery of life and death, I might find the cure I was seeking. But, for the immediate future, this was merely speculation on my part.

THE PSYCHIATRIST
IN SEARCH OF A
NEW MODALITY

As the years passed, I continued to use hypnosis as a therapeutic tool in my practice. At times I combined it with behavioral modification therapy as well as psychoanalytic psychotherapy. But the pressure to conform to more accepted methods intensified, and most of my colleagues in psychiatry moved to somatic approaches, such as medication, to treat psychiatric ailments. They were quick to explain that we live in a society that is becoming more accountable for the deeds of others. Therefore, we as physicians must also become accountable to the general public for the services we render. As a consequence, they said psychiatry must reorient itself into the mainstream of medicine, where concrete methods of diagnosis and treatment are used. As a result, I invested more time and energy into studying specific organic therapies. I began to treat more patients with medication, according to what I was taught in school. However, after a while I seriously questioned what I had learned throughout those long years of studying medicine and psychiatry. I believed sincerely that psychoanalysis was a wonderful tool for many people, but it is a lengthy therapy involving great financial sacrifice, and all too often patients do not learn all they need to know about themselves for an effective cure.

Eventually I realized that there was a great deal more to hypnosis as a therapeutic tool than I had previously thought. After years of application, I discovered that certain habits such as smoking, nervous tics, lack of self-confidence, minor psychosomatic ills, and the like can be removed through hypnosis. In one dramatic case, I helped a crippled young woman walk again by utilizing a deep hypnotic trance and the suggestion that her legs were strong, that they could sustain her weight, and that she could walk and enjoy it. An understanding of the healing powers of hypnosis came to me after many painful experiences. I began to feel that much of the time, money, and energy I had invested in other systems of treatment were, in many cases, wasted effort. Then one day, while making notes on one of my dreams, I experienced a strange, almost eerie revelation. I felt as though I were in a state between sleep and waking, that I was a middle-aged woman doctor or healer, unmarried, unattractive but with a good heart. I knew that this past self liked to help her patients. My father was a carpenter. In this state I could see him most clearly, and after a while I even realized the name of the country in which I lived (Iran) and my name (Thelma Sangiavi). I had an impressive emotional experience at the time of my death (from a form of cancer). I could see a bright, glowing light and I sensed myself leaving my body. Then everything was gone. I opened my eyes and found it difficult to believe what I had experienced. Almost immediately it occurred to me that this must have been a past life, and I began to search within myself for other lives.

Through self-hypnosis I regressed myself over a period of several months into other lives, in some of which I had been male and others I had been female. I began to trace a noticeable pattern throughout these past lives that was remarkably similar to my behavior in this life. I was able to identify initially a total of 24 past lives, 11 of them as male in different non-medical or non-healing occupations and thirteen as a healer or medical doctor. Two of the latter were as a female. I had begun a tentative exploration into the subject of reincarnation sometime prior to these experiences. I decided to read more in the literature to separate fact from fiction.

Life after death is universally accepted in the Orient; philosophers and religious teachers seldom felt the need to prove this belief. Hindu and Buddhist writings are never quite the same, but their mutual agreement on rebirth clearly communicates a central theme of eternal growth. In a boundless universe, they aver that there should be innumerable possibilities for growth, wisdom, self-realization, and the attainment of higher levels of consciousness. According to Hindu belief, *Manvantara* is the period of evolution stretching from the beginning of time to its end, and it consists of a journey not only from birth to death but throughout millions of years. Since the Hindus consider man to be a spiritual being, the continuity of his existence is uninterrupted. Experience through the ladder of reincarnation extends from the very bottom to the top. In one life a man may be wealthy and powerful, but in another a slave or a pauper.

In the Judeo-Christian belief, I also found references to reincarnation. A biblical reference that may imply reincarnation is found in Psalms 90:3–6, which emphasizes a thousand-year cycle between incarnations. In one of the most controversial passages in the Bible, Christ offers a strong indication of having lived before: "Who do men say I the son of man am?" he asked his disciples.

"And they said, some say that you are John the Baptist, some Elijah, and others Jeremiah, or one of the prophets." (Matthew 16:13–14)

Another striking instance of a Biblical reference to reincarnation again occurs in the Book of Matthew, when Jesus is transfigured before Peter, James, and John:

> As they came down from the mountain, Jesus charged them, saying, "Tell the vision to no man until the Son of man be risen again from the dead."

And his disciples asked him, saying, "Why then say the scribes that Elias must first come?"

And Jesus answered and said unto them, "Elias truly shall come first, and restore all things.

"But I say unto you that Elias is come already, and they knew him not, but have done unto him whatsoever they listed. Likewise shall also the Son of man suffer of them."

Then the disciples understood that he spake unto them of John the Baptist. (Matthew 17:9–13)

The Jews expected the return of their great prophet, and according to scholar Rabbi Moses Gaster, the belief is that Adam returned as Noah, Abraham, and Moses. There is also one claim that Adam was reincarnated as David and will still come back as the Messiah. In the New Testament there is strong evidence of an expectation among the people that the prophets would return in future lives.

Isaac Myer's noted work on the Kabala provides a long list of Europeans who believed to some degree in reincarnation. This includes Jacob Boehme, Ficino Pico, Pope Sixtus, Raymond Lully, Cornelius Agrippa, John Raechlin, Spinoza, Leibniz, Ralph Cudworth, Henry More, Francis Bacon, and Isaac Newton, as well as the philosophers Schopenhauer, Hegel, and Schelling. We know that other distinguished men of that era, such as Leonardo da Vinci, Paracelsus, and Jordano Bruno, believed in reincarnation.

Among the doctors of the mind, American psychologist and philosopher William James was one of the most significant to share an interest in reincarnation. At Harvard in 1893, he delivered his famous Ingersoll lecture, *Human Immortality,* in which he affirmed that physiological psychology did indeed accept a scientific basis for immortality. These findings, he said, rested on the reductionist view that the brain functions only in a protective thinking capacity. But he stressed that the brain can just as easily transmit ideas that have an origin elsewhere. He argued that when the brain finally ceases to function, it vanishes from the observable world but that the sphere of being that supplies consciousness still exists.

Another modern voice to join the controversy over immortality and rebirth is that of C. G. Jung. In his commentary on an old Chinese book, he said: "Death is psychologically just as important as birth, and . . . an integral part of life. It is not the psychologist who must be questioned as to what happens finally to the detached consciousness. Whatever theoretical position he assumed, he would hopelessly overstep the boundaries of his scientific competence. He can only point out that the views of our text with respect to the timelessness of the detached consciousness are in harmony with the religious thought of all times and with that of the overwhelming majority of mankind. He can say, further, that anyone who does not think this way would stand outside the human order and would, therefore, be suffering from a disturbance in his psychic equilibrium."

The first revelation of Jung's interest in reincarnation comes from a lecture entitled *Concerning Rebirth* that he gave in 1939, and which he later revised in 1950. He began with an introduction to metempsychosis and reincarnation, and defined reincarnation in these words: "This concept of rebirth necessarily implies the continuity of personality. Here the human personality is regarded as continuous and accessible to memory, so that, when one is incarnated or born, one is able, at least potentially, to remember that one has lived through previous existences, and that these existences were one's own, i.e., that they had the same ego-form as the present life. As a rule, reincarnation means rebirth in a human body."

Jung continues, "Rebirth is the affirmation that must be counted among the primordial affirmations of mankind. These primordial affirmations are based on what I call archetypes. . . ."

This was all well and good, but as a scientist I needed more concrete proof. I found that in the research of Dr. Ian Stevenson, the leading scientific investigator of his day in the field of reincarnation. He first became publicly known in 1960, when his *Evidences of Survival from Claimed Memories of Former Incarnation* received the winning prize in an American Society for Psychical Research contest. Prior to writing the essay, Stevenson had studied hundreds of cases in which children and adults appeared to remember their past lives. With only one exception, the claimed memories on which Dr. Stevenson bases his conclusions happened spontaneously in normal stages of consciousness. Stevenson claims that reincarnation is the most plausible hypothesis for explaining the cases of this series. He does not conclude that they prove reincarnation either singularly or together; indeed, he is quite sure they do not.

In 1966, Stevenson published *Twenty Cases Suggestive of Reincarnation*, which is now considered a small classic in the field of reincarnation. Stevenson traveled to South America, Alaska, Europe, the Near East, Asia, and many parts of the United States to conduct on-the-spot research into reported cases. His book is considered by most to be thoroughly scientific. Dr. Albert Stunkard, chairman of the department of psychiatry at the University of Pennsylvania, said, "Stevenson's present work . . . seems queer to many conventional scientists. It is certainly controversial. But he is the most critical man I know of working in that sphere, and perhaps the most thoughtful, with a knack for building into his research appropriate investigative controls." The article reports that Stevenson became interested in reincarnation because of a "growing feeling of dissatisfaction that available knowledge of heredity and environmental influences, considered either alone or together, often didn't account for personality as we see it."

In summation, it should be stressed that Dr. Stevenson emphasized that his research had brought to light evidence suggestive of reincarnations, but not final proofs. When asked in an interview if he himself believed in reincarnation, he stated—in the spirit of true science—that he did not think his own belief of importance. What he did believe in is the truth of the cases he investigated. Reincarnation, at least for him, was the best explanation he has been able to present.

Stevenson has noted that a rational man can sensibly believe in reincarnation on the basis of scientific evidence alone, although it appears that Dr. Stevenson, in spite of his remarkable contribution to the subject of reincarnation, did not experiment much with hypnosis in past-life regression. In addition, the cases he presents that lack such results from hypnotic past-life regression were most probably cases needing a specialized approach in order to elicit data.

A British psychiatrist, Arthur Guirdham, tells the following case of a woman patient which left him no other explanation but that of reincarnation. He first met "Mary" in 1961, when he was chief psychiatrist at Beth Hospital in England, where she consulted with him about persistent nightmares. These were accompanied by such loud screaming that she and her husband were afraid they would wake the neighbors. Dr. Guirdham writes that Mary had been suffering since she was 12 from horrible dreams of murder and massacre. At first he suspected a neurosis, but he could find none. Mary was a perfectly sane, ordinary housewife. Nothing wrong could be discovered with her mental faculties. After a few months, she told him that when she was a girl, she used to write down the dreams. She had also written down things that occurred spontaneously in her mind, things she couldn't determine about people and names of which she had never heard. She gave Dr. Guirdham the papers and he began to examine them. He was amazed to find that the verses of songs she had written as a schoolgirl were in Medieval French, a subject of which she had no knowledge.

Guirdham sent a report of her story to Professor Pere Nellie of Toulouse University and asked his opinion. Nellie shortly wrote back that Mary had presented an accurate account of the Cathars, a group in Toulouse that subscribed to a Puritan philosophy during the thirteenth century. Mary also described for Guirdham the massacre of the Cathars and unveiled a horrid account of being burned at the stake. Dr. Guirdham was astounded. He had never really thought of reincarnation, never believed or disbelieved in it. Mary also told him that in her previous life she had been kept prisoner in a certain church crypt. Guirdham found that some religious prisoners were taken to such places when there was no room for them in regular prisons, and that some of them had indeed been kept in the specific crypt Mary mentioned.

In 1967, Guirdham decided to visit the south of France to investigate other of Mary's assertions. She gave him names and descriptions of people, places, and events, all of which turned out to be accurate in great detail. He even found in the archives four of the signs she claimed to have written as a child. Word for word, they were as she claimed them to be.

In this account, Dr. Guirdham accumulated considerable evidence of the woman's knowledge of thirteenth-century life. Upon his request, she had made accurate drawings of old French coins, jewelry, the layout of buildings, and so forth. She was able to correctly identify persons whose authenticity was verified by an examination of records of the Inquisition.

In her book *Reliving Past Lives: The Evidence under Hypnosis*, Dr. Helen Wambach wrote about her research into the lives of 1,200 volunteers. Her findings were impressive. Dr. Wambach first regressed certain groups to the time periods of 1850, 1700, 1500, 25 BC, and 500 BC. In following sessions, she regressed the same group to various time periods ranging from 2000 BC and 1000 BC to AD 400, 800, and 1200. Next, Dr. Wambach began evaluating the statistical information on classes, sex, geographical location, and other variables. To her surprise, she found only 11 data sheets out of 1,088 with clear evidence of a discrepancy. An important finding was that the subjects shared equally both male and female past lives. This was considered quite remarkable, since most of Dr. Wambach's volunteers were females.

The steady increase in world population is explained simply by Dr. Wambach: More souls choose to incarnate on Earth as conditions here are more attractive than in earlier periods of history; here people have the opportunity to experience—to live out—the purposes they have created for themselves.

Dr. Wambach regressed some 750 people in this group. Through her they relived extraordinary moments, days, and months before they actually emerged into the world. One of the questions she asked them was whether a person chooses to be born. This was usually answered affirmatively (though they were sometimes advised by those on "the other side" to make the choice.) Another question she posed was why they choose to reincarnate in the twentieth century. Although answers varied, most people emphasized that greater learning was possible in this time of change; others expressed a wish to repair a relationship they had not worked out in a past life.

Dr. Wambach asked whether one chose one's own sex for the next incarnation. The answer was often that this had to do with the degree of completion of one's experiences on the Earth plane. Does a person know who was one's mother in a previous incarnation? Yes, most of the time. In this connection, many of the volunteers reported that they met a number of different people from previous lives in their present existence in order to complete an unsuccessful relationship—or because of a certain attraction. Another interesting question was whether an individual was incarnated in the fetus prior to birth. Although varied, the major response was that only at the time of birth did the soul enter and stabilize itself in the body; during pregnancy it would often enter and re-enter intermittently.

Are the poets correct in their claim of love's immortality? Some researchers into past lives would have us think so. One psychic researcher used regressive hypnosis to return people to their past lives to prove that they lived together in earlier lifetimes. Many of those regressed had been attracted to each other for several lives, for both the good and the bad. In many cases they had not learned their lessons in previous bitter experiences, and so they had to be reborn together to correct their "errors."

Reviewing the literature on reincarnation, it dawned on me that proving it to the scientific community and the general public could be of great benefit to a suffering humanity. If trauma from past lives continues to trouble people in the present, a therapy that allows patients to remember and integrate emotionally troubling incidents under hypnosis or in an altered state could offer an alternative when modern psychiatric medicine failed to elicit a cure. This emboldened me to embark on the most ambitious and daunting project of my life, to prove reincarnation is a fact to the skeptics and disbelievers. But, more importantly, from the bottom of my heart, I wanted to help people to overcome haunting and, in many cases, disabling emotional afflictions from the past. I realized how damaging this could be to both my professional and academic careers, but as a scientist and a man of conscience I had little choice.

PAST-LIFE REGRESSION THERAPY

Being able to place my past-life recall into a broader philosophical perspective, I was now ready to test the validity of my experience by conducting a broad-based research study. While still an assistant professor of psychiatry at Rush Presbyterian St. Luke's Medical Center in Chicago, I asked for volunteers for this study into past lives and conducted more than 700 regressions. Those who participated came from all walks of life, including people from the hospital, corporations, different stores, acquaintances, and referrals from those in the study. Participants ranged in age from 8 to 80 years and most were of Christian faith or descent, though some were from other religions. Their level of acceptance of the study results varied, but the majority were open and cooperative, though some of them were initially skeptical. A small minority denied the results, while others thought that they just made it all up. However, many of the latter became more accepting when their phobias, depressions, anxieties, panic attacks, headaches, and other psychological and physical ills remarkably improved or cleared altogether. Most of the participants benefited from the study with immediate positive therapeutic results.

The study was conducted in my Palatine, Illinois, office from 1977–1980. The technique I used was more or less uniform in order to eliminate any possible differences in the way I obtained the information. Most of the time, I had the research subject sit on a reclining chair or lie on a couch. The room was soundproof and the lighting minimal. A microphone was attached close to the subject's mouth for recording. The hypnotic induction pattern was also standard but with some deviations tailored to each individual's history. The history taking of about one hour preceded the whole regression process, since it allowed me to screen the mental stability of the subject and determine if they could withstand intense probing of the psyche. It also gave me clues on what questions to ask.

Of the more than 700 regressions, 110 of them showed significant results and about 30 percent were charged with high emotional responses from the vivid reliving of their past-life experiences, with a pronounced therapeutic cathartic or abreaction effect. Many of these subjects entered a somnambulistic stage of hypnosis, tantamount to being injected with sodium pentothal (commonly known as "truth serum"). The advantage of such a state of very deep hypnosis is that it allows the subject to access and relive the past-life experience as if it were happening right then and there. Consequently, its beneficial effects are more immediate and lasting, while the information obtained is more accurate, truthful, and reliable. The other 70 percent were divided into three almost equal groups. The first group entered a deep hypnotic trance, the second a medium trance, and the third a superficial trance. The medium and superficial trance groups required more regressions followed by spontaneous associations to retrieve and understand past experiences. Some individuals did not require hypnosis at all to experience significant past-life recall. I have since come to the conclusion that very spiritually evolved subjects either can reach a somnambulistic stage of hypnosis with great ease and/or have no trouble associating and remembering a past life without it.

In 1980, one of the most significant cases in this study changed the course of my professional practice, and my life for that matter. It was the healing of a young woman who became a patient of mine and submitted to regression therapy after standard therapy failed to cure her. Due to profound depression, she had attempted suicide several times in the preceding year (drug overdoses or wrist slashing). This was in spite of the commonly accepted up-to-date psychiatric treatment she received at one of the finest hospitals in Chicago, Rush Presbyterian St. Luke's Medical Center and Medical School. I was on the medical staff at that time, an attending psychiatrist and an assistant professor of psychiatry. After several regression sessions, she was able first to relive with emotional outbursts episodes from a past life that were the source of her conflict, and then to free herself of them. In the following months, she became a very vibrant, functional, and happy individual who did not need psychotropic medications and who underwent only three months of follow-up psychotherapy. Years later she had not experienced a relapse.

Despite these results, the reaction of my colleagues at the hospital was very adverse. They would not sponsor and finance my study, and I was instructed to completely relinquish my past-life research and treatment project or face disciplinary action: being removed from the academic roster and losing my admitting privileges. (This was partly due to their close-mindedness and partly due to medical politics. Hospitals and doctors have a vested interest in cooperating with pharmaceutical companies and maintaining their medical "standard" practices and procedures. Anything that deviates from these guidelines is a serious threat to their very survival as professionals and institutions.) Soon after this I went into strictly private practice and, in effect, fell off their radar.

In the last 25 years, I have conducted literally thousands of past-life regressions in my private practice. I have found this therapy to be a great adjunct to my therapeutic practice as a psychiatrist. I have gleaned from my many case histories the following cases that have aspects relevant to the subject of this book: Sherrie Lea Laird's past life as Marilyn Monroe.

Perhaps the most amazing case I had encountered at that time was of Doris G., a 22-year-old woman who first came to me seeking help for depression through hypnotherapy. Despite a number of treatments, she failed to improve. Eventually, she became suicidal and was hospitalized. She suffered from a depression that did not respond to either psychotherapy or anti-depressive drugs. After several months, Doris's suicidal tendencies lessened and she became functional enough to be discharged; however, her functioning was still marginal. She found it difficult to maintain a job, relate to her family, and to live either by herself or with friends. In short, she experienced a great deal of hardship in her relationships.

I asked Doris if she would submit to a past-life regression, and she agreed. She could not always enter a deep trance when hypnotized; she appeared to have difficulty in maintaining her attention sufficiently to focus on my suggestions. The first time she volunteered, she was quite afraid. In spite of my determined attempts to hypnotize and regress her, my efforts proved futile. But I continued to encourage her, explaining that in the beginning the subconscious may be quite unwilling until it gets used to the idea and feels safe enough to permit the experience to happen.

Eventually I hypnotized her. Initially, she reached only a superficial trance, but during the course of regression it gradually deepened and she was able to offer the following information:

She once lived in Cornwall, a town in Orange County, New York, during the early 1800s. Her name was Lisa Arthur, and she was eight years old. She mentioned that she was a student in the third grade at Middletown School, a private female boarding school in Middletown, New York, some distance from Cornwall. She gave the teacher's name, Mrs. Pfeiffer. Her father took Lisa to school by carriage. Lisa could describe Cornwall and her house. She described the grass, the trees, the Hudson River, and a town that may have been near their house. The house was gray with some pink and black. The rooftop was black. She was living on a farm, and this was a farmhouse. Also she could see in her visual field other farmhouses.

She described the people in the household: grandfather Samuel Arthur (58 years old, a farmer); grandmother Mary (decreased when Lisa was four); father John (35 years old, a farmer); her mother, Sara or Elaine (29 years old, a housewife); and brother Tom (six years old). Lisa thought she also had one older sister and other two sisters who probably died before she was eight years old (Mary, three years, and Alice, eight months). Her grandmother was buried near the house, the grave marked with a cross. Lisa used to go to St. Theresa Catholic Church in Cornwall. Lisa claimed she was baptized there. There was a store in Cornwall, the Merchant's Store, and there was an older salesman there. Lisa died on April 18, 1812, at the age of 12. She committed suicide by jumping from a fourth floor window, as she was unhappy with her life. It seems that she was alone and was spending a great deal of time at Middleton School and away from her family. Lisa claims that after her death, there was an announcement in the newspaper that she fell from a window and could not be saved, as she subsequently died due to a head injury. She was buried near her grandmother's grave, close to the house. On the grave headstone is the inscription: "Lisa Arthur, 1812." She mentioned no karmic connection. Lisa reported another lifetime in Blarney, Ireland, in which she committed suicide as a teenager by banging her head on the walls of a room to which she was confined by her family.

The interesting therapeutic result of these past-life regressions was that Doris began functioning better and integrating the knowledge of her conscious discovery of herself. The idea of suicide became futile; it had not solved anything in her past lives, and the problems continued in her current life. As a consequence, she has been gradually improving in her mental status and outlook on life and has completely relinquished the idea of suicide.

The remarkable results through investigation, by myself and genealogist Nancy Fredericks, led to establishing that Lisa gave accurate information with regard to her hometown of Cornwall. In the census population of 1810, the name Samuel Arthur appears only in Orange County. Also, it is clear that Samuel Arthur, a miller, was the head of his family because documents state him to be a witness in court at one time regarding an inheritance. The other people in the household were a female who fits the mother's age, a younger boy (six years old), and an older sister. The two younger sisters were probably deceased. Another interesting finding is that Lisa was the only girl between the ages of ten and 16 at the time of the census. She described quite well the location of her house, the farm, and a pond that can only be Arthur Pond. At one time she described the Hudson River, which she could have only seen from Cornwall, and not in Middletown. Middletown is quite far from her home, and her father used to take her there by carriage. The name of the teacher, Mrs. Pfeiffer, appears in the census population of that area, and at that time there were only two persons with this name near Middletown, and one of them was a woman. Also, it appears that Middletown School was a private school for girls in 1812 (it turned public in 1813). Though there were no records kept prior to that date, it appears that Doris's account of life as Lisa was genuine and she had no reason to commit fraud. In any case, it appears there is enough information given, up to now, that cannot be explained except by reincarnation.

If this was true, as a physician and psychiatrist I felt compelled to make some philosophical reflections about the meaning of this extraordinary finding. At the time it changed a great deal the way I looked at illnesses, the way I looked at current existence. It changed the way I was to understand my patients from then on, as well as people in general. It opened up horizons in terms of diagnosis and therapy, and, if put in the context of helping humanity and suffering people, I thought that efforts in verifying these truths could be worthwhile.

Another type of research that proved to be quite fascinating concerns the recollections of an eight-year-old girl. Her name is Mary F. Without hypnosis, this girl could go into a past existence and give very detailed accounts. The session was tape recorded, like the others. She just covered her eyes, sat down, relaxed and printed on "the blackboard of her mind" that her name was Pavrah Lemgap, which she corrected later to Paula Liborio, age 23 or 24 years. The year was 1886. She said she was born on February 18, 1862, in Tala, Mexico. She printed these names on the "blackboard of her mind," too. Her occupation was horseracing. I asked her the cause of her death, and she said she was killed in a horse race when she slid and fell from her horse, fatally striking her head. She died on May 8, 1886. I continued and asked her how long she waited until she was born again in this lifetime. Without hesitation or deliberation she replied immediately, "Eighty-six years." She described the house in Tala, Mexico, as being of a "funny" shape, very small. (She would draw it later.) It was made of logs and ropes that held tile logs together. On the roof a string held together the two slanting pieces, and ropes were along the sides. She also described a window, some simple draperies, and one door. The terrain and landscape consisted of grass, dirt, and hay. There was a forest on the left side of the house with very tall pine trees.

Later Mary drew for me the houses of her neighbors, which were arranged in a circle. She said that in the middle of the circle of houses there were some small rocks and that nearby there was a big sea, or lake. She began spelling the name of the body of water: "Chapara." Looking at a map we find there is no other name for a big sea or lake in Mexico that would fit that description and location except Chapala Lake.

When Paula died she was buried like her grandparents were, in a grave close to the houses. Mary described to me a Mexican coin of the time, and later she drew it. On one side it shows a village with several houses and on the top is printed the word "Mexico." On the other side is a palm tree and again on the top is printed the word "Mexico." Mary said she prayed that she would have "a lot of money" by winning the race; she "tried praying a lot so God would help," but it did not work. She named her subconscious Paula and said, "Paula entered the wrong body in Mexico." This lifetime, "Paula entered the right body." This time she wants to live and have the abundance that she missed in the previous lifetime. This is true, as she was born this time around to parents who can give her a life of abundance. She chose them this time because she claimed she was "fed up being poor." Mary described, under my questioning, a special alcoholic drink called Pequira. She said it looks orange or yellow and it is sweet, containing lime juice and pineapple.

Investigating the findings from this little girl, Mary, it appeared that a great deal of her information was authentic. First of all, it was striking that she gave the name of "Tala" as the place of her birth. This town fits her description, as it is on mountainous terrain with pine trees and is close to Guadalajara, Mexico, at an elevation of about 5,000 feet. Chapala Lake, the largest lake in Mexico, is quite close to the place where Paula lived, located as Mary described "on the right" of her house—east and south. Her simple-minded account seemed so natural that it is hard to believe it is made up. As it turns out, the Registrar of Baptism in Tala, Mexico, confirmed her birthday.

This was another amazing case that suggested reincarnation as a plausible hypothesis. This girl does not have unusual psychic abilities, nor is she a medium by any means, and she had no way to acquire this information in her current life. In her former life, she was Catholic. In her present Jewish family, she was never exposed to Mexican culture. Her information is simple and accurate, and comes right from the source: the memory bank in her subconscious. It was made accessible through this exercise of past-life regression.

The most interesting comparison between these first two cases requires a brief digression at this point. In my desire to help my patients, my research has taken me far from my education as a psychoanalytic therapist. Since most past-life regressions reveal a relationship that in the East is attributed to karma, or the belief that one's actions have a consequence in this life or a future life, my further research on this subject brought me to esoteric astrology. This is based on reincarnation: that this present life span is not unique but part of a long cycle of experience that stretches far back into the past and, even today, prepares itself for the future. Numerous times are we born into a new physical body, and we experience the joys and sorrows, the struggles, failures, and successes of life. We are not on this journey alone; instead, we reincarnate with those we have loved, those we have hated, those who have helped us, and those with whom we have suffered. We may find ourselves in different or even alternating relationships—at times as master or servant, at times as parent or child, at times as husband or wife.

The doctrine of karma, though originating in the East, has become increasingly better known and appreciated by the Western world over the past 50 years. Everything in the universe is brought under the influence of karma, the law of cause and effect. It explains the kind of experiences one can expect during one's lifetime—and, more importantly, how the mistakes of previous lives can be corrected. Through the study of esoteric astrology, I gained a better understanding of karma and the lifetime to lifetime relationships I was seeing in my regression work with patients. One astrological aspect in a person's birth chart proved very revealing. By studying the position of the South Moons Node, we learn those aspects of our character brought from previous lives. We follow through in this lifetime by developing the traits of the North Moon Node to guide the current life in order to overcome negative karmic effects from the past.

The moon nodes should not be confused with the sun sign of an individual. The sun sign indicates the planetary position as related to the sun at the time of birth. It is one of the 12 positions, or signs, and has its respective name (e.g., Taurus, Libra, etc.). For example, the sun sign Taurus and its respective divisions generally give an individual his personality traits in this lifetime, but it does not necessarily indicate where he came from in terms of past-life experiences or where he is headed. The South and North Nodes of the moon, as well as the astrological signs in which they are placed, are directly opposite from one another, which is a logical way of karmically balancing opposing character traits over time.

In my current study I found out that a majority of my past-life regression subjects related former-life birth dates within the past 200 years that correspond to their birth dates in this lifetime. In both lifetimes, the past one and the current one, these dates coincide with the same North or South Moon Node positions. This statistical finding (odds of two in 12) suggests a plausible continuity between the two lifetimes, which are in temporal proximity to each other.

Returning to these first two cases, Paula Liborio's birth date was February 18, 1862 (sun sign Aquarius), which corresponds to the Capricorn North Moon Node. In her current life as Mary F., she was born on July 22, 1972 (sun sign Leo), which also corresponds to the Capricorn North Moon Node. In many past lives she was therefore experiencing in the Cancer South Moon Node. This implies that in both lives this girl has been learning the same life experience—the experience of Capricorn. This logically makes sense, as in the previous life she died prematurely. Therefore, she apparently did not get sufficient time to experience in the Capricorn North Moon Node. That is why in this lifetime she is to repeat the same experience. This karmic astrological concordance in Mary F.'s case is another proof favoring the validity of her reincarnation.

Doris G.'s birth date in her current lifetime is June 7, 1958 (sun sign Gemini), which corresponds to Libra North Moon Node. As Lisa Arthur, born on December 11, 1799 (sun sign Sagittarius), she was experiencing in the Aries North Moon Node, which is 180 degrees opposite to Libra North Moon Node. It is fascinating in Paula's case that there was no shift in the life experience (Capricorn in both lives), but there was a 180-degree shift in the sun sign from Aquarius to Leo; in Doris's case the shift from the previous life to the current life was 180 degrees both in terms of life experience (from Aries to Libra) and in terms of the sun sign (from Sagittarius to Gemini). In Doris' case another characteristic is impressive. The life-experiences sign and the sun sign belong to the same element: fire in the previous life—respectively, Aries and Sagittarius—and air in the current life—respectively, Libra and Gemini.

Separate past-life regressions of a mother and a daughter provided me with further support for the validity of reincarnation and are particularly relevant to the subject of this book. Audrey G., the daughter, an attractive 23-year-old woman, confessed before she went into hypnotic regression that she had had a tremendous fear of blood since she was a young child of three. She told me that she faints at the sight of blood. Ironically, she served in a clinic in one of Chicago's large hospitals. She told me that whenever she sees blood samples, she feels faint and repulsed. I asked her if she knew of any significant occurrence in her current lifetime prior to the age of three that could explain her morbid fear of blood. She could offer none.

During her regression, Audrey reported being a three-year-old living on a farm in a small mountain village in the 1600s in Germany, near the Swiss border. One day she witnessed her mother being beaten by her drunken father. She then saw her father stab her mother with a knife. She could see the blood spilling over her mother's clothes and onto the ground. She ran to a nearby barn, where she hid trembling with fear. She told me that her present mother is the same mother who was killed by her father in that earlier life.

The daughter did not tell her mother anything that transpired in her past-life regression. The mother, Carmella G., reported under hypnosis that there was some time in either 1572 or 1672 in a small mountain village in Germany when she bled to death because of a beating by her husband. She could see her frightened, young daughter running to a barn. Carmella reported another lifetime as Mary Mueller, born on September 12, 1832, in a place called Ogellaff, Switzerland. A map of Switzerland reveals that the only place close to that name is the town of Ogellingail, on the border between Germany and Switzerland. She said she married Paul Mueller at St. Joseph's Church on August 12, 1882. They had a daughter, Ann Mueller, born to them in 1856. Mary died on April 9, 1894, of "a cold." She claimed that the karmic connection again was Ann, who is her daughter Audrey in her present lifetime.

After all these findings, it is clear why Mary had such a strong fear of blood. The tremendous emotional pull towards her mother, due to fear that she might lose her again, can be explained as well. In turn, the mother began to understand the strong emotional attachment to her daughter.

A similar type of corroborative regression was found in the case of Linda A. and her daughter-in-law, Cindy A. Both women are intelligent individuals who realize the importance of not contaminating the research by communicating with one another about their own regressions.

Their two successive and separate regressions revealed the following: 1) both Linda and Cindy shared multiple previous lives together (eight to 14 lifetimes); 2) gender roles were changed as were the types of relationships; 3) both women experienced emotional closeness throughout all the lifetimes shared together; 4) both women share an affinity for certain countries (China, Egypt, Africa, India, England, and the United States); 5) in their common life spent in Africa, Cindy was Linda's wife; and 6) in Egypt, Cindy was Linda's mother. Their relationships in other lifetimes revealed similar interchanging of roles, all of them close, which accounts for their strong emotional attachment to each other in this lifetime.

Another case, that of Joan D., illustrates a physical condition that stems from a past life and is again relevant to our study: in this case, nearsightedness. In her current lifetime, Joan had been complaining of nearsightedness and pseudotumor cerebri, and had been treated for many years by neurologists and other doctors without major success. Pseudotumor cerebri is a condition in which the tissue of the brain is swollen due to the accumulation of liquid. This happens especially in women who are on birth control pills, are pregnant, or are on certain medications. This condition may be life threatening and its etiology is unknown.

During her regression to her lifetime as Arthur Tucket, Joan reported that he was born November 1, 1918, in Osaka, Japan, where his father was serving on a U.S. military base. They returned to this country when Arthur was four years of age. Eventually Arthur became a horse trainer and worked at various racetracks. The father, Arthur Tucker Sr., died when Arthur Jr. was 18. His mother, Mary, had died when Arthur was seven. After his father's death, Arthur worked with horses on the grounds of different racetracks, lastly in Baltimore, Maryland. On May 4, 1940, when he was 21, a fire broke out in the stables at the track and the horses trampled him to death. When recounting this, the subject became very emotional. She began to sob and her whole body trembled, as she experienced again the legs of the horses trampling her to death.

Joan reported another life as a 20-year-old female in the year

AD 16. She was condemned to die in a lion's cage, but she felt she was not guilty. It is not clear whether this was because of her belief in Christianity. In any case, she saw again a lion tearing her head with his paw. At this point, she began to cry and scream. This event was the one that triggered her current affliction of pseudotumor cerebri and nearsightedness. Obviously, related events reported in other lifetimes also contributed to the trauma to the head at close range.

Apparently the subconscious fixated in those situations. Since the above conditions were made conscious for the first time, reprogramming was possible by positive-repetition programming. Joan's nearsightedness is a desperate attempt on the part of her subconscious to contain the deadly object or situation at close range, to stop it from becoming lethal. Obviously it was without success, but it seems to establish a pattern where physical traits based on a psychospiritual complex are "passed on" in future lives for their resolution.

Other such cases that are relevant to the subject of this book are explicit in problems, relationships, and career pursuits that are intertwined from one lifetime to the next. This brings me to the case of Stacey M. It was September 1990. I'd just moved with my family to Los Angeles. I have been attracted to this city since my days in Jerusalem in the 1960s. There is something magical about California, by far the most progressive and free-minded state in the union, and it attracted me and my unorthodox approach to psychiatry.

I opened an office in west Los Angeles. at the Cedars-Sinai Medical Office Towers, adjacent to Cedars-Sinai Medical Center where I was accepted on the medical staff. Also, I began teaching psychiatric residents and medical students at UCLA Neuropsychiatric Institute as an assistant clinical professor of psychiatry and approved by the UCLA Board of Governors.

After I resumed my professional work as a practicing psychiatrist, a new patient appeared in my office. Stacey M. was 35 years old, tall, slender, and beautiful. Smiling, she spoke with a soft and sweet melodious voice and radiated a mysterious and romantic aura. Certainly, her sex appeal was undeniable. She moved her head so sensually and her dark blond hair caressed her beautiful cheeks, sometimes enigmatically eclipsing them completely and revealing only a pair of enticing, beautiful green eyes. Everything about her spelled S-E-X. But why? It appeared that it was her subconscious way of asking for love. Anybody who has to go to that length to ask for love is starved for love. But this kind of sexual façade can be misleading. Deep in her heart, it was not sex she was longing for but great love with no beginning and no end. I listened to her story.

"I'm an alcoholic diagnosed as suffering from major depression. I've been taking uppers to stay awake since working as a waitress while going to high school. I've been through many psychiatrists and I'm now on desipramine." Big tears were rolling down her face. She continued as her voice weakened and trembled. "At age three my maternal grandfather molested me, and at nine one of my half brothers. After that I've continuously gone through rapes and abuse by both men and women. I think I have a great mind, but I'm destroying it with chemicals. I'm self-educated and have an unbelievable gift for survival."

I induced hypnosis and Stacey entered a somnambulistic state. I asked her to describe what was happening after suggesting to her to relive one of her most meaningful past lives. She described a life in England in 1732 as a wealthy noblewoman named Tessia who ruled over a town and its people. She was in love with a married man, a prince, and engaged in a clandestine love affair with him, but something happened to keep them apart. She and her family were falsely accused in a court of law of wrongdoing to the people of the country. She was stripped of her ruling power and was disgraced. She was made out to be a whore and was blamed for taking the prince away from his wife. Tessia fought to regain her ruling stature but was unsuccessful. She felt lost and worthless. Over the next five years, she drank heavily and finally hanged herself.

Stacey benefited therapeutically from this past-life regression and the many others that followed. Her depression lifted and she no longer needed the desipramine. She began to better utilize her very bright mind in her business. She could now master her anger much better and her relationship with her husband largely improved despite many ups and downs. However, Stacey continued indulging in alcohol until at my advice she embarked on a 30-day detoxification and rehabilitation program for alcoholics. She is now very successful in her own business, but Stacey sometimes regrets not becoming a movie superstar in this life. Maybe in the next life . . .

In the 1990s I continued my past-life regression research and therapy practice. I ran into intriguing and compelling new proofs of the validity of reincarnation, including xenoglossy (i.e., speaking a language not learned in this life) and the presence of biometric markers that are transmitted from one incarnation to the next. These mainly consist of facial similarities. In other words, the shape and proportions of the face remain consistent from lifetime to lifetime, though the skin complexion and the appearance of the teeth may vary greatly. Hand gestures, posture, and types of attributes may be the same from life to life. Thus, even photos or portraits are strikingly similar from one lifetime to the next. Body type is often consistent though the size may be different. An individual may be physically weak in one lifetime and strong in another; or tall in one life and short in the next. Character traits seem to persist from lifetime to lifetime, and while we retain negative traits we need to work on we discard others we've sufficiently redeemed. The same applies to physical and mental illnesses.

We change gender, social, racial, and national roles in order to learn the golden rule: Don't do unto others what you don't want to be done unto you! Thus, Christians can reincarnate as Jews and Jews as Christian. A Nazi German may reincarnate as a Jew and vice versa. A black person may reincarnate as white, and a white as black. An Arab terrorist may reincarnate as an Israeli, and the other way around. This makes it fairly silly for people who are different to hate each other.

I've also found that individuals are often attracted to a certain geographical location where they reincarnate. They tend to come into lifetimes in groups to fulfill previous emotional attachments or to share karma. And what I noticed occurring with great frequency from one lifetime to another are synchronicities regarding events, symbols (such as numbers and letters), and names that are similar or that have the same number of syllables or rhythm. Ear shape, voice, and iris recognition are three biomarkers that intrigued me quite a bit. I've copyrighted these ideas in my Past/Present Life-Iris Recognition Comparison Test (PPL-IRCT).

As referenced earlier, Ian Stevenson, M.D., has been investigating children who can recall their former lives. Walter Semkiw, M.D., in his book *Return of the Revolutionaries*, refers to two of Dr. Stevenson's cases where photographs of the individuals from a previous lifetime were available. These photos indicate that the adult physical appearance is consistent from one lifetime to the next. These two cases originated in Lebanon and are summarized in another book about Dr. Stevenson's work, *Old Souls* by Tom Shroder.

One of the cases is of Hanan Monsour/Suzanne Ghanem. Hanan, born in the 1930s in Lebanon, was 20 when she married Farouk Monsour, from a distinguished Lebanese family. She had two daughters, Galareh and Leila. After she gave birth to her second daughter, Hanan developed a heart condition. She was advised by her doctors not to have any more children. She went against medical advice and gave birth to a third child. That was two years before her death. Farouk said that Hanan told him then that she was going to be reincarnated and have lots to say about her previous life.

Ten days after Hanan died, Suzanne Ghanem was born. Suzanne's mother told Dr. Stevenson that shortly before the birth she dreamt that she was going to have a baby girl; that a woman about 40 years of age told her that she was going to come to her. Later, when Suzanne's mother looked at Hanan's photograph, she thought it looked like the woman in her dream. Basically, Suzanne's mother dreamt that she would have a daughter who looked like Hanan. The dream came true. At less than two years of age, Suzanne took the phone off the hook and repeated many times, "Hello, Leila?" The family was unaware of who Leila was. When older, Suzanne related that Leila was one of her children. She denied being Suzanne and called herself Hanan. By the time she was two, Suzanne/Hanan could name her other children, her husband, and 13 other names (including those of her parents and brothers).

Eventually the Monsours were located and met with the Ghanems. The Monsours, initially skeptical, became believers once Suzanne recognized and named all of Hanan's relatives. At age five, Suzanne would call Farouk repeatedly during the day. Suzanne visited Farouk and would sit on his lap, resting her head against his chest. Even at the age of 25 she still calls Farouk, a career police officer. He has accepted Suzanne as the reincarnation of Hanan, his deceased wife. What is really amazing is how similar the facial appearances of Suzanne and Hanan are. This is a very important biomarker backed by Dr. Ian Stevenson as valid proof of reincarnation.

Certainly my understanding and practice as a physician and psychiatrist completely changed over the years from 1977 through the 1990s as I amassed more information through past-life regression research and therapy. I've evolved more through the royal road of unlocking the secrets of my patients' and my own past lives, and I have discovered the spiritual healing hidden in the mysterious recesses of the psyche. In September of 1998, while I was preparing to write another book on reincarnation, I received a shocking e-mail from Sherrie Lea Laird, a renowned singer from Toronto, Canada. She claimed to be Marilyn Monroe reincarnated. She came across in a very convincing and genuine fashion. She described to me in detail her flashbacks and night-mares since childhood and implored me to help her overcome the compulsive self-destructive behavior carried over from this past life.

My initial assessment of Sherrie's claim and the nature of my response to her were very casual, though I couldn't help but acknowledge on my part a déjà vu experience. At the time I could not understand it, and I decided to remain unbiased in my conclusions and recommendations. However, my preliminary assessment was that this case sounded very legitimate. Most people making such claims are apt to brag about it; here's something that makes them special. But in this case, a sincere cry for help from someone plagued by compulsive patterns and who claims disgust and repulsion about her famous past-life persona rings much more true. I decided to be open and began an e-mail correspondence with Sherrie as preliminary background to possible past-life regression work with her.

MARILYN REMEMBERED
By Sherrie Lea Laird

The years before I got in touch with Dr. Finkelstein in 1998 about my Marilyn flashbacks were a nightmare of ups and downs: more depression, sleepless nights, feelings of emptiness and love-lessness, and constant thoughts of suicide. The only thing that kept me from going over the edge was the thought of leaving my little baby Kezia alone. I think all of this was triggered back in 1992 by a past-life memory of Marilyn dying, forcing its way out of me, and the only thing I could relate to it was an intense feel-ing like being born and having my chest crushed.

I was in an abusive relationship which really wasn't one at all, with a guy named M Kennedy[1] who was lying to me and hiding his drug addiction. That part of my life was an absolute night-mare. I had a dream about it before he first hit/choked me. Prior to this incident, M and I were such good friends and we shared a real love for the '50s. He was born in 1955 and swore that in a pre-vious life he had slept with Marilyn Monroe. The incident was near Christmastime, and we had slept over at my parents' house. We woke up at my mum's and over breakfast I said, "Gee M, I had the weirdest dream that you choked me in this strange, small, yel-low bathroom. You wouldn't stop, and my dad and brother came to my rescue." We all laughed because everyone liked M. He had us all fooled.

So the next day I was at home, and it turned out that M had been out buying drugs that day with a friend of mine, who wasn't so secretive about it and told me. I didn't know about his addiction, and I confronted him about it that day. Well, we had planned to go out with Kim from across the hall, and when she came to the door, I said, "Listen Kim. We're going to go out by ourselves, just you and me, 'cause M's on drugs." I told her I'd be down in a minute. No sooner had I closed the door and gone to the bathroom than I was being choked and held off the ground in my yellow bathroom. I was naked, and M threw me into the bathtub. He then grabbed me by the hair, dragged me out to the living room, threw me on the couch, and punched me in the head repeatedly. I was finally able to get him off me, get dressed, and get out of there. This episode was all the more alarming because M was the first man I really loved. I felt a connection to him as soon as we met; it was as if we instantly recognized each other, and in hindsight he looks just like Stanley Gifford, Marilyn's real dad.

This led to another alarming episode. Because of my attraction to the '50s, I had painted my kitchen turquoise and M had helped me put down black and white tiles. While M was supposedly at work, I had this bizarre and horrible flashback. The kitchen actually frightened me for some reason. I thought it could be the paint fumes, but in the end it wasn't that. That day I was so scared of my kitchen that I said to my aunt downstairs, "Something's wrong. Please come with me and Kezia to the movies." I felt these incredible crushing chest pains. It was as if the world's strongest man were holding down my arms at my sides and crushing me around my arms and chest. I was sure it was the paint fumes and eventually it subsided, so we left for the movies. The pain started up again every 20 minutes or so. After a couple rounds of these, I went to the lobby of the movie theater and said I needed an ambulance and that I was having a heart attack. In the ambulance I told the drivers that it felt like I'd already done this with them. I felt like I knew what they were going to say next: It was déjà vu, a constant stream of familiarity. And it was a constant off and on squeezing of my chest.

I was then lying in the hospital and being tested and the doctors were sure they were going to find cocaine or something but didn't. The nurse approached me with something in her hand, and I felt like I was falling backward into another time and place. I didn't know where I was. I started screaming, "Don't let them touch me, don't let them touch me" like this was some sort of insane asylum.[2] The nurse said, "Relax. I'm just going to put this pill under your tongue." When I felt calm enough to talk, my aunt was there at my side. We were/are best friends. I said, "Anne, the only way to describe it is that I'm going through the birth canal. I mean, what else could feel like every 20 minutes you're being squished around the chest. It's such a horrible feeling, grotesque and creepy, perverse even. It's really a bad feeling."[3] I also remembered having these same feelings, not with as much pain but definitely with lots of remorse and feeling perverse and guilty, as early as age seven. I didn't know what they were, but I felt them coming in waves. And I'd just try to bide my time until they would leave me alone. This time the doctors kept me in the psych ward overnight. No matter what I said, it came out sounding crazier and crazier. I told my doctor, "I hope you don't get too spooked when I tell you this, but I think I'm reliving a past life and I've just come out of the birth canal." It was just crazy talk to him, and the next day I had to sneak out of the hospital.

From then on it was a battle of drinking and drugs and just trying to stay alive.[4] I was now, finally, pursuing my singing career.[5] I had a very late start for a singer. And I would often have flashbacks of names, faces, and places that looked familiar but weren't from this life, like Frank Sinatra singing in a club in the '50s.[6] I already knew who I was in my past life because I'd been through the mirror thing two or three times, where I said, "I'm Marilyn Monroe" and then saw her image in the mirror. Once when I went to Jamaica, I said, "Ah-hah. I was black. I've been here before and I love this place. I'm staying here." But near the last night, I was tipsy and had on a little knitted beret, and I went into this very

'50s-looking bathroom at the Seawinds Hotel and stared at myself in the mirror. I said, "I'm a black singer. I sound black for a white girl. And I can really sing. I can almost will my face to show up. In fact, when my face shows up, I'm going to have more soul than any other white girl in the world." And boom, the face of Marilyn Monroe popped up because by then I looked exactly like her in this life but never noticed it. The hair length and color were just right, the little beret, even the country I was visiting.

Back in Toronto I pursued my singing career, and at times I found that I really loved and needed to mix pills with alcohol. It wasn't long before I was a walking pharmaceutical store. I instinctively knew what worked well with what, and how pills are nothing on their own compared to when you mix them. I started to notice that everything I did, especially my reactions to things, was sometimes wild and always supersensitive, super-flirtatious, ambitious to the point of having no feelings for others whatsoever.[7] I recognized that I was becoming mentally unstable, more like what I remembered being like before, in another life, like it was forcing itself out of me. I tried to keep it under wraps, but I knew that the way I walked and talked was increasingly like Marilyn Monroe, even though I'd only seen bits and pieces of her movies.

At the time, I told another doctor at the same hospital, Dr. Golden or Goldenberg, that I needed stronger pills. He asked me to write out two pages of what I thought was wrong with me. I listed my depressions, my ambition, and at the bottom of the page I wrote, "I think I was Marilyn Monroe." They sent me home with some pills and at first they worked because I mixed them with alcohol. But eventually I hit rock bottom again. By that time, I had an Internet connection at home and started looking to see if there was such a thing as past-life doctors. Dr. Finkelstein's picture came up on the screen. Not only did I love his face right away, but he also looked familiar and like he was the right man for the job.[8] And I sent him my first e-mail. It was September 1998. In preparation for talking with him, I went back to the beginning of my recall of being Marilyn Monroe, or Norma Jean Baker.

When I was little I felt smart for my age, much the way you can see in little girls who play with tea sets when they've never even been to a tea party, but blown way up in my case. Some little girls are just old souls, I guess. My dad remembers me telling him, "Don't call me Sherrie. I'm someone else." He doesn't remember me saying who, but he says I seemed to know. But this was just in passing. My dad was busy trying to make a living and boxing on the side. He would just pooh-pooh it away. But I did sense that this other person, this grown-up woman, was very powerful and set in her ways. Even then it felt like my mind was already made up for me. I already had lots of likes and dislikes as a little girl that didn't come from my own experiences. Even my love for animals was just too much for my parents.[9] I'd get hysterical in a movie theater if an animal was hurt or taken away. Of all the other kids, I'd be the only one screaming, and it frightened them. Also, I had a dollhouse that folded down and had this outside patio and pool attached to it. It reminded me of something and I wanted to live there, or I just knew I had in some other time. What I'm trying to say is that I felt at an early age that my path was already cut out for me and that I was doing what this "other" person wanted of me.

The more I shut out the other person the more often that creepy, perverse, and choking feeling came back, like Sherrie was being pushed out of me. I found a way to just let it ride, meaning let it come: feel it and then ignore it. I just wanted to be with my animals and friends, and to sing my heart out. All I did was sing. Sitting there playing on Gram's floor when I was three years old, I knew that's what I wanted to be. I saw a commercial, I think for Wrigley's gum. People were wearing those funny Styrofoam hats you see during presidential campaigning, the ones with the stripes. It all had such a nostalgic feeling. There were three men singing, and the commercial was in black and white. It was harmonies, and I don't know if it was from this life or another, but it was very old-fashioned. And I said to myself, I'm going to be a singer. I seemed to acknowledge that other existence and accept it much in the way a psychic can sense things.

I don't remember everything that was going on in my child-hood other than our move from Scotland to Canada. I was just growing up and being parented and trying to be a child. But I felt like I was acting all the time.[10] If I was playing in the backyard, it wasn't just playing; it was always something more . . . dramatic. It was as if I were being filmed or playing to a camera. How can I describe to you what it feels like being an old soul, an old person in a little person's body? This feeling just never went away. It was there all day every day, whether playing outside, walking to school, or going shopping with Mom or to the zoo with Dad. Everything felt nostalgic, and I was constantly play-acting without trying. I just wanted to pet animals and be with my parents, but that's how I got through it. And singing was always on my mind. The radio would carry me away; no one listened more closely to songs than I did, to every nuance of voice and inflection. I was absorbing everything. I didn't really care about the secret other person. I was going to be a star on my own, and so she needed to MOVE over.

When I was 11 or 12, I was sitting on my aunt's knee and we were talking about the beauty mark just above my lip. I asked what it was. It looked stupid to me. She began singing, "A kiss on the hand may be quite continental, but diamonds are a girl's best friend."[11] The lyrics just echoed in my head, as if coming down a long corridor of sound from the past. I asked, "What's that?" She said it was a song from an old movie, sung by someone famous: Marilyn Monroe. My aunt only said that she was a singer, but I had this coy, sly feeling and said to myself, "Why do I feel like she's talking about me?" I felt a little embarrassed by this thought, but I kind of knew who she was and felt proud, too. And then I got distracted because I was starving and breakfast had taken too long. Later, I remember feeling important after hearing her name, like I had great, great things in store for me. I was going to be famous, too. My aunt hadn't said much at all; it was all internal, an instant recognition. It was probably one of two times I ever heard of Marilyn Monroe while growing up. The other time was much later, when I was around 18 or so. Someone yelled out Marilyn

Monroe's name, like someone had called to me. I was looking into a mirror, and then I said, "Oh yes? That's who you were. You've been driving me nuts all my life, haven't you? Why don't you leave me alone? There's nothing I can do for you."

Junior high and high school truly felt like an ongoing failure. I always thought, "What am I doing here? I won't use any of this stuff. I'm going to be famous." I just didn't fit in at all. The other girls either loved or hated me. They'd make fun of my walk or gossip that I thought I was beautiful or glamorous or something. Later I was voted Most Likely to be a Playboy Bunny. But, in fact, the opposite was true. Those girls were just afraid that I was going to steal their boyfriends, since the boys were always asking to walk me home. Sometimes I let them kiss me, but nothing more. At the shopping mall grown men would hit on me, ask me out, and I'd be shy and speechless and terrified. I would stutter and shake my head no. I later found out that they thought I was 20, not 14. Actually, I was feeling more and more isolated, losing myself to a daydream world of fame and riches. The older I got and the more I filled out and became "womanly," the more the other person asserted herself. I felt like I couldn't get any peace and that there was only enough room in my body for one of us. I realized ONE of us would have to go, but which one? We were one and the same. My battle was to find myself, my own voice at this age and based on my own talents, with her fighting to mold me into her image.

Sherrie began to lose that battle. After age 14 I found that I liked the effect I had on men; I almost thrived on it. I started to notice that when I was around men something would happen without my effort. Later, I learned how to just "apply" it to get a response. I just loved it. I could walk into a restaurant and stop the room by just twirling my head. My aunt noticed it, even if my parents didn't. People would say everywhere I went, "What is it about you that electrifies men?" In my late teens, I realized that I could maximize this effect by modeling and acting, on top of my ambition to be a singer. I sought out and did some modeling at the time and took drama classes in school, and I got an A + .[12] I had an order of how to proceed and would daydream about it as I walked to school. I didn't know where it came from; no one told me how to do it. And I was the most secretive person you'd ever meet. Only my aunt and my best friend Kim had any idea of my ambitions, and they were both sworn to secrecy.

After high school I did some modeling but nothing really jelled, and I think everybody, my parents in particular, were concerned about me being aimless. Kim lived next door to me, and her brother D had joined the army as a paratrooper. Both of our parents encouraged me to write to him because "he's very lonely and needs our support." When he'd come back to visit, I would go on dates with him. I discovered he was more advanced than the boys I'd been with, more street smart and stuff, and I thought it was so fun. But these were only short dates because he always had to go back. His mum would say, "If you two got married, you could travel the world together and have a PMQ's private married quarters." This went on for a while, and after he went back in August of 1982, I missed him. D came back the next December and asked me to marry him. I thought about it, and then in February I said yes and we made wedding plans. He came back in April of 1983 and we got married.[13] I went on my honeymoon with all my Scottish relatives, and my mum and I had so many fights because, when we were down in South Carolina, I was flirting with guys and taking their phone numbers. I just didn't know how to love anybody, and I now had an eating disorder because my new husband said I was fat. Anyway I didn't care really because I was going to travel the world, and if it didn't work out there'd be other army guys.

We moved to Calgary, as D was based there. But he would go away and I would grow very despondent. It was the first time this young girl with so many hopes and dreams actually started thinking of suicide.[14] I would literally be left in our apartment with no food (didn't care during the anorexia spurts, but did care during the bulimia times) and no hydro. No TV. No phone. I was definitely going to kill myself. I told him, "You TOOK me from a loving home and family FOR THIS!" Oh, how I hated him. My dog and I would travel back and forth to Calgary regularly, costing my parents a small fortune in plane tickets. I guess I was just as bad a daughter as he was a husband. And then on March 11, 1984 (I remember that date vividly), I was talking to my aunt on a pay-phone at a convenience store, joking about my suicide. I told her to have that phrase put on my headstone. She thought I should have a baby, that maybe that would cheer me up, but I didn't think I could get pregnant. But by June of that year, I was again alone in a little PMQ while D was off God knows where, and I didn't love him and I wanted to go home. I had missed my period for a while and was now obviously pregnant. I gave birth on December 11, 1984. I was going to call my daughter Natasha, but I had recently read *Passion's Promise* by Danielle Steel and named her Kezia after one of the characters.[15] My in-laws gave me a hard time about it, but I didn't care. This child was mine and mine alone.

I left D after the birth, and Kezia and I moved back in with my parents, who now lived on a farm outside of my hometown. After I got my health back and felt like me again, my old ambitions flared up, especially since, according to everybody, I looked like and acted like Marilyn Monroe more than ever. But I had never even seen a Marilyn movie. Maybe I had seen the last half of *Some Like It Hot*. This was around the same time I was dating my "Tony Curtis" boyfriend.[16] I needed to know. And then, checking my teeth in the mirror one night, her image was reflected back at me. I could feel a prickly sensation up my spine and around my neck. Time stood still. It wasn't so much everybody saying I looked like Marilyn, as it was me inwardly agreeing with them, and feeling ever so smarty-pants about it. It was like: YEAH, I KNOW. But this irritated me because WHAT did I really know and why won't this stop? So Kezia and I took a quick drive into town and I asked the guy at the local bookstore, "You got any Marilyn Monroe books and have you ever heard of her?" He looked at me kind of funny and said that he didn't have any Marilyn Monroe books, but had one about Norma Jean. The book didn't even have a cover. On the way home Kezia asked, "Mommy, don't you think when you read this, you're reading about you?" And I thought the way she said it was very spooky.

I read the book and what I cared about most was how she really felt; all the details of her movies meant nothing to me. I could identify with everything that Norma Jean was feeling at every turn. It was a big YES and I would talk back, "Leave her alone, why don't you. Don't try to tell her what to do." I felt immediately uncomfortable when she would have to be with Jim. I knew of the good times and the bad times with these men; I could feel it all, every last detail, and it got on my nerves. It was always the emotions I identified with most. Well, this book showed me that there was something deeper going on, and I didn't know whether to pursue it further or to just let it be. I decided to let it be for now, but there were just so many "coincidences," plus I had that continuous man thing going on. At times, it would really come oozing out again. It all just started adding up and I thought some time later that I already believed in reincarnation, though I was never taught about it, and it could be possible that I was Marilyn.

And I would off and explore this after I'd get "triggered" by some coincidence, and then I'd forget it and just go about living my own life. Then something else would pop up, and it would start all over again. I'd see her movies, or bits and pieces of them, or glance through a picture book here and there over the years and I'd feel embarrassed for her. I'd say, "Well, that's not what I thought it was going to be. I thought it was going to be much more glamorous and worth it." She just looked so fat at times. I couldn't see the benefit in me being her, but I could still identify with her mannerisms and, more importantly, I would feel her attractions to the other actors and people in her life. That's when I'd most feel I was her, because it wasn't Marilyn I cared about per se, but what she cared about . . . the attractions were the same. Personally, I don't think JFK was so attractive but I do think Bobby Kennedy and Arthur Miller were. I noticed we had the same taste in men for the most part. I like Italians with big noses and big families, but I also liked the looks and brains of an Arthur Miller type.[17]

It was so easy just to slide into being Marilyn. We were the spitting images of each other, and then I started wearing her like an old sock. It meant nothing to me, though, and I said, "Okay, good. That's a great piece of information, but it's not going to do anything to help me now." But, something told me that I wasn't going to get away with leaving her behind that easily. And without prompting or any good reason, my life would fall into pits of depression. At first I could climb my way out of them, but each time the pit seemed deeper and it was harder and harder.[18] This horrible weight I carried with me was taking Sherrie down, and possibly Kezia and my whole family with it. I tried ignoring it. I tried drinking it away. I tried to outrun it and outlive it by building a new life, but the harder I tried to leave it behind, the more confirmations and coincidences would appear. I had opened a can of worms that I could no longer handle. And now I could see very clearly why WE AREN'T supposed to remember our past lives. I felt God was saying "HAH! See what you get? You wanted to know, and look what you've done. You could've had a happy life and a new future, but you had to tamper with something that was none of your business." I felt nothing but punishment for it.

But, amidst all of this despair, a sign of hope came. God hadn't deserted me after all. I read somewhere that Marilyn's mother, Gladys Baker, had died on March 11, 1984, in Calgary, Canada. (That was the night I had talked with my aunt on the phone and she had suggested I have a baby.) I said, "NOOOOO! It's too good to be true. It can't be that simple." And I said, "I'm going to count the months now, and if it adds up to nine, I'm going to FAINT." And boom, it did: March 11 to December 11. Every fiber, every molecule in my body was vibrating and alive. Kezia was the reincarnation of Marilyn's mother, Gladys Baker, who'd come back to take care of her little girl, me.[19]

Deep down I had always suspected as much. It was the things Kezia would say as a little girl, like "don't call me Kezia," and be really adamant about it. From around three years old she was always telling me what to do, giving me advice, and just knowing things. She was very close to my mum, so I thought it was something they were concocting together. But it was all her. From the beginning she's always been the boss of me; her being the mother in our relationship started early and stayed that way. So, it's probably something that goes farther back in time than just one lifetime. It did cross my mind that she might have even said to call her Gladys early on. This realization was truly a gift from God. I felt that in spite of my suffering over being Marilyn, this was Him saying, "See? I love you. I've not left you alone. I bring you not only my love but your own love over and over."

In the following years, Kezia and I jockeyed between living at the farm with my parents and helping them with their horses, and living in my Gram's building, where there was an assortment of musicians but also whores and pimps. I was always singing and working on my music, taping myself and refining my vocal style. Kezia and I hung out with my aunt and were very close with her beautiful cousins: the twins Shelli and Ryan, and Kristy Lee. We had lots of fun and plenty of laughs. I would still tell everyone that I was going to be a famous singer, and they knew I was practicing all the time, but I was getting a slow start.[20] I worked odd jobs to pay the rent, like at an aircraft parts place called Garretts,[21] and I did a stint as waitress but got fired. I worked as a bartender, faking I could make drinks and then learning how to on the job. I did office work at an airline called Ward Air. The last year at Gram's building (she had always been controlling and it was getting worse), it was Kezia's birthday a few weeks before Christmas, and I decided not to pay the $700 rent, but to instead give her a great birthday and Christmas. I had already made last month's rent and planned to catch up again, in halves. But we got evicted on December 29 and went back to the farm to live with my parents again.

After I dumped M, I took up with a musician, C, who got upset with my flirtatious behavior. I really worked hard at calming it down, but it would come out very strongly when my guard was down. My Marilyn side would make me feel like a drag queen with all of her exaggerated feminine traits. Sometimes I would go into the bathroom, lock the door, smoke marijuana, and really play out the body movements and facial things. I'd say things in her voice as if to purge myself of her. During the depressed times, I still needed to mix pills and alcohol. I have no tolerance for being upset whatsoever; I'm not addicted during the good, healthy, productive times, but if Kezia (Gladys) or my parents upset me, this is the worst. With C it's more normal; I'll just need to drink or spend money.

For a while after my first suicide attempt, I had issues with my parents and I ended up stealing and living in my Aunty May's car. I would sleep in the car with the dogs, and then out of the blue I took off to Nashville[22] with the two dogs for a month. I said I wasn't coming back until I "made it." This all happened over a fight with Kezia. There's a thing about Kezia, a coldness, and sometimes she doesn't seem to know who I really am. We love each other dearly, but there are these issues. Anyway, during another suicide attempt, I apparently had thrown a chair and some dishes out of a hotel window and I ended up naked on the front lawn, which I believe happened to Marilyn during one of her bouts.[23] History really does repeat: another arrest, another psych ward. But, as I said earlier, I began to realize that I needed help from another source, not from the doctors with their white coats and drugs.

I just inwardly knew, call it psychic, call it faith, that there had to be help, a doctor who could heal my soul. I begged for it. I was taught that God is a compassionate and loving God. Did he really want me to die? I would if I didn't get help. I just knew in my heart that God's love energy wanted me to thrive, and that I would be led to my salvation.

NOTES FOR CHAPTER 4

1. It is interesting to note here two meaningful synchronicities: A) M Kennedy has the same last name as John and Robert Kennedy in Marilyn's life; B) M Kennedy physically resembled Marilyn's biological father, Stanley Gifford, who abandoned her and her mother, Gladys Mortensen Baker. It is worthwhile noting that the men in both Marilyn's and Sherrie's lives, who were emotionally and/or physically abusive, happen to be the ones these women loved and/or missed the most. It is a well-documented fact how much Marilyn missed her father and how she looked all her life for a father and his love.

2. Sherrie experiences a frightening déjà vu "asylum" flashback to when Marilyn was psychiatrically hospitalized at the Payne Whitney Clinic, the psychiatric division of New York Hospital, where Joe DiMaggio bailed her out.

3. The feeling of her chest being crushed is a somatic past-life memory that Sherrie has experienced repeatedly since early childhood. This somatic flashback comes from Marilyn's traumatic pre-death-state period of about 15–20 minutes caused by the gradual infiltration of her vital breathing center in the brain stem with the narcotics Nembutal and chloral hydrate. Coroner Thomas Noguchi, who investigated Marilyn Monroe's suicide, cited death due to respiratory failure.

4. Mixing alcohol (especially champagne) with drugs and abusing drugs and alcohol are other striking similarities between Marilyn and Sherrie.

5. To maintain her "sex symbol" profile, her promoters fallaciously portrayed Marilyn as not having singing talents. Besides wishing to be a famous and serious actress, she always wanted to be a singer. Sherrie is a renowned Canadian singer whose remake of Sade's "No Ordinary Love" hit the top of the pop charts. This is a very revealing synchronicity, disclosing the truth of Marilyn/Sherrie's outstanding singing talent.

6. Sherrie has always had an affinity for the 1950s, during which period Marilyn became the greatest Hollywood movie star of that era.

7. It is common knowledge how self-involved and fiercely ambitious Marilyn was, to the point of showing no feelings for others. Sherrie duplicates these qualities at times.

8. This is indirectly related to Marilyn and one of her former incarnations, as will be revealed later.

9. Is it surprising that both Marilyn and Sherrie love animals so much that even those people closest to them cannot understand it?

10. Amazingly, from a very early age, Sherrie had the feeling that everything happening around her was like a movie and that she was "acting." It appears to be a continuation of a prematurely interrupted acting career in her previous life as Marilyn, who was working on the '30s-era film *Something's Got to Give* at the time of her death.

11. "Diamonds Are a Girl's Best Friend" is the song Marilyn sang in *Gentlemen Prefer Blonds*. When her aunt sang this song to her, it resonated in Sherrie's subconscious mind. As a child with no prior conscious knowledge about Marilyn, this déjà vu feeling is very revealing.

12. In her late teens, Sherrie, like Marilyn, due to being praised by

men for her good looks, enrolled in modeling and acting classes and there demonstrated her acting talent.

13. Marrying the army guy next door at an early age happened to both Marilyn and Sherrie. Marilyn married James Dougherty and Sherrie married D.

14. Marilyn suffered from depression and suicidal ideation and was psychiatrically hospitalized as a result. She even took too many pills mixed with alcohol immediately prior to her death. Sherrie not only contemplated suicide as often as Marilyn, but she attempted suicide several times and was psychiatrically hospitalized as a result. At one time feeling horribly guilty about the death of her agent and lover, Johnny Hyde, Marilyn took an overdose of pills. She was saved by her friend Natasha, who caught her in the act.

15. Marilyn's favorite drama coach and one of her lifelong friends and confidants was Natasha Lytess.

16. Marilyn had a crush on Tony Curtis, and as a young adult, Sherrie dated a man who looked like Tony Curtis.

17. Preferences for the same type of men remained unchanged for Sherrie.

18. Pits of depression, not necessarily accompanied by suicidal ideation or attempts, were prevalent for both Marilyn and Sherrie.

19. The fact that Sherrie's daughter, Kezia, was conceived on the same day or just after Marilyn's mother Gladys Mortensen Baker died, and in the same Canadian province, Calgary—most unusual for an American born and raised in Los Angeles—is one of the most compelling synchronicities of this comparison. This is further compounded by Sherrie's feeling that the role of mother/daughter has been reversed in her relationship with Kezia. Even today, as a young woman in her twenties, Kezia still exhibits the same motherly behavior toward Sherrie. Further, Kezia is not mentally ill, as Gladys was, and the motherly love she deprived Marilyn of is now being bestowed on Sherrie. This is a classic karmic compensation pattern often evident in the reincarnation record of people with close ties coming back to rectify a wrongdoing. (There is also a North/South Moon Node comparison between the two that I will delve into later in the book.)

20. Sherrie's unshakable certainty, despite continued setbacks, that she would succeed during this down period matches Marilyn's conviction.

21. The fact that Sherrie worked at an aircraft parts place and for an

airline compares to when Marilyn worked at the defense plant, where she was discovered by photographer David Conover.

22. Going to Nashville, Tennessee, to "make it" is a little further than going from West Los Angeles to Hollywood (as Marilyn did), but it has the same intent. Also, it is interesting to note that Marilyn visited Tennessee in the summer of 1944 for a brief stay with her half-sister, Bernice Baker. The intent in this case was different, but the location was the same.

23. Sherrie's temper flare-up throwing dishes out of the window and ending up naked on the lawn compares to the episode at Payne Whitney Clinic when a naked Marilyn threw a chair at someone.

FIRST CONTACT

It was the fall of 1998. I was still teaching UCLA psychiatric residents at Cedars-Sinai Medical Center while conducting past-life regressions in my Palatine, Illinois, office—commuting back and forth. It was fascinating therapy and the results were very encouraging. One of my patients was a high-ranking Christian cleric based in Chicago. Under deep hypnosis, he recalled one of his past lives as an aristocrat. He was wrought with anger over his heartless abuse of others in that life. He had hurt and killed many people. As a result of this regression, he abreacted very emotionally and expiated for his former sins. He felt a ton of grief lift off him, and for the first time he truly understood his religious vocation.

Off hours I spent quality time with my wife Shulah and my oldest daughter Drorit, her husband Barry, and their three children. We loved to watch Lakers' games, and I'd play basketball with the kids or swim with them in their pool. Sometimes we'd vacation at Big Bear in the San Bernardino Mountains. My youngest daughter, Sarah, single at that time, resided in Jerusalem. We'd visit her in Israel or she'd fly to Los Angeles. Both of my daughters had passed the California bar but did not practice law. I felt an unusually deep love for my wife and my daughters, and decided to write a book on soul mates. I knew from my prior past-life regressions that we had been together in many lifetimes, but I was obsessed by this strong inner voice to search further. As before, I didn't require a standard hypnotic self-induction; I just entered a state of altered consciousness in which I became oblivious to everything but my inner revelations. In this way I recalled 25 of my past lives, a few of which I'd already uncovered. It was like real life, clearly seeing and talking with my soul mates in these other lifetimes, experiencing such deep feelings of love that it moved me to tears. Many of these were with my beloved wife, daughters, parents, and brother and sister. Others were with people I had not met, or at least not yet, in the present.

At one point I experienced a past life in France as a noble physician. I was in a convent ministering to some of my patients. One of the nuns, Louise, was helping me apply a dressing on the chest of a wounded soldier. I was looking up at her. She had a beautiful face with big blue and very sad, slightly swollen eyes. She was dressed in a dark-gray nun uniform up to her neck. She appeared to be profoundly depressed. I took her aside and looked into her eyes. She burst into tears. I felt this inner urge to protect her, to help her. She finally confided in me. She had been a courtesan of the king, but due to royal intrigues had been banished to this nunnery for the rest of her life. Her story, our story, bears relevance to the subject of this book and will be explained later. I bring up this incident to account for my feelings of déjà vu and déjà attendue on being contacted by Sherrie Lea Laird shortly after this past-life recall of mine.

I couldn't retrieve the first e-mail from her in September 1998; this was the second e-mail, followed by others, as well as lengthy telephone conversations with her:

Sent: October 07, 1998
From: Sherrie Lea Laird
To: Adrian Finkelstein, M.D.

Subject: Reincarnation/M. Monroe, not even a joke!

Hello Doctor,

I've already sent one (September 1998). It may or may not get there from your own "e-mail and comments" section. If it does, just disregard this one please. If not, then I guess here it goes again. This second time around I'll probably be more blunt. However, this will sound crazy to you, as it also sounds crazy to me and I have to put up with these thoughts. I was hoping to have some direction from you as to where I could go here in Toronto to have legitimate hypnotherapy if you know of any. I will pick up a copy of your books as soon as I get a chance. The only past-life book I've read is June Avery's *Saturn and Past Lives.*

I firmly believe in reincarnation, based on a couple of terri-fying panic-caused flashbacks, which have even sent me to the psychiatric ward. They will have a record of [me from] four years ago. I was trying to tell my doctor "I'm not crazy; I'm just having past-life flashbacks!" However I'm not sure we were meant to remember. Perhaps for some people it would be too much. Then, on the other hand, perhaps we can right the wrongs and not make the same mistake twice. Even famous people in previous lives have to go somewhere. What if a per-son who was famous in a previous life, abused herself with drugs and let other people make her feel small and didn't give proper thanks for the beautiful life she had, [came back].

Perhaps this kind of thing explains why with my singing career and talent, I may not achieve my so called "success" and why I can do nothing to get cherished loved ones off of drugs in this life. I feel that past life, I think I'm aware of it, is so directly related to this life. I believe sometimes so fully and other times more skeptically, but it never completely goes away. I think I was M. Monroe, but who doesn't? And I should think they would want it to go away, the same way I do. And I'd feel strongly that they would be quite wrong anyway.

And besides my memories just within the last ten years, I've had countless coincidences happen to keep sending me on my path, which has now become as much as to eliminate, or con-firm and then eliminate, this idea. Of course by now I've read many books on this "person," but only to discover more and more similarities.

BEFORE READING UP on anything, I was so set on naming my daughter Natasha. Why? I didn't know. And the very first thing I had ever read about MM, within those first pages, made so many things come flooding back to me. Natasha, the drama coach. However, thank God, I named my daughter Kezia, whom I had by an Army guy who lived next door to me. If you did any homework at all on Marilyn Monroe, you'll understand what I'm talking about, but the point is that these were just the beginning hints for me; maybe they're just coincidences, but so many keep coming regularly. It was driving me mad at one point, and I asked God for a sign if it were true, and I walked a short distance to the _____ video store. This is within 15 minutes from my home. And the clerk handed me the movie called *Bus Stop*. Out of the blue and not only that, but MM's name in the movie was Cherie and she was a singer. I don't idolize her or want to be her. People used to tell me all the time I reminded them of her. Quite frankly, that kind of blubbering and misuse of one's own body disgusts me and a lot of it I find extremely embarrassing.

I was born July 1963, but because of the music biz I lie about my age and say '68. My boyfriend and music partner doesn't know anything about this, but one time when he'd seen some old footage he looked at her and said, "I've seen that face before" and said something about [our] striking similarity, but other than that only you and my daughter know about these thoughts. Doctor, please excuse this long letter if you have even read it. But maybe you can see why I need some kind of closure to this whole situation. Perhaps later I can laugh and say what a hoax nature plays on us and has made fun of me the whole time. Anyway, 'til then, I do hope you have time for a response. Thank you very much.

Sincerely,
Sherrie Laird

P.S. I am also truly hoping you won't think I'm a nutcase. Surely in your line of work you've heard it all and maybe even the same kind of story.

My initial character analysis of Sherrie, based on empathic resonance and routine psychiatric history taking, evoked a trust response. This was based on several factors that separated her from the usual pretenders claiming celebrity past lives, some of whom are in the psychiatric record. For one, she didn't attempt to edit or prettify anything in her exposé. On the contrary, she hurried to get it out of her system. An unforced flavor emanated from her writing style and linguistics. I felt she cared little about the form of her communication or writing and couldn't wait to pour out her very heart, and as soon as possible. And it was like an unending monologue overflowing the screen. She was very unforced and flowing with the information about herself. In other words, she came across to me as natural, not as fake or contrived.

Sent: October 09, 1998
From: Sherrie Lea Laird
To: Adrian Finkelstein, M.D.
Subject: Sherrie L.

Dear Doctor,

How kind of you to: a) return my e-mail and b) return it so soon!

Yes I would love, and be quite scared at the same time, to talk to you. I'm quite relieved that you don't think I'm crackers. So many thoughts go around my head about this situation that maybe talking to a head doctor who understands could really help.

My biggest hope to come out of this is to either prove that I am not the reincarnation of you-know-who, or if it proves otherwise, then hopefully to see old friends and loved ones before they die. Maybe they would get something from it too, even if I don't look quite the same to them. But at least this is some sort of attempt to free myself. Though it is something that could be comforting to mankind (reincarnation), it's also absurd. And at least I am aware that the only life that counts is the one we're living right now.

Thanks ever so much,

Sherrie

As the correspondence continued, I noted that Sherrie wasn't making this claim for the purpose of self-aggrandizement. This was strictly an outpouring from a troubled soul, and the confession was purely cathartic in nature. She needed to dispose from her being all the emotional poison from a traumatic past life that still haunted her. To put it bluntly, she asked my help in ridding herself of the persona of Marilyn Monroe. She sincerely didn't want any part of it and desired to be only Sherrie and pursue her career as a singer.

On October 16, 1998, I phoned Sherrie in Toronto. As the phone rang, I was very curious to hear Sherrie's voice for the first time. It took many rings, and when I was about to hang up, I heard this melodious, warm, and plushy soft voice at the other end.

"Who is calling?"

I'm very experienced from my psychiatric work to carry on conversations with people, but this time I have to admit to a little stage fright. Patiently, the beautiful voice inquired again.

"Is anyone there?"

Finally, regaining my self-assuredness, I answered, "Yes, it's me, Dr. F."

"What a pleasant surprise. You must be so busy. I thought you wouldn't have time to call. But I'm glad you think I'm not crackers."

"On the contrary," I replied. "You're more sane and open-minded than most. Thank you for being yourself!" Then I continued, "Can you tell me how you feel about finally confessing you're Marilyn Monroe incarnated?"

"I feel relieved and at the same time very frightened," she replied.

I pursued this line of inquiry further. "What makes you feel relieved and what frightens you?"

She burst with refreshing exuberance. "Yeah, I'm relieved that you think I'm not nuts or a fruitcake. Ha, ha. All my life I was told I am different. My parents told me this, my other relatives, and the band musical guys. I've been feeling crazy. But I know I'm not. I completely believe in reincarnation. As I explained in the e-mail, I had a couple of very scary panic attacks caused by flashbacks, which sent me straight to the loony bin, the psychiatric ward. They have a record of me. That was four years ago. I was trying to tell my doctor that I'm not crazy; I'm just having past-life flash-backs. But I could tell from his reaction that he didn't believe me."

"You haven't told me what's frightening in all this," I insisted.

Bursting into tears she said, "Gosh, I can't take this. You know people, television people, will try to shoot us down. I'm so terrified to appear on a show as Marilyn reincarnated. That's unless you're there and do all the talking. I'm afraid you don't know what you're getting into. You seem to be so nice. They may tear us apart."

"Don't worry. If this pans out, I'll stand by you," I reassured her. She calmed down. And the rest of the conversation was my reassuring her that I'll protect her against the falling sky.

At this time I might note that during my lengthy professional work as a psychiatrist, I had to assess and treat thousands of patients who sought my assistance to rid themselves of their own demons. No one among them sought my expertise in past-life regression therapy due to a claim of being Marilyn Monroe rein-carnated—or, for that matter, any other celebrity in the last 200 years. Most were regular people. Occasionally I would get famous people from the very remote past, but I had no way to prove the validity of their information through past-life regression. Some were so genuine and emotional, like Sherrie. As they say, "When you cry, you don't lie." Moreover, when the crying is done under very deep hypnosis (tantamount to truth serum), no one in my experience has been able to "fake it." At the time I had hoped that Sherrie would come to Los Angeles, at least for a few days, so I could regress her and probe into her psyche for any recent past-life recall under hypnosis. This was to confirm or disprove her intuitive claim of having been Marilyn Monroe, and, if she really was this tortured soul, to thrust her demons out, once and for all.

Of the 35 or more individuals on record claiming to be Marilyn Monroe's reincarnation, none of the others has come to my atten-tion or other professionals in the field, to the best of my knowl-edge. True, there are many Marilyn impersonators out there, but

I haven't come across evidence in my research in books, scientific journals, or magazines that even remotely proves that any of these Marilyn claimants are authentic. On the contrary, some of them appeared to make claims of a psychotic proportion, i.e., being completely detached from reality. As a matter of fact, Sherrie and I had more verifiable proof in the first six months of our research back then, even without past-life regressions, that she was the reincarnation of Marilyn Monroe than any doubter could disprove.

What greatly added to Sherrie's credibility in my assessment was that after questioning her about her singing career, I understood her reluctance about making claims that might destroy that career. This only added to her reliability. From the very beginning of my correspondence via e-mail and telephone, I took the initial steps to set up a preliminary research investigation into Sherrie's case. I included in this study Sherrie's real birth information, which confirmed that she and Marilyn have the same North/South Moon Nodes and North/South House Moon Nodes. (This was a prime indicator in other past-life regressions where there was also a lot of physical evidence, such as birth records and the accuracy of historical names, places, and events, to corroborate under hypnosis.) I also took photos of Sherrie and made a preliminary comparison of her facial resemblance to Marilyn Monroe, which proved uncanny.

During that period, many more telephone conversations ensued. Unfortunately, they weren't recorded. Using my recollections and notes, I can say that they consisted mainly of me giving Sherrie enough support to continue with our research into her claim of being Marilyn Monroe reincarnated. She needed lots of encouragement and expressed immense gratitude to me for rescuing her from her lion's cage, so to speak. On the other hand, as a spiritual psychiatrist, I explain my part was merely as a facilitating instrument for God's grace. God brought Sherrie and me together for a reason, and we needed to place our trust in that wisdom. Sherrie was very curious about my work, having found my listing on a website as a world-class expert in past-life regression therapy. But there are other pioneers in this field as well. The question came down to, why me? I told her that would probably come out in the course of our research and that we should just have trust in the master plan.

In late December of 1998, I had a phone conversation with Sherrie in which she again expressed concern that our research, once made public, could endanger her singing career. She was afraid that people wouldn't understand, or that they would ridicule and debase her in the public forum and call her a fake. This frightening possibility had to be weighed against the evident therapeutic relief she felt as we delved deeper and released more of her Marilyn demons. At the time she also told me in confidence some family problems that seemed strikingly similar to those of Marilyn Monroe. The difference was that Sherrie had both her parents and what Marilyn had so desperately wanted: a daughter to love. Kezia was then 14 years old, and their roles remained kind of reversed with Sherrie being the rock-and-roll girl and Kezia the "mum." (At that time we hadn't discussed the possibility that Kezia may be Marilyn's mother, Gladys Baker, reincarnated.) A great deal of our discussion focused on Sherrie's drinking problem and her combining upper and downer drugs with champagne, so much reminiscent of Marilyn. I strongly advised her to enter a drug and alcohol dependence program and to seek out a local therapist in this field. She had already done both and they had failed her: The doctors would mainly prescribe antidepressant medications that didn't work and treat her past-life claims as pure fantasy.

Coincidentally, and we may also call it a synchronicity, during the holiday season of 1998–1999 I met and began a friendship with Ted Jordan. I didn't know at the time that there was a connection between Ted and Marilyn. We met at the Christmas party of Cedars-Sinai Medical Center, Department of Psychiatry. He was there with his lady friend Susan, who was a nurse on the psychiatric staff. Ted, 74, was a retired Hollywood actor who used to play cowboy roles in movies and on television, and is best known for his work on the hit TV show *Gunsmoke*. Since my office at the time was located at Cedars-Sinai Medical Towers and he lived only a block away, Ted and I would meet for lunch occasionally. I was curious about his life as an actor, while he was interested in psychiatry and solicited some free counseling regarding his relationship with Susan. One day, since he had worked in Hollywood during that period, I confided to him that I had an inquiry from a Canadian singer who was having terrible flashbacks about her past life as Marilyn Monroe.

Ted's facial expression changed immediately. He jumped up from his chair and said, "Wait a minute! I didn't tell you this, but I had a romantic relationship with Marilyn Monroe, or Norma Jean when I knew her. I was a lifeguard at the Ambassador Hotel in Beverly Hills when I met her. She was 18 and I was 19. That's where her model school was located. I wrote a book about our relationship, *Norma Jean: My Secret Life with Marilyn Monroe.*" I didn't know this at the time. When we next met, Ted handed me the book and urged me to "Read it!" After reading it, I understood so much more about the life and the tragic death of this great star, Marilyn Monroe. I could also compare bits and pieces of information from her life with what I knew about Sherrie's, which put her claim into a new perspective. They both had the same low self-esteem, extraordinary ambition, the champagne and drug addictions, and the raw sexual energy that turned heads (as Sherrie claimed from age 14 onward). Both Sherrie and Marilyn had the same breathless, little-girl voice and their conversations were intermittently spiced with a special giggle that could disarm anybody.

In the interim, Sherrie had sent me a video of herself performing as a singer in Canada in order to prove to me that she wasn't somebody "from the street." She looked so beautiful, and again a déjà vu feeling surprised me. By that time I had also seen several of Marilyn's films. Ted wrote descriptions of Norma Jean and talked about her in conversations with me, and what he said fitted with Sherrie. There was a unique way she threw her head back like Marilyn. She moved with that same sinuous glide, and her big blue eyes gazed in that special way while her mouth was slightly open. At times Sherrie, like Marilyn, would act like a scared teenage girl. And as Ted saw in Norma Jean and later in Marilyn, I too sensed in Sherrie the same extremely vulnerable and fragile child-woman incapable of hurting a fly, but who was also hardheaded and consumed by an unending ambition to succeed. Ted once told me that Marilyn "moved through life in a soft, unfocused daze but could be manipulative and uncaring and even cold at times," which also seem to fit Sherrie. At the same time, like Sherrie, she could be the most loving and warm person, hoping to be loved in return. I could easily see and sense all of these traits in Sherrie. I was looking for dissimilarities as well but I couldn't find any, except some minor physical differences genetically inherited in this lifetime from her parents. She is slightly taller than Marilyn, has somewhat larger hands and feet, and her face is a bit fuller.

It was obvious that Marilyn, in this life as Sherrie, had retained most of her sex appeal. At this point I talked with Sherrie about her sexual history and her intimate relationships. She confessed to having had many boyfriends. It was easy for her to fall in and out of love. Like Marilyn, she was fiercely independent and ambitious in pursuing her career, but at the same time was overly dependent on men as she sought that ideal love that always escaped her. Sexually, like Marilyn, Sherrie could easily "turn it on" at any time and be highly orgasmic, while at other times she could be cold and unyielding, as she told me. She could be very sensitive and have her "awful" moods. I learned later that, when it came to her performance on a set, on stage, or in a studio, Sherrie was very hard on herself—a real perfectionist. But she usually pulls it together and acts like a real star when required.

According to my notes, Sherrie and I spoke on December 21, 1998, and exchanged Christmas greetings. After the holidays, Sherrie said that she would be very busy with her concerts and could not say when she would reconnect with me. She said that it would probably be some time in February of 1999. But, after I hadn't heard from her, I decided to write to her about our mutual acquaintance.

Sent: February 18, 1999
From: Adrian Finkelstein, M.D.
To: Sherrie Lea Laird
Subject: Reincarnation/M. Monroe, not even a joke!

Dear Sherrie,

I hope you are well. Thank you again for your past inquiry into my work with reincarnation (my web page: www.past lives.com). You asked me at the time if you could be M. Monroe reincarnated. My answer was indicating such a possibility and I suggested we talk on the phone. I enjoyed very much the conversations with you. It was not clear if you could come to my office for past-life regression due to your geographical location, concert schedule, and financial considerations.

Recently, I met by chance and was befriended by a very charming elderly man in L.A. He agreed that I mention his name to you because if you were MM before, you would certainly know him. His name is Ted Jordan. Obviously I did not tell him your name, as your permission would be needed for that. In case you wish for me to put you in touch with him so that the three of us might research the possibility that you were MM in your previous life, please let me know via e-mail or telephone. If you prefer the latter, what is the telephone number where you can be reached and at what times?

Love and God bless you,
Adrian Finkelstein, M.D.

Sent: February 21, 1999
From: Sherrie Lea Laird
To: Adrian Finkelstein, M.D.
Subject: Hi, From Sherrie

Hello Dr. Finkelstein,

I'm sorry it took so long to write back. I tried to find a good time to call, but I've had some shows and rehearsals as well as we won a songwriting contest which means a great deal to our career. This is Sunday at 3:00 our time and I am just reading your e-mail now.

I had a rush of energy go thru me when you said Ted's name and, as usual, told myself that I am being silly. But this could be very good for us to start connecting in some way, hopefully by telephone at least. Does Ted think this is crazy? Would he know me still? I could send a photo down and see if he feels more interested or not. The picture shows me singing and I had blonde hair, but just last week I colored it in dark with bangs.

I would love to be regressed, as some of these things need to be dealt with and put to rest. I have dreams that I am MM all the time. As I mentioned before it was quite a jolt to my system to have these ideas out of the blue and feel it so strongly (as I have kind of an affiliation toward black people I was thinking this was the case but so many small things seem to prove otherwise). I am so excited about seeing Ted or talking to him. How will this be made possible? How did you run into him and how did you bring up this subject? Was he excited at this possibility or scared like I am? Please call me any time if I am home. I check messages right away and I will call back immediately.

Thank you for not giving up on me and having an open and educated mind.

Sincerely,
Sherrie

P.S. Did you know that MM played a singer named Cherie? I keep meaning to get some of the movies to keep, and I definitely will but sometimes I don't like watching them. Some of it is embarrassingly melodramatic and sometimes it's funny. I haven't told anyone about this except my daughter, one other lady, and yourself because I don't want them to think I'm mad. This is not the kind of thing to just blurt out, and it could hurt my career. But it is worth knowing why this is happening, don't you agree too?

So, with their permission, I arranged for Sherrie and Ted to talk with each other on the phone in March of 1999. They talked almost daily and for hours at a time. Most of the memories they shared were commonplace, but they also discussed numerous private moments such as making love. At times, Sherrie would get frustrated as Ted would remember an incident from his present life, while she had to remember it from her life as Marilyn. It was difficult for her to get the details right. They called me almost immediately after their conversations, gushing with recognition. Or, if they talked at night, they'd wait to report to me the following morning. I took notes, making a list of potential questions to ask Sherrie during her past-life regression. Ted was convinced that only Marilyn could know some of the unreported episodes in their romance and friendship that Sherrie remembered. For instance, Ted reported to me that one time while Norma Jean and he were making love, she forgot and left open her lipstick on the bed's linen. They made wild sex like acrobats all night long. They fell asleep exhausted to find out upon waking up toward the middle of the day that the linen as well as their naked bodies were surrealistically painted in bright red. Sherrie totally confirmed this incident.

I also found jotted in my notes the following dramatic telephone conversation with Sherrie.

March 9, 1999

My telephone rang. I picked up the receiver and heard at the other end of the line Sherrie crying and sobbing.

"He died," she hardly could utter.

I inquired, "Who died?"

Between sobs she replied, "Joe."

"Do you mean Joe DiMaggio?" I asked. "When?"

"It happened yesterday. Now I feel so alone. He was the only one I loved, who loved me, believed in me, and stood by me. Silly me. I'm talking as if I'm Mar. But I feel and I live her. She is me! Or isn't she? I'm confused. But then why do I feel so strongly about him?"

"What do you remember about him? Any fond memories of him?"

"We planned to remarry and go to Hawaii," she replied while still sobbing. "But it didn't happen." She paused. "No, it didn't. It's as if I'm in a daze. I'm floating. But now . . . now . . . I feel like I'm suffocating. I feel this crushing in my chest . . . I cannot stand it. It hurts so much . . . ." She half screamed as if even the scream were obliterated by lack of air. I immediately intervened, as it was quite clear to me that Sherrie was having a flashback to the time just prior to Marilyn's death.

"Sher, I want you to forget all this and relax completely. Breathe deeply through your nose three times. Breathe out negativity; breathe in all the beautiful energies surrounding you and just let go and relaaax! Take your time! Take all the time in the world! I'm here to help you through this."

After about a minute Sherrie calmed down. "I feel better," she said.

"I'm glad. You will stay well and have only positive effects from this experience." Eventually, we planned to have another telephone conversation in a week.

March 16, 1999

This time I initiated the telephone call. "Hi, Sher! How are you?"

"I'm busy with my music. But, you know, I'm so excited that the only soul alive from the oldies of my past that I care to meet, Ted, is planning to come to Toronto. Yea, I'm so excited! Yea!" She giggled.

"Does that mean you aren't coming to L.A. for regressions? You know you almost had a regression on the phone the other day."

"Yes, I know. But now I'm afraid to lose Ted. All my old friends have a tendency to die on me. I would've come myself to L.A., but I can't leave my gig rehearsal for many days and I don't have a passport."

I talked with her some more. Sherrie appeared rattled by these phone conversations with Ted, which only made Marilyn's presence in Sherrie's life more tangible. Earlier, when I began to organize Sherrie's trip to Los Angeles to meet with me and Ted, I began to notice her increased emotional response. However, after this phone conversation, I felt very disappointed that she couldn't come. At least she would meet with Ted. Unfortunately, later that same month I was sorry to hear that these plans were dashed as Ted was severely disabled with back pain, needing hospitalization. Ted was devastated and told me that his cowboy movie parts, riding and falling off of horses, had taken their toll on him. I reassured him, wished him a speedy recovery, and said that he and Sherrie had plenty of time to meet. Little did we know.

Sent: March 18, 1999
From: Sherrie Lea Laird
To: Adrian Finkelstein, M.D.

Hi, Dr. Finkelstein,

Just got my e-mail today. I've been a combination of not home for a few days, busy with recording, and also working at my mother's work, all day every day and late into the evening. You know the old adage: When it rains, it pours.

No, no, about Ted, I would love to spend hours talking to Ted and you, so many of the same topics we would love to discuss together. The pictures are packed and sitting on the shelf in my cupboard, as yet unsent but will be sent. If I have hesitated it must be my subconscious fears cropping up. But I haven't meant to ignore the situation. I am very upset to realize Ted's wife, or ex-wife, I don't know, has passed.

And of course one of the major reasons I wished I had pursued this earlier is that Joe D., as you know, has passed and I almost feel at a loss for words. I feel cowardly for not trying to find you sooner, especially when I had ample time to pursue every angle of my situation. Perhaps I was not mature enough to handle it. But I kept thinking of my past loves and acquaintances and knowing time was moving on, but of course not really realizing the full effect the age difference has.

Dr. Finkelstein, I have some fears because I am so close to God and I count my blessings every day for this beautiful life I have this time. My family is so great and I'm afraid to shock them. They've always thought I was so different but this would really put me up there with the birds. (I realize, too, that MM wanted a great father who looked like Clark [Gable] and that is what I have. My father is very suave, an ex-policeman, and has those same type of looks. Sorry, that was off topic.) But don't get me wrong; this would never stop me from meeting with you and investigating my past. My biggest problem is time and my career.

The thing I share with MM in this life is that my ambition is unstoppable, and I have the same narcissistic qualities. And I felt it all come back when I spoke with Ted. What I felt was that I was dying to see Ted and I wanted it for his sake as well. But a similar feeling of being too busy came back. Will you ask Ted if MM was kind of unreliable when it came to the needs of others, when it would interfere with any career situation? I so want to pursue all of these unique things in our little circle we have formed. I suppose I'll have to make the time, won't I?

Talking to Ted on the phone definitely didn't feel one bit strange; it was instantly comfortable and I felt we could talk endlessly on everything. He mentioned Bob Slatzer and how ridiculous his claims were. Some things may have been exaggerated by Bob, etc. but I didn't feel animosity on this topic. Actually my gut instinct was to say some of it was true and that I had some compassion for Bob, who I feel was simple and had found a subject (MM) to make his life feel livable and important. But all this would come out (or not, if I'm actually crazy and not MM) in a regression session.

How could we move forward in such a manner that is safe and productive and not intrusive to my present career? Speaking of my singing career, I'm just now battling some mysterious throat situation. I guess I have been pushing my voice too hard. I also had an airway endoscopy on March 11. I'm not supposed to talk at all for some time but thank God there are no nodules as of yet. I once watched *River of No Return* and was fascinated how exactly our voices sounded alike. And it still bothers me today that people said she (me) couldn't sing. I've definitely heard worse voices even on the radio. I shouldn't take up your time like this. I am sorry for this huge letter.

Yes, please send my love to Ted. If he has e-mail give him my address. I hope you also have found a friend in each other. I would like to act very fast upon our secret, before anything happens to Ted. And, if it works out to be accurate, there are some others we could find.

My record company is supposed to release a single (a song) and follow up immediately with another this spring. In the meantime we are recording a full album. Perhaps we can make a tentative arrangement for the late spring, early summer. Perhaps you may come out this way, in which case it would be a lot easier for me to slip out without being gone for a week to explain where the heck I've been. Write back soon. I will mail the pictures to Ted tomorrow or this weekend at the latest. Thank you for all your efforts on my behalf.

Sincerely,
Sherrie
God bless you, too! XOXO

Sent: March 19, 1999
From: Adrian Finkelstein, M.D.
To: Sherrie Lea Laird

Dear Sherrie,
 Today I met with Ted Jordan and he expressed some con-cern that you hadn't sent the pictures. He thought he may have said something during your telephone conversations that made you indecisive. Ted is a fine fellow, as you probably know. He said he had no intention for that to happen. In any case, I hope you are doing well and making progress in your pursuits.
 I am just completing a book based on my lifetime work with reincarnation. The book is tentatively titled: *Soul Mate, I Love You Forever*. Otherwise, I continue my office practice and am looking forward to the time you would feel convenient for me to assist you in exploring some of your other lives.

Love and God bless you!
Adrian Finkelstein

Despite my leaving many phone messages, Sherrie didn't return my calls. It was as if she had all of a sudden grown cold and distant. In a way I felt rejected, but I understood this was my own countertransference or projection onto my patient—or in this case, my research subject. After all, Marilyn had a history of suddenly breaking ties with people, and apparently that trait had carried over to Sherrie in this life. Marilyn's history included first husband Jim Dougherty, her young lover Ted Jordan, later husbands Joe DiMaggio and Arthur Miller, and many others. After all, why would I be any different? I'm only a psychiatrist poking my nose into her private affairs. Then I realized that this was the result of a deep-seated subconscious conflict. She had sought me out in the first place; I didn't initiate this contact. The only conclusion was that Sherrie was terrified to face the truth. She wasn't ready yet.

March 21, 1999

Finally, I got a hold of her. "Hello, Sher! How are you doing? I bet you're pretty busy with your music."

"Yes, I am and I'm damn mad with my band. They treat me so badly," she yelled out.

At this point I remembered Ted telling me about Marilyn's temperamental, emotional outbursts. It again dawned on me how similar the two were in regards to their career goals. Also, from my limited experience I saw how Sherrie, like Marilyn, would immediately apologize after a fight, as if the apology were magic and erased what had happened.

"So, you can't come for regressions. What a pity! Maybe some other time. Also, I'm so sorry Ted had to cancel his visit on account of his health."

"Please, give him my get well wishes," she said. Then, referring to her band, she continued in a morose and angry voice. "You know they could go and f— themselves." After a pause and still in an angry tone, she said, "You know, it's out of the question, endangering my career with these regressions. They [the band] already think I'm a nut cake. If I tell them that I am Marilyn Monroe reincarnated it would be the end of my singing career. And believe me I'm no less ambitious than Mar when it comes to my career. I'm the same. No one can interfere with it. Not my boyfriend, not you, and not my band."

"What do you mean, me?" I curiously asked.

"Sorry," she replied, catching herself. "I don't mean you. It just came out of my mouth. I know you want to help me. Thank you so much, but I cannot do it. I have to go. I'll send you an e-mail. Bye for now and my love."

I said, "Bye!" Then she hung up.

Outside of a cursory e-mail from her several days later, this was the last substantial contact I had with Sherrie Laird for the next six years. Sherrie, Ted, and I eventually dropped out of touch with each other. Sherrie continued with her singing career and Ted moved to Palm Springs, California, near his older, retired brother, who is an M.D. However, I still felt that if Sherrie could've handled it, past-life regression therapy could help rid her of her "dragon," as she called it years later. It could free her and her family of Sherrie's "Marilyn obsession," and I had no doubt it would have, in retrospect, prevented the two suicide attempts in the years after we broke contact. As for me, I immersed myself in my medical-psychiatric practice, with emphasis on past-life regression therapy and spiritual healing, and teaching a new generation of doctors at UCLA these lofty principles. However, the Sherrie/Marilyn case never really slipped from my mind. Despite being busy with numerous other projects, I continued my research by seeking out books, magazine articles, and Internet websites in which Marilyn Monroe was mentioned. I viewed many of her films. Over the years I amassed a great deal of information about Marilyn Monroe and I tried on several occasions over this span of time to reestablish contact with Sherrie but to no avail. Eventually, I concluded that she was not ready to pursue our research and deal with her dragon, and I just let it drop. Or did I?

I maintained contact with Ted for a while, initially visiting him at the hospital and giving him Sherrie's get-well wishes. In our last face-to-face conversation, Ted reiterated with conviction that Sherrie came across to him so naturally and compellingly as his old lover and friend, Norma Jean. Shortly after his recovery, he moved to Palms Springs and our contact continued intermittently for more than year before his health deteriorated further and we lost contact with each other. Ted had encouraged me to write a book about our mutual experience with Sherrie, but at that time the record was too incomplete to contemplate such a project.

Part II

MARILYN/SHERRIE RETURNS

It was the spring of 2005. It had been six years since my last contact with Sherrie Laird. In the interim I had relocated my office from west Los Angeles to Malibu, which was closer to my home, because of the long drive back and forth—usually in heavy traffic. I was still commuting three times a week to the Medical Center to teach UCLA third-year psychiatric residents complementary and alternative medicine. The emphasis was on therapeutic hypnosis, including a preview into past-life regression therapy and spiritual healing. During this period, most of my professional work included past-life regression research and therapy. I continued seeing patients from California and other states, as well as others from Japan, France, Korea, Israel, United Arab Emirates, Russia, and China.

In January of 2000, I had taken on a case that reminded me of Sherrie Laird's case. This patient was a renowned French singer, Michelle L. (fictitious name), who had flown from Paris for a series of past-life regressions. At the time, her songs were being played on radio stations throughout Europe. And, for only the second time in my experience, she revealed under hypnosis a past life as an entertainment superstar. Her name was Jean B. (fictitious name). Interestingly, both Marilyn and Jean died in their thirties due to an overdose of pills and reincarnated relatively soon after their deaths. As I've mentioned, this is the pattern with premature, unjust, and tragic deaths. Marilyn apparently reincarnated after 11 months and Michelle after three years. The reason for their depression, ending with the taking of their own lives, was comparable: a broken heart from being abandoned by the love of their lives, Marilyn by JFK and Michelle by a very prominent French politician. In my mind, this kind of synchronicity reinforced both cases. In this lifetime they continue to exhibit similar physical and personality traits as in their former incarnations, including bouts of depression and anxiety along with alcohol and drug abuse.

In February of 2005, I finished writing another book on reincarnation in which I combine my professional research and therapy work into past lives and spiritual healing, and the insights gained over three decades, with the wisdom of spiritual sages down through time. I tentatively entitled the book *A Psychiatrist's Notebook: Practical Self-Discovery & Self-Help Spiritual Guide*. It was very favorably endorsed in manuscript form by Bernie Siegel, M.D., founder of The American Holistic Medical Association and author of the bestseller *Love, Medicine, and Miracles*. However, I decided to blend this manuscript with my previous unpublished book on soul mates.

In reviewing thousands of regressions, the first case that came to my mind was Marilyn Monroe's reincarnation, but I would need Sherrie Laird's permission to write about her story. I had unsuccessfully tried to reach her several times in the past six years to resume our research. Now her phone number had changed and I found no further listing for her in the Toronto directory. I had slim hopes of locating her through other means and decided to set the project aside for the moment. Then, on April 7, 2005, I received the following e-mail from Sherrie. It gave me goose bumps. This message was followed by a rapid series of e-mail and telephone exchanges over the next several days as we renewed our working relationship and considered resuming our research.

Sent: April 07, 2005
From: Sherrie Lea Laird
To: Adrian Finkelstein, M.D.
Subject: Hello, Dr. Finkelstein! How are you? It's Sherrie.

I don't know if you also check into astrology but apparently Mercury retrograde talks about someone from the past trying to get in touch with you, and here I am. Do you remember me at all: Sherrie/Marilyn?

I have a new video out. I'll give you the link. Once again they insisted on changing my hair (I also have long red extensions in it) . . . It's my dance remake of Sade's "No Ordinary Love." It's all over the radio. The video barely even looks like me, particularly the end.

I've only ever wanted success, to talk to the public, and also save animals. I'm in a band now and you can check out a pic there. I have a short blonde wig on, 'cause I'm in an Annie Lennox tribute band. But there's a pic if you click on, with one of the other members.

Unfortunately, don't know if life is so [doomed] to repeat itself, you have to really fight to overcome its forces. I did attempt a suicide with sleeping pills twice and was hospitalized. I still wasn't seeing the connections so clearly, that it could easily be from the past [life]. I was in a very lost state. But either from spiritual connections or just straight up family ones, I realize how wrong, wrong, wrong that is. Why would I hurt people who love me so deeply? I think this is the lesson, you know, to be less selfish with yourself. I'm not selfish with stuff or things. But I think I have a problem with sharing me.

I was hoping you still remember me. I didn't mean to drop all this right off the bat. But e-mails are so convenient to just spill your guts.

How are you in California? I was in a strange mood when Joe DiMaggio died and I thought of Ted and my contact with him. I was hoping he is still alive. If this all turned out to be true, in the end it's a really horrible deal of the cards because with people passing and my life and financials make it so difficult to prove it all. I would have gladly been the guinea pig for it all and undergone hypnosis of all kinds. I'm pretty sure inside anyway that it wouldn't disappoint. Maybe we are not to know, as it will fill us with cockiness. However, wouldn't it free us from fear of death? Is man really to know anything for sure? Have we learned to know aliens as a fact or Heaven as a fact?

I hope you'll find time to write to me e-mails. I've had computer failures at this time, so fingers crossed this gets to you.

All my love,
Sher
XOXOXO

Sent: April 07, 2005
From: Adrian Finkelstein, M.D.
To: Sherrie Lea Laird

Dear Sherrie,

Is it a coincidence? No! I don't think so. Yesterday, before receiving your e-mail, I was thinking of you. I was absorbed with thinking that maybe, with your permission, I could tell your amazing "Marilyn story" in my new book. Of course your real name, singing profession, location, events, and Ted's name would be changed for confidentiality. Isn't it weird?

You look fabulous and sing like an angel. It pained me to read that you attempted suicide, and twice. But, I am also glad you have concluded that suicide is not the right exit. I haven't heard from Ted since sometime in the spring of 2000. It has been a long time, more than six years since we have heard from each other, and five years since my last telephone conversation with Ted. I hope he is still alive. I'll look for him.

Above all, I think it is a sign that we have reconnected. It is at least telepathy. There must be a reason that we independently thought about each other at about the same time, after such a long lapse of years. Certainly, if I could somehow be a sounding board for you, or assist you in any way, do not hesitate to tell me. It is now six years later in your life. What happened in the interim that you have come back, in spite of your fear that it may jeopardize your career?

Until then, love, peace, and God bless you!

Adrian

The truth of the matter is that I was initially leery about investing time and energy into this research with Sherrie after her sudden break-off six years earlier. I still needed to know what had been happening with her to ascertain if I could be of further assistance. I needed to know at a deeper level why she had reconnected. Was she having more flashbacks, depressions, compulsive acting out? How had her life turned out in the interim? These questions were answered almost immediately. A couple minutes after sending the above e-mail reply, I received a call from Sherrie. The following is reconstructed from my notes of the call.

April 7, 2005 10:10 P.M.

"Who's calling?"

"Yea, Dr. Finkelstein." Sherrie sounded very excited and enthusiastic, "I love your e-mail. So, you aren't giving up on me?"

"I'm so glad you called. No, I don't wish to give up on you. I'm just a bit wary . . . I wonder if this time you mean it."

"Dr. Finkelstein, this time I'm totally ready. I can't stand my life any longer. The flashbacks and nightmares of being Marilyn Monroe are worse than ever. At this point, I don't care about my career. My nights are hell and during the day I sleep on and off. I'm exhausted and I feel that if I continue this way I'm gonna end it all." I could hear her sobs at the other end of the line.

"How can I assist you now? Do you really feel suicidal? Do you intend or plan to kill yourself?"

"No, not now," she answered still sobbing. "But I feel so miserable, so unhappy, a lot of pain that is unbearable. Please, Dr. Finkelstein, help me!" Then she continued, seemingly in one breath. "I attempted at first to get help locally, but I was needing you to be my doctor again. Now how can I ever convince this educated and open-minded but probably very, very busy man, that he MUST help me? I don't have two dimes to rub together. I felt doomed from the start, but I said, 'Hey I don't even know how much it costs, but surely it will be worth it.' But then I spiraled out of control with the people in my musical career. I was getting consumed by it. Them telling me what to do and not considering my creative input . . . my 100% downfall, even as recently as my last video for 'No Ordinary Love.'"

I interrupted her long monologue and asked, "What happened with your musical career that contributed to what you call your downfall?"

"Before I made contact with you again, Dr. Finkelstein," she said, "without even knowing why, I said this video needs to be about reincarnation, show scenes of Mark Antony, Cleopatra, further back and to present day . . . that to me is 'No Ordinary Love,' old couples, and John and Yoko . . . What I have now is a been-there done-that, ordinary love video that was mimicked after a Calvin Klein commercial. Didn't Calvin already do that? I wanted something out of the ordinary. Isn't reincarnation 'in' at the moment? Sure, it's not following their typical thing or their typical taught thing. Half of the world and maybe more is aware of it, believes in it, or is just about to believe in it. I'd like you to please picture my chilled-out mix to the thoughts of reincarnation. It's beauty, it's haunting, and it offers endless possibilities for a fresh and new wonderful eternal life."

"I understand," I said.

"So, would you help me?"

I felt moved by her sincere words. "I would wholeheartedly, but this time we need to thoroughly check the logistics as I'm very busy with my practice in L.A. I'm not sure if you got a passport; the last time you didn't have one."

"No, I haven't got a passport."

"Sherrie, let's put everything on hold until we verify the logistics of our meeting together and possibly performing past-life regressions on you. Meanwhile, let's keep up a correspondence and compare notes."

Sent: April 08, 2005
From: Sherrie Lea Laird
To: Adrian Finkelstein, M.D.

Hi! Isn't it quite amazing? Something must have whispered

to me because I had gotten so busy and also had some tough times. You surely can use whatever you need in regards to the story. If by chance it should come out, and may in fact come out along the way anyway, that's fine too.

I want to recall all the things I've felt and remembered and known that have been strange symbols or coincidences, our touching base included. How unique, I wouldn't even know how to explain it.

That's great! You are writing a book. You must have already. I should be more attentive. And if you have one, I have to get it immediately. What a great study you've chosen. How did you come by this and are you completely convinced of it? Did you ever meet anyone else saying they were Mar? How would we go about getting information or do you already have what you need to create the story. I'd love it.

I think mankind needs to think outside the box and take their minds off the everyday common struggle and think of the endless possibilities we possess and could do so much more with them.

Funny, but just talking to you, typing rather, I feel I slip back into a way of thinking and talking that I've blocked for so long. No one besides Kezia (who was almost Natasha) and my aunt know, though several very close people, boyfriends included, get a sense of it. Even my younger boyfriend, who doesn't know much of Marilyn, will say if we see her, "You are her, you look like her, you are her, I wouldn't be surprised." These are things I don't fish for, but I say to myself, "If he would say this, it would be another sign."

I'm here for anything you need in regards to the book or seminar. You can refer to or talk about what you have to do. I totally give permission for that. It might be even more interesting to one day meet me or bring me to an event. We would maybe regress first.

. . . My boyfriend is Hungarian. I had a real comfort with him when I read or re-read somewhere that one of Mar's closest friends was the Hungarian photographer, Andre.

Well, I guess so much is coming back. Do keep in touch. I'm here. And if you talk to Ted, tell him we should chat again, even better on e-mail. I'm trying to be private around family members who are around. They already think I'm different, in a good way, but I don't like to scare them.

Good luck! Keep well!

Forward me any discussions or seminars you've had in the past: articles, etc. I would love to read them.

XOXO
Sher

Sent: April 08, 2005
From: Adrian Finkelstein, M.D.
To: Sherrie Lea Laird

Dear Sherrie,

Thank you for your e-mail and your permission. However, now comes the hard nut to crack: convincing people that the story is true. You expressed your own doubts at times and so do I. But, you and I seem to have faith that it is real. My intuition, which is usually correct, coupled with my lengthy experience in this field, tells me it is true. It remains necessary to convince the skeptics and disbelievers. That is why more tangible proof is a must, if we wish to present your case as a fact and not fiction. I have to go now, but I'll return soon and continue. Meanwhile, if you happen to read this e-mail and come up with some ideas, please let me know! Until then, take care of yourself!

Love, peace, and God bless,
Adrian

I took many hours pondering on how to proceed with this research. That night after e-mailing Sherrie, I couldn't sleep because I was intently thinking about our situation. If I waited, she could waffle again and back out as she had done in the past. What it came down to was the fact that the only hope for this woman's recovery was a series of past-life regressions. It appeared from our last conversation that her psychological condition had worsened. I had no doubt that if her demons weren't unearthed and dealt with in this manner that continued drug and alcohol abuse would lead to a tragic end. And if she couldn't come to me, I would have to go to her. The sooner the better.

Sent: April 09, 2005
From: Adrian Finkelstein, M.D.
To: Sherrie Lea Laird

Dear Sherrie,

. . . I wanted to let you know that I've reached a decision. This time I'm not waiting for you to come to L.A. I am planning to be in Toronto probably in mid-May to visit with relatives. If it is okay with you, we may schedule a time and place for a research past-life regression.

Meanwhile, if it is of any assistance in facilitating your relaxation and thus enhancing your memory, visit my web page: www.pastlives.com. [Here I gave instructions on activating my streaming video, Time Travel, which enhances past-life recall.] Please, write to me of your experience!

By the way, our first contact with Ted was in March of 1999. It's been a while. Also, I thought I lost his information. However, only a few minutes ago stretching my hand over hundreds of folders and without looking at the alphabetical order, I picked up exactly Ted's folder. Coincidence? I don't think so . . . I found both his telephone number and his brother's, Dr. Benjamin Friedman. I tried Ted's number, but I got a fax sound. Then I tried his brother's and left a message on his answering machine. Hopefully, he will return my call. I'll keep you informed.

And now, not as doctor to patient, but as friend to friend, I would like to share with you an insight that occurred to me, and forgive me if it does not apply. I had a dream and immediately upon waking, it hit me that you may feel threatened by revisiting M's life. Her life was fraught with pain and suffering. Also, any time you make strides forward toward M's level of success, you may feel again threatened and troubled—like you become Marilyn again. Following this, you retreat or even go to the extreme by contemplating in desperation doing away with yourself, as you told me it happened twice since 1999.

My recommendation for your consideration is to be aware of this possibility, and thus not let it disturb your present life because now you are in charge of your destiny. You are Sherrie, not Marilyn Monroe. God loves you and you love yourself. As you inquired of me to give you information about my work, I recommend you read the attachment, *A Psychiatrist's Notebook: Practical Self-Discovery & Self-Help Spiritual Guide* (60 pages), before we proceed with our plan.

Love, peace, and God bless you!
Adrian

Sent: April 09, 2005
From: Sherrie Lea Laird
To: Adrian Finkelstein, M.D.

I love your idea. I think this is an amazing way to start, and that you're coming to Toronto. This is amazing.

Funny, but I live on a street called Avenue Rd. and several of the places look very '50s, and I wondered, is it just my connection to the '50s, or have I/Marilyn actually been thru it? Why would she come to Toronto?

. . . So I'm going to get started on that as soon as possible. I'm both excited and terrified. Yes, it's true what you said. In previous attempts I felt threatened by [my past life], and thought only bad could come of it. But, perhaps with my very fortunate realization, that if nothing more it's cruel to hurt your loved ones. I wouldn't hurt myself again.

I felt safe with the words of comfort you gave me to get started and I will use those and print them out, too.

I can't wait for Ted to get back to you, and I also remembered a trip to Montego Bay, where I had a flashback. There are things that we can ask Ted; he must know if it's accurate or not.

I'm scared that I will not come thru for everyone, but I know it's time and this should be done. One shouldn't take this kind of thing with them, without finding out the truth. I surely would have backed out before now, if I wasn't at least 85–97% sure. People are just meant to question themselves, whether they are right or not, I presume. We will do all we can to get this information correct and out.

So, God bless you, too, and I will see, talk, or write to you very soon.

Good luck!

I'll be ok.

XOXO

Sher

P.S. There just was an eclipse on the 8th. Astrologically, it brings a massive change and decision for career and life. Without even thinking of this happening within a matter of four days to a week, suddenly it's upon me. And I have to say, absolutely with no pre-planning from me, so we are surely being guided by something. I don't know what.

We continued to e-mail each other. During these communications, I urged Sherrie to meditate on her Marilyn flashbacks and nightmares, but also to strengthen herself in preparation for her past-life regression work. She agreed and said, "Okay, yes. I think we should do that. For instance something I remember, though I admit suppressing it for the last four years or so, maybe less, and lately it erupts more than ever and terrifies me, being Marilyn, feeling Marilyn, thinking and acting Marilyn." She said that while she had her kitchen painted turquoise, she felt an overwhelming "past-life thing." Sherrie would say, "I still have it for turquoise color of paint. It just takes me way back."

Then Sherrie continued by enumerating other "coincidences," which I call "synchronicities," this term being more precise. Sherrie described a flashback of being at a concert, perhaps at Carnegie Hall. Sitting under a chandelier, she was watching a performance by Frank Sinatra back in the '50s. But, awhile after she'd seen pictures of that place in her mind's eye and thought there were seats, there was no longer a chandelier.

She also had a picture of being escorted up a flight of stairs by perhaps two nuns and maybe a man. It's a place that looked older though new for the time, and she could see a huge water tower.

These flashbacks could have been from the filming of Marilyn's first successful movie, *Niagara*.

Sherrie was very much relating to Marilyn's pregnancies and her burning desire to have a child. There were many other striking resemblances: the neediness of her personality, the vanity, the makeup skills, the drinking—especially in combination with pills. Others were her choice of art, her concern over the plight of blacks, her love of animals, her needing an older man—the daddy figure. When overwhelmed, she would exclaim, "Oh God! So many things. If I wasn't her, I am her complete clone. She was a good singer and people didn't think so. I even walk around naked in the house like her." She would complain. "I'm not comfortable around most women, but when one is loving, absorbing that and feeling it is even better than the love of men, as it is more complete."

She related, "My dad looks like Clark [Gable], but also I recognize many of the faces (Hollywood actors and actresses, and producers, directors, and cameramen) from that era. Not knowing why, I love Donald O'Connell, the face of Zanuck [studio boss at 20th Century Fox, where Marilyn made many of her movies]." Sherrie would feel attracted to several people in old films without knowing why, and then discover that Marilyn had been in a movie with them.

One time Sherrie described a rather morbid vision. "I have a vision of a casket. Maybe this would help, but it used to be a very strong vision of black and maroon. A Kleenex box used to remind me of it, but I see a place. The casket is on an angle near a front window. Very nice black. Very nice deep maroon. This is something I would have no way of knowing; I've never read anything about it." Was she referring to Marilyn Monroe's casket?

On other occasions, Sherrie reminded me how much she would like to reconnect with Ted. "Wouldn't it be the most wonderful thing to come and sit in a room with Ted? I feel that if I was in a calm and relaxed state, I would remember everything." Unfortunately, Ted's brother still had not responded to the voice message I left on his answering machine.

Meanwhile, I arranged my flight to Toronto. I was scheduled

to arrive by Air Canada on Tuesday, May 3, and my departure flight was on May 5. As agreed, I notified Sherrie in order to coordinate the time and place of our meetings. She suggested I stay at a nearby hotel, the Holiday Inn, Yorkdale. She didn't know what it looked like inside, but thought it should be pretty good. She offered to pick up my wife and me at the airport.

A few days later, I finally found out that Ted Jordan had died on March 30, 2005, a week prior to the day Sherrie e-mailed me. It was very strange and a major synchronicity that after six years, Sherrie should contact me only seven days after Ted's death. I had finally got in touch with Ted's brother, Dr. Benjamin Friedman, who was broken up by his beloved brother's death and found it difficult to pass the news along. I immediately called Sherrie to inform her. I did remind her that in her April 7th e-mail she alluded to Ted's possible death. "I was in a strange mood when Joe DiMaggio died," she said. "And I thought of Ted and my contact with him. I was hoping he was still alive. If this all turns out to be true in the end, it's really a horrible deal of the cards, because with people passing and life and financials make it difficult to prove."

Sherrie's reaction to the news of Ted's death was devastating. She began crying on the phone and had to hang up. Later that day she e-mailed me about her reaction.

Sent: April 12, 2005
From: Sherrie Lea Laird
To: Adrian Finkelstein, M.D.

Oh, so sad, so sad, as I feel he truly needed to talk to me. And so now [I see that] I was frantic to talk to him! As soon as I've heard your words about Ted, I gulped and I also had the feeling that "if only," and this must have just happened shortly ago. It does make sense as we're being propelled to further it.

I've been having frights for the last two nights. Since using my new mantra, "I am one with perfection," I'm looking forward to the relief of any bad dreams. However, I'm not having bad dreams, but bad things [happen] just before sleeping.

Recently I had pneumonia, and around January 12th I had

a terrible near-death experience. It was blackness and I felt my chest being crushed, and I was surrounded by dark figures, and my soul was being pulled out of my solar plexus area. I was being lifted. I was pulled upward, but it couldn't be sucked out. So, I'd fall backward.

I told the nurse before I was admitted, "I will die if I'm not seen soon." Her quote: "It's just the flu; go home, blah, blah, blah . . ." However, the last two nights [I experienced] the same squeezing that happened with the turquoise paint and/or the pneumonia. So, you are right. There is much resistance and great fear of going prematurely, or while sleeping, for sure. I've got to find a way to calm myself from it being so frightening. Could I end up dying from doing research? No! Right? Well, obviously, I was thinking of Ted and was probably thinking of him even more so around that time.

I decided to go onto the Internet to try to see if anyone has come forward saying they were M. Couldn't find anything, but I did find that M . . . was wearing the color of her casket. It does not spring forth any memories of a bronze casket with satin, as when I see a flash of a casket of that period of time I see dark maroon, black. However, I do link it to a Kleenex box that is half and half, and I've seen her tombstone and I definitely feel, just a calm indifference that she's not in there at all. I'm seeing there is work to do here on earth. There is something more she/we/me are meant to do . . .

I had some more things to tell you but am needing some time to think of Ted and what it all means and what to do next. I feel utterly saddened, as I think our friendship grew even deeper post mortem and that now it's my turn to miss him. Tears are coming to my eyes.

Keep well, Doc! You are an important ally. I hope I do not let you down.

P.S. Just wanted you to know, I realize that I've read so much about the past, but two things occur to me: A) that I think of things first and then they are confirmed, and B) I seem to know what is true (what feels right or feels wrong and untrue). So, I think we are safe.

At this point the difference between working with Sherrie as a research subject and working with her as a doctor treating a patient had reached a critical point. I wasn't licensed to practice psychotherapy in Canada, and while regression work there would be therapeutic, it was still research and not therapy. What I could offer was my continued support as a spiritual mentor of sorts, as opposed to her visiting Los Angeles, where I could treat her as a patient. In that capacity, I immediately responded to her call for help.

Sent: April 12, 2005
From: Adrian Finkelstein, M.D.
To: Sherrie Lea Laird

Dear Sherrie,

Yes, think about Ted! However, as you've realized it is no problem in our research, but only Marilyn dreading while Sherrie knowing that "dying prematurely" is not true. Sherrie knows that life goes on and that there are many positive wonderful things to be done. One of them is to practice that strengthening awareness—that the casket's or grave's color doesn't mean anything because you live forever. You most probably are that immortal witness from the grave, Marilyn, and this is what she offers you in a positive way. Otherwise, you are S in this life with a different learning curriculum than M, in a way.

The similarities between you and her that are negative must be unlearned (i.e., let go of them); the ones that are positive should be cherished. This is the way to save and love M, by saving and loving S, for you are the same person. God is good and gracious. It has offered you a safety net to fall in, S, so use it wisely. We've already done some research footwork and many dots can be connected at this time. It just may require some additional so-called "coincidences" (which I call synchronicities) that fit together like a glove. See, it is not always necessary to go through a formal past-life regression to come to these proofs.

Coincidences: 1) Ted passed on March 30, 2005; 2) A week or so prior to your e-mail to me, I began writing a query letter for my new book which would cover your case, and I was planning to ask your permission to make it public, though I also wanted to reconnect with you for more research on this story; 3) Your e-mail to me on April 7, 2005, after more than six years of no contacts between us; 4) Your North Moon Node in both of your lives, as M and as S, is in the Sign of Cancer, which my 30-year past-life research experience confirms as one of the proofs in a majority of people who died prematurely, tragically, and unjustly . . . ; 5) I just happen to meet Ted Jordan at Christmas party in 1998, only months after you contacted me the first time. While alive, Ted confided to me the validity of many common memories revisited by you and him during your discussions with him six years ago. In lieu of regression work at that time, more than anything this convinced me that your claim was legitimate, and that is why I've hung in there.

Unfortunately, now Ted cannot be the witness on paper, but I am and my credentials speak for themselves. However, we may need more factual proofs, including the past-life regressions, which I promise to facilitate to the best of my ability and make it a pleasant experience for you. Think of Ted, then let me know of your thoughts. By the way, you are one with perfection when you go to sleep, as well as during your waking state. Toward the end of *A Psychiatrist's Notebook*, more precisely page 57, there is a question people often refer to: What is the most important spiritual guide you recommend? Wisdom's answer is BE AWARE OF GOD WITHIN, ALWAYS! Act constantly as if God were within you and you will witness so-called "miracles."

God be with you!

The following day Sherrie called to say she loved my encouraging words and promised to try to think of the positive. She added that she was losing the fear of proceeding with the past-life regression. I thanked Sherrie for her offer to drive me from the airport and recommending Holiday Inn, Yorkdale. My wife and I had made reservations there from May 3rd through May 5th, including transportation to and from the hotel.

Sent: April 14, 2005
From: Sherrie Lea Laird
To: Adrian Finkelstein, M.D.

Hi A,

I know I really should stop searching on the Internet, but this is something. After all this time, I've barely even thought of doing it. I decided to try to find M's teddy bear.

I also wondered about bulimia/anorexia in itself and if related to her or anything as I notice sometimes I go thru bouts of this and at certain times it really acts up, like now. However, I did stumble on this link: http://edition.cnn.com/SPECIALS/views/y/1999/10/tuchman.monroe.oct28/#2/. [No longer active.]

Apparently, there was a piece of paper—our writing has always looked the same as I noticed ages ago. But it says, "He does not love me." It was a very strong thought. When I first went back and thought of what could be the Lawford party evening, I had a very strong feeling of devastation and betrayal. It just felt like I had put all my eggs in one basket, and dealing with the deep truth that this man, JFK, did not love me back.

What's funny is here and now I don't find him [JFK] handsome at all. I don't like his hair. Whatever was going on there was almost a fantasy world. M just seems to be fixated on something, there must have been thoughts, more of, to be associated with a president would allow for more intelligent conversations and I'm betting it was also based on needing a podium to speak up and be smart and help the world. I do not see M as being any happier in that relationship coming to fruition. I think there has to have been a bigger goal/cause in [sight]. Plus, combined with the need for love, his love, to be a supportive force to carry on and of course the need for a child with him.

I'm feeling quite mad that all this attention for a man who, at the root of it all, was just a man, and perhaps a selfish stubborn, arrogant one. Part of the memory, where a man in a suit is sitting there, is that I see myself writhing around on the bed while he smiles. And I believe that there is at least one person outside the door. I also do believe there were in fact times that drugs were administered to M. That tidbit does seem accurate.

Back again,
XOXO
S

As Sherrie was still apprehensive about the regressions, I reassured her again on April 14 not to worry, that I'd be gentle on her and that I felt everything would be all right. I further emphasized during this phone conversation that the regressions should not be approached as a performance, but that they require for her to be and act herself naturally.

She was giggling and bobbling with enthusiasm at the other end of the telephone line, saying she couldn't wait to see me and my wife. She expressed her gratitude for my being "a rock" in our very ambitious project. She added that she needs a lot of healing, no matter the outcome. She asked me to take care of myself. A few days later I received from Sherrie a CD with her professional musical recordings as a gift. It was April 19, 2005. I called her and complimented her for her angelic singing voice.

I was in the process of preparing step-by-step our upcoming encounter. By this time Sherrie confirmed to me that she reserved the days I'd be in Toronto to be free from musical rehearsals or concerts in order to follow unabated with our research plan. I dropped her a few lines to touch base with regards to some tentative times when we could meet and proceed with our common research pursuits during my stay in Toronto. I gave her the proposed meeting times, in the hotel room for the regressions, as well as meal times that could also serve as informal processing time for Sherrie and me. I asked Sherrie to let me know her thoughts about this plan. Then I advised her to believe in God within and everywhere, in herself, and in the Higher Power working through her and me; thus, everything will be "a piece of cake." I reassured her again not to worry, that I'd be gentle with her and that she would be perfectly safe. I concluded by expressing my feeling our mission would soon be accomplished. Sherrie replied that the schedule was perfectly fine with her.

On May 1, two days before my scheduled trip, I was putting together the research I accumulated from books, magazines, and movies about Marilyn Monroe. Based on this information, and with Sherrie's life history and our communications, I derived a past-life regression questionnaire for our session work.

I planned this upcoming first round of regressions to mainly verify the authenticity of Sherrie's claim to be the reincarnation of Marilyn Monroe. The prepared questionnaire was mostly composed of "memory" questions. Sherrie had to remember from Marilyn's life names of people, specific events and experiences, family, friends, and films, as well as the corresponding stories and feelings associated with them. Therefore, the emphasis was to test Sherrie's "Marilyn memories," rather than to bring forth her most profound emotional experiences as Marilyn. In other words, I had to first prove that Sherrie Lea Laird is the reincarnation of Marilyn Monroe before moving to the second part, the real reason of our work together: the Marilyn/Sherrie healing process. (But even these question-oriented regressions, with the memories that surfaced during them, would start the healing process.) Once that was established, and after Sherrie had processed these regressions, I was considering a return to Toronto for a second round of regressions, mainly cathartic healing sessions. My primary interest was in the healing aspect rather than proving that Sherrie was the reincarnation of Marilyn. Therefore, I was intent on the depth of the emotional clearing in these sessions as well, probing such areas as Marilyn's death, her relationship with the Kennedys, other significant relationships, and also to heal Kezia of her own fixations as the reincarnation of Gladys Baker.

During this time, I was also considering and pursuing other avenues of proof. They consisted of the following: personality traits, physical and emotional problems, linguistics, writing style and graphology, and biometrics (voice; fingerprint; face, body, hands, and feet architecture; and hair analysis), and possibly DNA analysis. All the above potential proofs would establish resemblances, or the sameness, between Marilyn Monroe and Sherrie Lea Laird at many levels, which I felt would complement the regression work.

But in my experience of 38 years of practicing hypnosis, I knew that past-life regression performed during a somnambulistic state would be sufficient to prove whether Sherrie was the reincarnation of Marilyn Monroe. In the course of such a deep hypnotic trance, selective amnesia could be induced. Even before meeting Sherrie in person, my lifelong psychiatric professional work had sharpened my diagnostic skills. Thus, I could say with a high degree of probability that Sherrie would be a very good hypnotic subject capable of entering a somnambulistic state of hypnosis. As proven later on, I was correct.

Somnambulistic trance is tantamount to being injected with a truth serum: The subject follows the hypnotist's suggestions exactly. Therefore, during that altered state of consciousness, the hypnotist can suggest and thus induce selective amnesia; in other words, forgetting a select group of memories, usually only for the time the subject is under that deep hypnotic state. In Sherrie's case, such selective amnesia or forgetfulness would be necessary in order to erase, as it were, all memories, experiences, and feelings pertaining to Norma Jean/Marilyn Monroe acquired from books, magazines, films, the Internet, and any other sources of public record. Instead, Sherrie would be able to reveal to me—if she is really Marilyn Monroe reincarnated—only authentic memories, experiences, and feelings of her life as Norma Jean/Marilyn Monroe.

A Modern Hypnosis Dictionary by Tom Connelly, a prominent British hypnotist, gives the definition of selective amnesia as follows: "Inability to recall memories about a specific thing. Often used as a demonstration of hypnotic phenomena where a subject might be told to forget a number between one and five and then asked to count the fingers on his hand."

In the hypnosis specialty book *Hypnosis: Questions & Answers*, by Bernie Zilbergeld, Ph.D., M. Gerald Edelstien, M.D., and Daniel L. Araoz, Ed.D., specific (or selective) amnesia is described very clearly on page 177:

> Sometimes specific amnesias can be very compelling to a patient and provide an experience that teaches flexible control over memory processes. For example, it is suggested that on a television screen the subject will see numbers from one to ten randomly displayed.

As you begin to count the numbers aloud you will find that one of those numbers has been erased and it is gone. It has disappeared from your counting system. You can't find the number 'six' anymore, it is gone from your counting system, and in a little while, as you search for the numbers on the television screen and read them out to me, you will be able to find all the numbers . . . 1, 2, 3, 4, 5, 7, 8, 9, 10 . . . just like that.

Teaching a specific amnesia for specific neutral information may later provide the basis for teaching the patient to block out for therapeutic purposes specific real-life experiences that he may want to forget for a time period. It is especially useful as a method to teach the patient he has control over memory processes.

This suggestion under hypnosis would obviate any contamination from Sherrie's conscious knowledge of Marilyn Monroe during the regressions. But, as a point of clarification, Sherrie has always appeared candid and trustworthy to me when she communicated her curiosity, after a flashback of being Marilyn Monroe, to research that particular personal experience. Like Marilyn, Sherrie proved to be a sponge when it came to knowledge. Being very bright, Sherrie would look constantly for answers to understand her plight. That is why at times she would read books about Marilyn or view one of her movies. But, in my professional opinion, this inquiry wasn't to copy but rather to confirm the truth of her flashbacks and nightmares of being Marilyn Monroe reincarnated. Or, Sherrie would experience her own trait of personality, behavior, facial expressions and bodily postures, likes and dislikes, and then later she would check out and be amazed that Marilyn had the same trait or preference. By that time she had only read one or two books about Marilyn and watched only the movies *Bus Stop, Niagara, River of No Return*, and a few others.

On May 3, I was at the Los Angeles International Airport preparing to board the Air Canada flight to Toronto. I was very excited and had this heartfelt desire to help this very troubled woman. Finally the plane took off. I was on board with my wife and was so happy that she was supportive of me in this very difficult undertaking. However, I momentarily forgot about the difficulty of my mission, that it was like the "mission impossible" of past-life regressions. Instead, there was a second wind carrying me to an unknown destination. It felt like I was no longer traveling through physical space and time; it was as if I transcended all barriers and limitations and felt in "good hands." I believed my fervent faith in God would help guide us through this difficult terrain, not necessarily where we wanted to go but rather where we needed to go . . . so many synchronicities.

We arrived at Holiday Inn, Yorkdale, on schedule. It took only a few minutes to install our luggage in the room, and then, I immediately called Sherrie, wearing my heart on my sleeve. I didn't bother this time to control my enthusiasm, my positive emotional outpouring. It was contagious, or Sherrie felt the same way, because when she and Kezia appeared in the hotel lobby we had a very emotional get-together. We instantly recognized each other and hugged. Then we went to the hotel's restaurant and I ordered dinner. Shulah came down from the room and got acquainted with Sherrie and Kezia, and then she left to have dinner with my cousin Anca, who lived with her family in Toronto.

After dinner we went up to the room on the tenth floor, and I explained to Sherrie about the room arrangements. I had my video camera available and Kezia had hers. The room was luxurious and spacious enough, allowing the three of us to sit comfortably. We had rented a non-smoking room so the air was fresh. Also, it was soundproof. There were two queen-sized beds; the one closer to the window was more suitable for Sherrie to lie on during the regression, as the video camera could be placed on a small round table adjacent to it. The heavy curtains were closed for privacy. However, Sherrie could use a thick, plush, comfortable armchair as well. Now we were set up for the first regression. After all of us used the amenities, we were ready to proceed. In the first regression session, Sherrie relaxed on the bed while Kezia sat nearby, focusing her video camera on Sherrie's face. I stood at the foot of the bed with my handheld video cam.

"Truth Serum"—Somnambulistic Hypnosis Past-Life Regression Conducted by Dr. Adrian Finkelstein on Sherrie Lea Laird; May 3, 2005; Toronto, Ontario

Sherrie was wearing a Kabalistic red string for protection on her left wrist. She signed the informed consent after I explained the facts about hypnosis to her. She said that she underwent hypnosis in the past for stage fright and that she is a very good subject. Nevertheless, I reviewed the usual questions and answers about hypnosis with her: Hypnosis is not sleep, though a person may fall asleep while under the hypnotic trance. If I use the word "sleep" at any time, I'm not referring to the natural sleep state, but sleep of the nervous system and the whole body. Hypnosis is a state of different degrees of one's conscious mind being tuned in to the subconscious. The subconscious is programmed to control the physical body, giving it illness or health according to its false or true beliefs, respectively. Therefore, consciously tuning in to the subconscious can influence it to faster and better accomplish positive goals. The subconscious also contains the memory bank, where memories are stored in the form of pictures or word clusters. Once we are tuned in to it, we may retrieve memories, emotions, and experiences from this life and past lives, inter-lives, and future lives.

The subconscious contains the seat of emotions (emergency and welfare) and desires (assimilation and elimination). Addictions to alcohol, drugs, work, television, people, and so forth occur at this level. An addiction is an exaggerated emotional attachment that hurts us. The subconscious, with the mentality of a young child, does not know how to let go of addiction. It requires better tuning of the conscious mind and its adult intelligence to convince the inner little child, the subconscious, to release the attachment. Increased demands of our conscious mind on the subconscious, without considering its abilities and limitations, result in destructive stress. Then, the inner little child may say, "I've had it. I'm going to check out of here." First it may give warning signs, such as anxiety, anger, depression (which is internalized anger), and other negative reactions. This negativity may induce different physical ailments. The extreme could be heart attack, stroke, or cancer. Thus, by being better tuned in to the subconscious, one can understand and cultivate this inner little child. According to behavioral studies, a vast majority of people mostly act on automatic pilot (i.e., their inner little child level). Ironically, the mentality of this child in our society is of a three- or four-year-old. Therefore, it's no wonder that there is so much misery and unhappiness in the world.

Then, what is the solution? It is to consciously tune in to the subconscious and deprogram it of the negative and reprogram it positively. The subconscious contains the psyche, or lower intuition, to preserve its life. Through better tuning we can unleash this ability to our benefit. The automatic pilot got contaminated by bad habits, biases, prejudices, false beliefs, principles, and pride, and programmed by authority figures such as parents, who were in turn programmed by their parents and so on. Parents are generally not to blame, as they did not know better. It is not difficult to figure out that better conscious tuning in to the subconscious enables us to identify and thrust out of our lives all this nonsense; it really liberates us. It results in deriving more joy and happiness from our lives.

I emphasized to Sherrie that past-life regression work means nothing unless it liberates her from emotional blocks by consciously recognizing them and explaining them kindly and firmly to the little child within, thus releasing them. These blocks consist of anger, depression, fears, jealousy, and envy; hatred against the self and/or others; false beliefs; and all other kinds of negativity. Then, I explained to Sherrie the rules of time travel; namely to "let go and let God," followed by the withholding of judgment, critique, and analysis during the whole process of the regression. In other words, let the brain rest and the heart speak. The heart tells the truth, and the truth will set her free. Another rule is to allow impressions to flow freely in from her five senses (sight, sound, smell, taste, and touch), her inner intuitions, and physical sensations: one or a combination of those. Whatever comes, or does not come, she should accept. A well known axiom of wisdom dictates that we get in life not necessarily what we want, but for sure what we need. And still another rule is that the first impression is on point, usually correct, and then the subsequent impressions follow, as accurately as the first. Naturally, do not question any of these impressions. Just accept them.

As the mind is multidimensional in time and place, one may be here and now in this room with me while at the same time somewhere else and in a different time period. Thus, don't be turned off and deny the experience because you are also here and now. Some people are afraid that regression is a time machine and that they may get stuck in a past life. This does not happen. It is like going to a concert. When the concert is over, you leave the concert hall. Another concern is the fear of experiencing a horrifying episode from a past life. In such cases, one always has the option of stepping back or floating away from the disturbing situation and watching it from a distance as a spectator. If the experience is very disturbing, one also has the option of opening one's eyes and coming out of the hypnotic trance with only positive effects. I encourage people to stay with the experience if at all possible and if they can tolerate it. Often one can understand the past life better through intense feelings and thrust its present negative consequences out of one's life once and for all, especially through emotional abreaction. Get it out of the system, as one might say.

Following these explanations, I proceeded with instant hypnotic induction. Standing by the side of the bed, I asked Sherrie to place her right hand palm down on my right hand. As I looked at the root of her nose, I asked her to look into my eyes. Then I instructed her that I was going to count to three. At the count of three she was to press down on my hand with her hand as hard as she could and hold it. At that point I suggested to her that her eyes were growing tired, droopy, drowsy, sleepy; that they want to close and rest; that they should close. As she closed her eyes, by surprise I suddenly retracted my hand from under hers and fired the suggestion: "Sleep!" It was obvious that she entered a deep trance. I then instructed her to count backward from 100, noticing that after two or three numbers the rest of them would grow dimmer and distant before completely relaxing out of her mind. I further instructed that the numbers would literally be erased, together with all the acquired information about Marilyn Monroe from books, movies, and any other source of outside information. Instead, if she really was Marilyn Monroe reincarnated, she would remember only unadulterated memories, feelings, and experiences arising from her inner self. She was then in a somnambulistic state, as evidenced by her waxy looking face and total amnesia and anesthesia, as tested by pinching her forearm hard, which her daughter Kezia witnessed. No pain. The information to be obtained from her from this point would be true. This state is even more informative than being under a "truth serum" since we aren't chemically numbing important brain cells, which can hold even more precious memories. This is why in this somnambulistic state the subject obeys the suggestions from the hypnotist exactly. Thus, my suggestion to erase all acquired memories about Marilyn Monroe would be followed by Sherrie.

After the hypnotic induction, the regression session began.

Finkelstein: I'm going to count backward from five. When I reach one, you will experience a pleasant childhood event. Number five, go back in time as your body is growing smaller! Number four, your body is growing smaller and smaller and smaller. Number three, people around you appear younger. Number two, pay attention to details! Number one, be there and experience this event as if it is happening right now and here!

Laird: [Smiling, apparently enjoying playing with her toys. Her lips are moving as if uttering some words, but her voice is too whispery and imperceptible.]

Finkelstein: [After about a minute] I want you to remember this positive experience as a child, and during times of meditation in a safe place, get tenfold or more impressions around this event. This will help you to understand yourself better, ridding yourself of any block. Thus, you will be able to derive more joy, love, happiness, and success in all your endeavors.

I want you now, only if you wish, to go back in time to when you were in your mother's womb, just prior to being born in this lifetime. As I count backward from five, you will gradually recapture your experience in your mother's womb. Allow impressions to freely flow in from all your senses—sight, sound, smell, touch, and taste—your inner intuitions, your physical sensations: one or a combination of those. Whatever comes or doesn't come, you totally accept. It is perfectly okay. If you feel uncomfortable, you always can float away and watch it from a distance as a spectator. If you feel very uncomfortable, you can even snap completely out of your trance, be filled with light, and feel well. But if you don't, I urge you to stay with the experience. This way, you can better identify the blocks consisting of negative emotional experiences, thus thrusting them out of your life once and for all.

Now I start counting. Number five, returning to your mother's womb. Number four, you are sharply focused on your womb emotional experience. Number three, by this time you may become aware of things happening outside the body. Number two, pay attention to details! Number one, be there and complete your experience! I'll talk to you in a while.

Laird: [Smiling, comfortable.]

Finkelstein: What's your experience?

Laird: [Moving her lips in contentment, but the words uttered by her are still imperceptible.]

Finkelstein: It appears you feel good.

Laird: [Affirmative facial expression.]

Finkelstein: Now I want you to experience, without any undue discomfort or pain, that you are being born.

Laird: [Begins sobbing, very frightened; her lips are moving more intensely, but her words are like whispers and are imperceptible.]

Finkelstein: [After several unsuccessful attempts to elicit a perceptive verbal reaction from Sherrie, I start to comfort, reassure, and calm her down.] Enough! You're just fine now. You're completely detached from this experience. You are safe, calm, and comfortable. How do you feel?

Laird: [Calming down, obviously feeling well now, as suggested; still with a whispery and hardly perceptible voice.] I'm okay.

Finkelstein: What made you cry and be scared?

Laird: [Voice still whispery, but more perceptible.] I felt separated from my mother and not placed on her body . . . as I did with Kezia.

Finkelstein: Okay, I want you to relive being born this very moment, and you are placed this time on your mother's body. How does it feel?

Laird: [Smiling, evidently feeling safe and comforted; uttering with the same very soft voice.] I feel good.

[This is an example of what is termed in hypnotic jargon "corrective experience." When the subject goes through a negative experience the hypnotist has the option to correct it, which brings about a favorable therapeutic result for the subject.]

Finkelstein: And now I want you to see, sense, or feel in front of you this beautiful door through time and space. I'm going to count backward from five. As I do, this beautiful door will slowly open, and eventually you will step through to the other side into one of your past lives . . . And if you really were Marilyn Monroe before, you will relive her life as if it is happening right now and here. You will have already transcended all barriers of time and space when I reach number one. Thus, you will be able to remember everything you have ever experienced in that life to a "T" . . . because you are not merely in this life and in this physical brain and body. You are far, far greater. You are immortal, a beautiful being of life, light, purest love; always loved; never alone; and eternal. You are a multidimensional self in time and space.

Withhold the judgment, critique, and analysis! Let go and let God! Allow impressions to freely flow in from your five senses, inner intuitions, and physical sensations: one or a combination of those. Whatever comes or doesn't come you totally accept. The first impressions are on point, correct. Just accept them, followed by subsequent ones. If anything makes you feel uncomfortable at any time, float away and watch it from a distance as a spectator. If you feel very uncomfortable you can at any time completely snap out and emerge from your trance altogether with only positive, healthy, and constructive effects from this experience. But if you can, stay with the experience, as this way you can emotionally free yourself from the bondage of past blocks that prevented you from being your true self. In other words, cleave to God within you and everywhere and feel totally fulfilled.

I start counting. Number five, the beautiful door through time and space is gently opening, revealing a brilliant bright light on the other side. Number four, the light becomes brighter and brighter, and it attracts you like a magnet. And now you are stepping on the other side. Number three, a physical sensation, a thought, a feeling . . . Pretty soon you are going to join one of the most important events in that other life and will be able to speak loud enough for me to hear you, without disturbing your beautiful level but on the contrary enhancing it by verbally communicating with me. Number two, pay attention to details! Number one, be there! I want you to tell me now what is happening.

Laird: [Still with a whispery, soft voice] I am wearing white shoes and white shorts. I'm graduating. I'm 19. I wear this crown and a banner from the modeling school. But it's just pretending; I'm not really winning. They are pretending to clap and be happy. [This could be due to a movie portraying a beauty contest in which she wins; therefore, it makes sense to remember herself as Marilyn Monroe instead of Norma Jean.]

Finkelstein: What's happening next?

Laird: [Softly] I'm going onward, hard work.

Finkelstein: What is your name?

Laird: Marilyn Monroe. I'm 19. I'm with Ted Jordan, my boyfriend.

Finkelstein: Isn't your name Norma Jean?

Laird: Yes.

Finkelstein: What are you doing now?

Laird: Going out when I should be trying to find work. I'm trying to have fun. Ted, Ted is giving me drugs. I'm doing drugs, but I'm strong enough not to get hooked on them.

Finkelstein: Is Ted your boyfriend you've just mentioned?

Laird: Yes . . . No . . . He is a fat man. Also, he is also Ted.

Finkelstein: Could he be your boyfriend's uncle, Ted Lewis?[1]

Laird: Yes, yes, he is his uncle. He cares for me, but he is hurting me, giving me drugs. But I like them. I'm sad because I'm supposed to be working. I get depressed, but I take them to unwind and feel more confident.

Finkelstein: Is Ted doing drugs? [Referring to Ted Jordan.]

Laird: No, he likes to drink and he just wants to party. He wants everyone to have a good time and be happy.

Finkelstein: At one time before this session, you mentioned to me Montego Bay. Does it ring a bell?

Laird: Yes. I'm with Joe in Montego Bay. I'm with a husband. I'm dancing and playing and falling in the water.[2]

Finkelstein: What are you doing now with Joe?

Laird: I'm going with Joe to the opera or theater to see a play.

Finkelstein: What is the name of the opera?

Laird: I think it starts with M . . . M . . . Madam . . . I think, *Madam Butterfly*. [It could be *Call Me Mame*.]

Finkelstein: Did you enjoy it?

Laird: Oh, yes. Joe enjoyed it very much. I have these ticket stubs from the theater, which I keep them in my little case with a small teddy, it's my little baby.

Finkelstein: What case?

Laird: My little teddy bear I also keep there, in a small oval suitcase. A lady has it.

Finkelstein: You said before that you are Marilyn Monroe. But when I asked you if your name was Norma Jean, you said it was. Then, why did you say first Marilyn Monroe, when at 19 you were only known by the name Norma Jean?

Laird: [Having trouble speaking louder] I feel this numbness in my mouth and face. I'm Marilyn Monroe. I was Norma Jean. Now I'm Marilyn Monroe.

Finkelstein: Why is it that in your life as Sherrie you reincarnated, of all places, in Scotland?

Laird: My father now was a royalty in the remote past, 1145, and we had a relationship. I think because they are brave. [Hardly uttering the words] But now I'm Marilyn Monroe. My mouth . . . I cannot move it . . . It is numb. My face is numb. I feel this crushing feeling in my chest.[3] [Sherrie is very pale and obviously in great distress.]

Finkelstein: How do you feel?

Laird: [Hardly uttering the words] I feel awful . . . thick, like everything is too thick and suffocating. Like I'm sinking.

Finkelstein: Now you are Sherrie, not Marilyn Monroe, and you feel just fine. The numbness of your mouth and face and the crushing sensation in your chest are completely gone. You feel well now. How do you feel?

Laird: I feel good.

Finkelstein: Is there anything you wish to say before I ask you to emerge from the trance?

Laird: No.

Finkelstein: Then, I'm going to count to ten. As I do you are gradually emerging with every count. At ten you will be back to your usual alert waking state with only positive, healthy, and constructive effects from this experience. You will be able to remember everything that you have experienced today, and get tenfold or more memories, feelings, and experiences while meditating on this session in a safe place. Next time you will go deeper more quickly and achieve more. I start counting. Number one, beginning to emerge. Number two, emerging more and more. Number three, feeling great. Number four, emerging more and more and more. Number five . . . Number six . . . Number seven, feeling wonderful . . . Number eight . . . Number nine, in full control of your body and mind . . . Number ten, fully awake and alert and feel good!

Sherrie was sitting up on the bed. She said, "I feel surprised and exhausted, also a little guilty that I haven't given more in this session. I would've liked to get more specifics, but I felt as if I was not deep enough under trance. Now I brought up more questions than answers."

I reassured her, "According to the clinical signs, you were in a somnambulistic state and it is normal to get the feeling that you weren't deep enough. Next time I'll demonstrate hypnotically induced anesthesia to show that you go very easily into a deep hypnotic state during which anesthesia is possible. You've done wonderful. The fact that at this time there are more questions than answers is good. What is typical is that in the end of the session, when your subconscious felt off the hook, so to speak, you revealed a very important piece of information. You revealed your experience of numbness in your mouth and face and the crushing feeling in your chest. These symptoms are the result of drugs."

She appeared unconvinced. "But in this life, since age seven and throughout my childhood and early adolescence, I've been experiencing these distressing symptoms. I surely wasn't on drugs during that time."

I explained. "It appears that you, as it often happens with many other people who are regressed into a past life, experienced the end of your life as Marilyn Monroe first. In other words, it is a customary event for subjects being regressed into a past life to not report it in chronological order, starting with the beginning of their lives. On the contrary, they start with the end. It is like a videotape; it ended and now it is being rewound from the end, which is close to death. That is why you revealed your name as Marilyn Monroe first, rather than your name in the beginning of that life, Norma Jean. Also, you encountered the sensation of numbness in your mouth and face, which prevented you from perceptibly uttering words.

"The feeling of your chest crushing is relevant as well. It tells us [as Sherrie confirmed in a later regression, and which my previous research bore out] that about 15–20 minutes prior to her death, Marilyn experienced a horrible crushing feeling in her chest and numbness in her face and mouth. The explanation is the many Nembutals, Seconals, and chloral hydrates she ingested with champagne. Being fat soluble, these drugs may take 15–20 minutes to be completely absorbed in the central nervous system, which is mostly made out of fat, to totally penetrate the vital centers in the brainstem, starting with the respiratory center. It is a rather gradual process until all these fat-soluble substances are completely absorbed. Obviously the crushing feeling in the chest is the result of a partially blocked respiratory center due to the partial absorption of the drugs . . . The numbness in the face and mouth is due to hyperventilation and hypercapnia [the excess accumulation of carbon dioxide, which can cause numbness].

"It is worth noting that Marilyn liked the color turquoise. In the end she apparently realized that she took too many of these drugs and could not return. At that moment it appeared that she really wanted to live and that last thought, plus the horrible crushing sensation in her chest, may have been associated with the turquoise color of the sky, but it was too late."

Sherrie agreed, "Yes, yea. That's true." She regained her confidence and conviction, "From childhood, just looking at the color turquoise gave me a crushing sensation in my chest and numbness in my face and mouth. It's got to be true, then. Yea, that makes me feel much better."

I took the opportunity to point out, "Sher, now you can see how the regression gives you more conscious access to your past-life memories. This can be scary as you proceed with them."

"Yes, it was scary. But why do I feel more relieved now?" she curiously inquired while smiling.

"You feel better because by thrusting out of your system some of the emotional poison from your past life some of the healing happens, some of the release you see after the regression session. After all, our main objective isn't proving your case as being the reincarnation of Marilyn Monroe but healing you as a research subject."

Sherrie began giggling, obviously enjoying what we were doing. She raised her hands above her head and with exuberance shouted, "Yea! Thank you, thank you, thank you! I feel so much better about the whole thing!" Kezia, who was sitting nearby all this time, clearly enjoyed her mother's positive reaction and was smiling from ear to ear.

NOTES FOR CHAPTER 6

1. Ted Lewis, the paternal uncle of Norma Jean's boyfriend Ted Jordan, was a famed Hollywood entertainer in the 1940s. According to his nephew and confirmed in Sherrie's regression, Ted got Norma Jean heavily hooked on drugs. Under regression, Sherrie first attributes Norma Jean starting on drugs to Ted Jordan though it appears that this is not the case.

2. Marilyn Monroe spent a memorable vacation with husband Joe DiMaggio in Montego Bay.

3. Marilyn Monroe died of respiratory failure according to Thomas Noguchi, the coroner who performed the autopsy. Immediately prior to her death, she likely experienced a crushing sensation in her chest due to the gradual involvement of the respiratory center in the brainstem by the barbiturates in her system.

MARILYN RECLAIMED

Past-Life Regression Conducted by Dr. Adrian Finkelstein on Sherrie Lea Laird; May 4, 2005; Toronto, Ontario

Before beginning this session, I wanted to prove to both Sherrie and Kezia the anesthesia state as one of the main signs of somnambulistic hypnosis; the others are very deep relaxation, a waxy facial appearance, and amnesia. I asked Sherrie to sit in a comfortable armchair. I placed her under a somnambulistic state of hypnosis using the same instant induction method as in the first session. Then I told her, "Now I'm going to work on your right forearm and I want you to tell me what you feel. Okay?"

"Okay," she whispered.

Sitting close as Kezia watched intently, I placed my hands on Sherrie's forearm and pinched it very hard. "What do you feel?" I inquired.

"Nothing. Just a little pressure," she softly replied.

"Now I'm going to count up to three, and you will emerge with only positive results and be completely awake with the full memory of what happened, and how you felt as I worked on your forearm. One, two, three. Completely awake!" I commanded. She opened her eyes. "How do you feel?" I asked.

"Good," she answered.

"Do you remember what happened?" I asked.

"Yes," she replied casually. "You touched my forearm."

"Did you feel any pain when I touched your forearm?"

"No, just a light pressure."

I said, "Now I'm going to work on your arm again as before. Only now you are in your normal waking state, not in a somnambulistic state of hypnosis." I again placed my hands on Sherrie's right arm and pinched it very hard, like before.

Only now Sherrie jumped and screamed, "Ouch!"

I released her forearm and apologized, "I'm very sorry!"

Awe was written on Kezia's face. She exclaimed, "That's amazing!" Then turning to her mother, she explained what happened.

Now it was Sherrie's turn to express her awe. "No kidding, I didn't feel any pain." It was very obvious that from this point on both Sherrie and Kezia were convinced that Sherrie did indeed reach a somnambulistic hypnotic trance state. This certainly made it easier to achieve the maximum benefit from the hypnotic regressions that followed.

After this experiment, I placed Sherrie again under a somnambulistic state of hypnosis by reiterating the preparatory suggestions from the previous session. Namely, I suggested that Sherrie erase all information about Marilyn Monroe that she derived from books, movies, and any outside sources. Thus, if she is really the reincarnation of Marilyn Monroe she will be able to recall and respond to my questions with only unadulterated memories, feelings, and experiences. During my 38 years of practicing hypnosis, I have found this method to be better than a "truth serum," Pentothal, or Amytal. Pentothal can obliterate important memories and it indiscriminately numbs brain cells. Contrary to a Pentothal interview, an interview under somnambulistic hypnosis makes use of all important memories; it isn't indiscriminate, as the chemical tends to be. Moreover, the depth of the trance ensures that the subject follows exactly the hypnotist's suggestions. In Sherrie's case, this brought accurate, valid reporting from her Marilyn life experience.

I checked to make sure that Sherrie was in a somnambulistic state as evidenced by her very deep relaxation. I tested this by lifting her arm and letting it drop, watching it plop freely onto her lap. Also, she had a waxy facial appearance; and amnesia, analgesia, and anesthesia were present. Thus, I decided it was now safe to ask Sherrie established facts about Marilyn and gauge her responses. I proceeded with my inquiry.

Finkelstein: What does the name Emmeline Snively bring to mind?[1]

Laird: [Anger, impatience.] I'm nervous. I don't think she likes me. I get a headache.

Finkelstein: Do you remember the Blue Book Modeling Agency?[2]

Laird: Yes.

Finkelstein: What comes to mind when you think of the Blue Book Modeling Agency?

Laird: Nothing. Appointments. Lunches.

Finkelstein: What about Emmeline Snively?

Laird: The second name is right. The first is not. I think I call her Miss. I have to do what she says.

Finkelstein: Why?

Laird: Because she won't book me. She tells me what to do.

Finkelstein: What does she tell you to do?

Laird: How to sit, how to stand, how to be. Everything.

Finkelstein: What do you remember about Haig Nightclub?[3]

Laird: Business suits. Scotch.

Finkelstein: What about Eddie Friedman?[4]

Laird: [Laughs] It's funny.

Finkelstein: Why?

Laird: Ted, he doesn't like it. He wanted a handsome name. He doesn't want that name; people will think things.

Finkelstein: How about Slapsy Maxie?[5]

Laird: [Laughing] Is it a man? Is it a place? We call it something different. Someone that works there. [It turns out to be a man, a boxer, and a place.]

Finkelstein: Any feeling about the Earle Carroll Theatre?[6]

Laird: Curtains, singing, choirs.

Finkelstein: Have you heard of Mocambo?[7]

Laird: Is Lili there?[8]

Finkelstein: Yes, Lili is there. How about Brothers Club?[9]

Laird: Yes, they're always telling jokes and pranks; playing tricks on whoever is around.

Finkelstein: What about the Brothers Club known for music?

Laird: In a different connotation, yes.

Finkelstein: Red Dragon, does it ring a bell?[10]

Laird: It's a product. I don't know; I think so. It's a label.

Finkelstein: Didn't you work there as a waitress?

Laird: Oh, yes, but it was for a short time. Not really so.

Finkelstein: How would you describe Grace Goddard?[11]

Laird: Aunty Grace. She was skinny, nice . . . kind . . . she's good.

Finkelstein: What do you remember about Gladys Baker?[12]

Laird: She's something else. She is something else. She doesn't know how to love me. She doesn't really want me. I would have taken care of her. I tried to love her.

Finkelstein: Who is she?

Laird: My mother.

Finkelstein: Do you remember the white piano?[13]

Laird: Yes, I love it. My mother got it. I think it belonged to someone, a lady and son.

Finkelstein: Does the name Mortensen evoke any memory? Is he your real father?[14]

Laird: No.

Finkelstein: Have you heard of C. Stanley Gifford?[15]

Laird: Yes, he is my real father.

Finkelstein: Do you recall Tijuana, Dr. Law, Gomez?[16]

Laird: [Laughs] It's about Groucho.

Finkelstein: What about Tijuana the place? Is it dirty?

Laird: Yes, I don't like it there. I don't feel I can go there for an abortion.

Finkelstein: What does Revival Meeting bring to mind?[17]

Laird: It is about life, about being, healing.

Finkelstein: Who are Damon Runyon and Walter Winchell?[18]

Laird: Is he a politician? Churchill? Yes, gray suit. Helping me with my work.

Finkelstein: As an actress?

Laird: Yes.

Finkelstein: Who is Leon Shomroy?[19]

Laird: A doctor? No, an assistant. He is helping me.

Finkelstein: Have you associated or had a relationship with Bugsy Siegel?[20]

Laird: I see him there. No, we didn't. But just flirting. I get called away to work in time. I leave for work. And it saves me. He's kind of not nice.

Finkelstein: Can you say something about Johnny Hyde?[21]

Laird: He's the kindest person I've ever met so far. He's always nice to me, taking me places, making me sit with him so people see me. He's trying to help me.

Finkelstein: Did you love him?

Laird: [Crying] I loved him as much as I could.

Finkelstein: What makes you sad?

Laird: 'Cause I have to start over and I'm all alone.

Finkelstein: How does he die?

Laird: He has chest pain and respiratory illnesses.

Finkelstein: Any feeling about Nembutal, Seconals?

Laird: I'm dying . . . I'm smoking . . . I'm taking them. I feel lost when he is gone, alone . . . I don't care about anything.

Finkelstein: Who is Harry Cohn?[22]

Laird: He is nice but firm. I like him. He cannot show he is nice to me in front of others. We don't always get along.

Finkelstein: Would you tell me about Lili St. Cyr?

Laird: Beautiful. Everybody loves Lili. She shows me how to move my hips, and she tells me how to be with men, to treat men, and how to fluff up their egos. And lips.

Finkelstein: Yes, what about lips?

Laird: She shows me my lips . . . how much lipstick to put on, and to make it heavy on the outside.

Finkelstein: Who is Joseph Schenk or Shank?[23]

Laird: He is the boss to make movies. People look up to him.

Finkelstein: How about Darryl Zanuck?[24]

Laird: I like him more than he likes me. He thinks I'm trash. He has no romantic personality. If only he would like me more.

Finkelstein: How about Jean Norman?[25]

Laird: [No answer]

Finkelstein: Can you tell me something about Helena Sorell?[26]

Laird: Fashion . . . She is making my hair look nice.

Finkelstein: Do you know Laurette?[27]

Laird: She is telling me about my name.

Finkelstein: What name?

Laird: Marilyn Monroe.

Finkelstein: Who taught you how to fix your eyebrows, how to accentuate your mouth more by opening it slightly when a picture is taken, making you look a thousand times sexier? Also, who taught you to look in the picture like you're half asleep? Who told you men go crazy over that? Who showed you how to move to accentuate your best parts?

Laird: Lily St. Cyr earlier and Whitey[28] too. But I know myself.

Finkelstein: Amazing, Lily St. Cyr appeared to me in a vision and told me she did it.

Laird: Yes, in the beginning. Then, was Whitey.

Finkelstein: Who was Bruno Bernard?[29]

Laird: I'm standing at a party with my Bernardi.

Finkelstein: Can you tell me about Peter Lawford?[30] Was he perverse in any way?

Laird: He is my good friend.

Finkelstein: Is he doing weird sexual things? Did you sleep with him?

Laird: No. He is only like that 'cause of alcohol and drugs. He's more normal. People only think that 'cause he's pretending. He doesn't like his dad. He's very nice to me.

Finkelstein: Any word about *Ladies of the Chorus*?[31]

Laird: It's a song and a movie. Nice! Singing. I like it. They're jealous, 'cause I got to sing more.

Finkelstein: What do you play in it?

Laird: A girl. I'm more snobby. They don't like me.

Finkelstein: Tell me about Fred Karger. Did you have a relationship with him?[32]

Laird: Karger.

Finkelstein: Ah, you know him?

Laird: Yes, he's leading me on. I don't know why. I feel so foolish. Why didn't he just tell me he's getting married to someone else, Laura Lei or Jane, or someone he thinks is better than me?

Finkelstein: Can you tell me about your relationship with Natasha Lytess?[33] Did she try to touch you?

Laird: Well, I think she is alone, too, and she is sad. But no, Natasha would not, would not dare to approach me sexually. She knows I wouldn't like that. It would upset me. She is my everything: my friend, telling very funny stories.

Finkelstein: How about *Love Happy*?[34]

Laird: Not very long . . . fun . . .

Finkelstein: How about your nude pictures displayed in barbershops?[35] How do you feel about how much money they make later on?

Laird: I don't really care. I don't care about money. I'm annoyed. It's worth so much more. Not fair, but I let it go.

Finkelstein: What do you care about if not money?

Laird: Comfort. I care about comfort.

Finkelstein: Who called you "Woo-woo girl"?[36]

Laird: Ted is calling me that to tease me.

Finkelstein: Why does he call you that?

Laird: Something lopsided and tipsy, 'cause of my boobs.

Finkelstein: What do you remember about *The Asphalt Jungle*?[37]

Laird: It is about unhappy people. People in conflict, crime. I play a secretary, maybe. No, a girl.

Finkelstein: What memories are evoked by *All about Eve*?[38]

Laird: It's a movie. I had a small part in it. It was a success.

Finkelstein: The Red Diaries.[39] Any thoughts?

Laird: It isn't one. I don't know. What is it? It is not what I call red. It was brown, maybe reddish brown. I don't think so. I wrote down what I ate, drank; my thoughts; poems.

Finkelstein: Spyros Skouras in 1951.[40] What does it bring to mind?

Laird: He is the boss. He decides where, how much. He is strict, promoting, demanding. In the end he wants it to work.

Finkelstein: What do you remember about Sidney Skolsky?[41]

Laird: He is good. He's one of the nice ones.

Finkelstein: Yes. Did he help you, like you?

Laird: He promoted me big. He supported me.

Finkelstein: Was Jerry Wald convinced by Sidney Skolsky to put you in the movie *Clash by Night*?[42]

Laird: Yes, but I got a minor part. But it helps me.

Finkelstein: Did you love Joe DiMaggio?[43]

Laird: Yes. He is tall and handsome and my body type. But he is dull. He never talks.

Finkelstein: Why did you marry him?

Laird: I thought it would work. I thought that's what everyone wanted. But it's boring, he never has fun. Everyone loves Joe. He's a man's man. He gets along with the men.

Finkelstein: It is 1952. And there is *Niagara*.[44] What memories does it evoke?

Laird: Yes, very exciting. It's about me, but they make me to look older. I don't like that younger people are in the set, or they make me look older.

Finkelstein: How much did you earn a week? [$750.00]

Laird: $742.00. Sometimes more . . . 5 . . . because if I need stuff. I don't have things. For things I need.

Finkelstein: It is 1954. *Gentlemen Prefer Blondes* is on theater screens. Can you tell me about it?[45]

Laird: Very big. Big production. Lots of people. Glitter. I am the movie. It is too late. Inside, something is missing. I don't care. I want to care.

Finkelstein: How is it working on the movie? Is it hard, easy, medium?

Laird: Sometimes hard, sometimes medium. It's a lot of work.

Finkelstein: "Diamonds Are a Girl's Best Friend."[46] What does it mean to you?

Laird: [Laughs] They are and they should be.

Finkelstein: Whom did you call "the cunt?"

Laird: Bette Davis. I said she was a mean bitch.

Finkelstein: How about Joan Crawford?[47]

Laird: Yes, I call her "the old cunt." Nobody likes her. She is nasty. I don't know why men like her.

Finkelstein: Did you feel disappointed about Ted Jordan and Lili St. Cyr's marriage?

Laird: Yes, at first. Then I was fine with it, 'cause she is my friend, too.

Finkelstein: What do you remember of *The Seven Year Itch*?[48]

Laird: With Tom Ewry [Ewell]. Fun, very fun. I enjoyed it.

Finkelstein: Have you heard of Jerry Giesler, the divorce lawyer?[49]

Laird: Yes, he was very smart, strict. I wouldn't want him to be against me.

Finkelstein: Is he your lawyer or someone else's?

Laird: Yes, he is my lawyer.

Finkelstein: Does he help you with a divorce?

Laird: Yes.

Finkelstein: From whom?

Laird: From Joe. He keeps papers for separation, protecting me legally from Joe DiMaggio.

Finkelstein: Would Sherrie refrain from being successful in fear of the same things happening to her? Does she resist?

Laird: Yes, I don't want to feel it again.

Finkelstein: Can you tell me what do you feel about Lee Strassberg and his wife Paula?[50]

Laird: Teamwork. Best for everyone. They love me.

Finkelstein: Why become Jewish?

Laird: Yes, I'm half Jewish. I feel Jewish.

Finkelstein: Why becoming Jewish?

Laird: I like studying, and traditions; the possibilities of eternity.

Finkelstein: It is 1956. *Bus Stop* is released. What occurs to you about it?[51]

Laird: I like him, Murray. He's crazy in the movie. They make up. Just funny.

Finkelstein: It is 1956. What business deal did you make with Fox?[52]

Laird: I bought the rights to have my own production company.

Finkelstein: How do you feel about *The Prince and the Show Girl?*[53]

Laird: Very frightening and fun. Laurence is so important. Very good and loving moments.

Finkelstein: Is Laurence Olivier a spoiled person?

Laird: Sometimes, but he has earned it. Sometimes we are happy and sometimes we are apart, not talking.

Finkelstein: Who is Ralph Greenson?[54]

Laird: My doctor.

Finkelstein: Referring to Dr. Greenson, did you express yourself at one time that you want to be cured, not to find out why you are "crazy"?

Laird: He is trying to help. He doesn't know what to do. He wants me to have rest. But then I cannot be successful. He knows. Too many different pills.

Finkelstein: Does he say that "you don't need a man to feel whole"?

Laird: Natasha says it and he says it, too.

Finkelstein: *Some Like It Hot* brings to mind what?[55]

Laird: I feel fat, ugly. I don't like it. Very terrible.

Finkelstein: Fat and furious? [Laughs]

Laird: Yes, fat and furious.

Finkelstein: Do you believe Tony Curtis meant it, saying that when he kissed you he felt like he was kissing Hitler?[56]

Laird: No, he didn't mean it.

Finkelstein: It is 1960. What do you have to say about *Let's Make Love?*[57]

Laird: Not myself in this movie. I don't get to be me. No, I think he [Yves Montand] is the real star. It's his movie. No one seems to really care properly.

Finkelstein: Did you have a love affair with him?

Laird: Yes.

Finkelstein: Did Arthur Miller, your husband, call you a "no-talent pill popper?"[58]

Laird: It is very true. He and many people. If I don't find my talent, I take pills. It hurts.

Finkelstein: What do you think about Clark Gable[59] in *The Misfits?*[60] That he died?

Laird: He is beautiful. He has not had it easy with a younger wife. He is not happy. He is lost. He tries to cheer me up, but he is not happy. Like the blind leading the blind.

Finkelstein: What about Payne Whitney Psychiatric Clinic?[61]

Laird: Not good. I don't want to stay. Joe is getting me out. I'm too far gone, out of control. I cannot feel emotions. I'm messed up. I'm in a fog because of the addiction.

Finkelstein: Have you heard about the Rat Pack?[62]

Laird: Peter and Sammy and Dean.

Finkelstein: Do you recall the meeting with someone, facilitated by Peter Lawford and Pat Kennedy Lawford at Bing Crosby's house in Palm Springs?

Laird: Peter is there and Pat.

Finkelstein: Yes, Peter is there. Who else?

Laird: Jack is there, he comes there . . .[63] [referring to President John F. Kennedy]

Finkelstein: What did you help him with? Did you fix his back?

Laird: [Laughs] Well, sort of. I fix his hair and help him with a speech. But they are just joking. I didn't really fix his back.

Finkelstein: So, you didn't really fix his back.

Laird: Jack joked that I fixed his back. I pushed it with my knee. I've been with Jack for several years before he became president. I have a crush on him. Peter makes me meet him. So exciting; very exciting. Being with him is wrong for the country. I thought we would make the most beautiful couple for America.

Finkelstein: What is Dom Perignon?

Laird: Champagne.

Finkelstein: Is it your favorite champagne?

Laird: Yes.

Finkelstein: How do you feel about "Happy Birthday to you, Mr. President"?[64]

Laird: One of the biggest nights of my life.

Finkelstein: Have you discussed JFK with Jacqueline Kennedy? Talking about her with your friends, did you call her "the statue"?

Laird: I don't like that woman at all. She is ugly. Her bulging eyes.

Finkelstein: What is your relationship with Elizabeth Taylor? Did you physically fight with her?[65]

Laird: She is snobby. [Laughing] I provoked her to get angry. Just a push. No fight. A little struggle, it was silly. I can be . . . kind of manipulative, too.

Finkelstein: Any thoughts about Natalie Wood and Warren Beatty?[66]

Laird: She is a goody two shoes. He is very young. Cute; all the girls want him.

Finkelstein: Were you carrying Jack's child and have an abortion when you were two months pregnant?

Laird: I told him I was pregnant, but I saw his face. For a while, I pretended, but then I felt sorry for him. Bobby Kennedy asks me if I'm pregnant or not. I am late. I tell him I'm pregnant. His reaction is one of panic.[67]

Finkelstein: Your doctor, Ralph, tried to teach you that you don't need men to make you feel worth it. You are worth it on your own right. Is that true that you thought God made a truly sick joke with Marilyn Monroe and you prayed to Him to bring Jack back, and maybe you'll feel Him more?

Laird: Yes.

Finkelstein: It is August 4th or 5th, 1962. Are you experiencing a suicide through an overdose of pills and alcohol?

Laird: Yes.

Finkelstein: How do you feel, now that is all ended?

Laird: I feel cheated. It went so fast. It all was such a short time, really. [Crying] I feel shame. I feel sorry for my friends and my doctor.

Finkelstein: Who is the person who advised you as you described in your diaries the following: "I must start feeling my self-worth and stop thinking I need a man to feel important"? [Advised by Dr. Ralph Greenson]

Laird: Natasha said it.

Finkelstein: How about Dr. Ralph Greenson? Did he say it?

Laird: He said it, too.

Finkelstein: Did therapy by your doctor really help you? You remarked in your diaries, "I'm a good person. I'm worthy of love. I'm good in bed. A million years of therapy sessions go down the drain."

Laird: Ralph did the best he could. He tried to help.

Finkelstein: Do you recall wearing a brunette wig, a little pill-box hat, and a conservative blue suit?

Laird: Yes.

Finkelstein: Did you meet with Jacqueline Kennedy while dressed like this?[68]

Laird: Yes. [Doesn't seem to want to talk about this.]

Finkelstein: At times you pronounced yourself that most of the time you cannot feel God at all. Is it true?

Laird: Yes.

Finkelstein: Who taught you about God's help among your good friends? [Jane Russell]

Laird: Jane.[69]

Finkelstein: Being Sherrie, can you say that Kezia is the reincarnation of your biological mother, Gladys?

Laird: Yes.

Finkelstein: Now, as you remain in the same level of hypnosis, open your eyes. I'll show you different pictures I want you to identify. Okay?

Laird: Okay.

Finkelstein: What is this? [Picture of neighbors Beebe and future husband Jim Dougherty]

Laird: They are my neighbors. And she is my cousin or sister through marriage. She is not really my cousin. Not by blood.

Finkelstein: Is it your husband Jim?[70]

Laird: Yes, but he doesn't look like that. He doesn't look good like that.

Finkelstein: Do you recognize the people in this picture? [Picture of Norma Jean, age 16, at a family gathering; beside her stand her two aunts]

Laird: [Smiling, with a happy look on her face] Yes, they are my aunts.

Finkelstein: Who else is there?

Laird: It's me. I am there.

Finkelstein: Can you recognize this picture? [Formal wedding group picture from June 1942 of Norma Jean and James Dougherty]

Laird: [With exaltation] Yes! This is my wedding to Jim.

Finkelstein: What about this one? [A rare snapshot of Norma Jean with her mother, taken at a Santa Monica Restaurant in 1945; also shown are Norma Jean's two aunts, guardian Grace Goddard, half sister Bernice, and Bernice's young daughter]

Laird: [Emotional] Wow, they are my family!

Finkelstein: Point them out for me!

Laird: [Pointing out] My mother, my sister, my aunts, myself.[71]

Finkelstein: Who is the lady in the rear center?

Laird: Aunty Grace.

Finkelstein: What is the occasion that the family is gathered for?

Laird: It is for my job as a model. I have my job now.

Finkelstein: Do you recognize this picture? [Norma Jean's first modeling shot, a shampoo ad from 1945]

Laird: It is my first ad. I'm a model. A shampoo ad.

Sherrie correctly identifies four more pictures of Norma Jean taken at the beginning of her career as a model.

Finkelstein: What do you think? [Nude picture of Lili St. Cyr]

Laird: She is beautiful.

Finkelstein: Who is she?

Laird: Lili St. Cyr.

Finkelstein: Do you recognize the man in the picture? [Ted Jordan and wife Lili St. Cyr]

Laird: Yes, [it] is Ted. Ted Jordan.

Finkelstein: Have you ever been lovers, you and Ted?

Laird: Yes, in the beginning.

Finkelstein: How about later? Did you remain close friends?

Laird: Yes.

Finkelstein: Also with Lili?

Laird: Yes.

I show Sherrie more pictures and she accurately recognizes the people in them. One is of Ted Lewis, Ted Jordan's uncle and a famous entertainer in Hollywood. He supplied Norma Jean with drugs despite his nephew's vehement protests. She did not like the nude picture Ted Jordan took of her. When I showed her a drawing of herself that she gave to her tailor to use to make her dress for JFK's birthday, she said:

Laird: That's me, that's me. That's the way I look.

Finkelstein: Anything more?

Laird: It's for Jack. No, it's not for Jack's birthday. It's not a black dress.

Finkelstein: It is not a black dress. It is for a very important night, one of the biggest of your life. Now, do you know more about this drawing?

Laird: Yes, I drew it for Jean-Louis to make me this glitter . . . this dress for Jack's birthday party. I am frightened. Singing for him in front of all these people. They hate me. Peter made it easier for me. He introduced me.

I continue my probing of Sherrie in her somnambulistic level of hypnosis.

Finkelstein: Now close your eyes and tell me, have you learned or assumed Marilyn's personality to defend yourself

125

against fears or insecurities in your life as Sherrie, or in order to advance your career as Sherrie to become famous as a singer?

Laird: Not at all. I never wanted to be Marilyn Monroe and suffer like her. I haven't been a fan of her.

Finkelstein: Marilyn, what made you love animals so much, a love you carry into your life as Sherrie?

Laird: Animals are the essence of pure love and life.

Finkelstein: Marilyn, I want you to say more about your relationship with Jack. How would you describe it?

Laird: Jack claims he doesn't love me. He loves what, who I am. And we are so different. He is organized and clever. I make him frustrated. With me he cannot concentrate. So much amusement to tolerate. So much work to do. He knows the country can be at war and he has to focus.

Finkelstein: What do you feel about Jack's younger brother, Bobby?

Laird: Bobby is our friend. Nice but strong. He could have been a great president. Everybody liked him. He would have been a better president than Jack, as he listens to everybody. He is younger than me, 34. I prefer Bobby—he is nicer and not married. He has a girl, a fiancée. I did lose interest in Jack. Not everybody knew that. I found Bobby more interesting. Jack was not as handsome anymore and got sick of me and pitied me. I hated that. I switched affection from Jack to Bobby. No time to marry Bobby and I'm falling apart. I created a persona I don't recognize. With friends drinking and having fun. I can't feel anymore. Good days are when I can get up and get dressed. Bad days when I cannot do that. Because what should I do? It's just not going to happen. I'm feeling very down and I stopped talking with Dr. Ralph Greenson. He comes by and brings me some replacement pills.

Bobby doesn't see me enough. He is very busy with a case. Very investigative. He is telling me how they are going to win due to a lot of information. I love Jack, if anything. Joe and I made plans to rescue me. I'm not married to Joe, but he is going to help me, if it is working. It will work. I don't stay. I have plans with Joe. He hugs me. I feel good with him. I felt good with Frank [Sinatra] a long time ago. I want to save my dogs. I didn't take into consideration I did wear fur coats. Sometimes I thought about it. It's Hollywood after all, no choice. I see it now as Sherrie. I knew at 80 Ted would stop. I knew I had to hurry. I felt it was an emergency when I connected with you.

Going to an event and asked to appear like in the picture *Hollywood Gala*. This event is different because of who will be there at the competition. I need to look better. There will be a man there. [Remembering the sketch she did, how to appear, her dress, her hair, the earrings . . . "for my tailor to take care of that"] I've drawn that before several times, for a movie gala to the Oscars. [She is talking of the celebration of JFK's 45th birthday in Madison Square Garden at which she sang "Happy Birthday, Mr. President".]

Finkelstein: Marilyn, would you tell me about the last days of your life?

Laird: Very lonely; very afraid of life. I don't see the outside world clearly for what it is with friends. My score of friends are in a similar state and cannot help each other. We're doing drugs and winding each other up. I got fed up and made a very big mistake, and I thought I would come back like before. I feel this crushing in the chest, half an hour and 15 minutes. I took all 15 Nembutals, champagne. Earlier I drank milk. I have taken ten of these chloral hydrates and maybe more again. I was calling Peter. I wanted to call several people, but I just got drowsy. I wanted to say I really did it this time. This crushing . . . Something is going to happen. Crushing feeling, I don't feel it. I took it. I see it away. No pain. Turquoise color, I see it on cars, a baby blue dove. It's my color . . .

Finkelstein: What's happening now? Are you still there?

Laird: Yes, close by the body. Hours go by. A Chinese man is opening the body. He does not care. In a life before Marilyn I had a vision of it. The Chinese man is in a hurry, Lee Noguchi. [Japanese by name; Marilyn saw him as oriental and said Chinese.]

Finkelstein: What's happening next?

Laird: People wonder what to do with me. I see Peter, Pat, the housekeeper, Joe. They don't get a chance to do something nice. Peter is very upset. He says, "it's all my fault." He feels guilty. He did not come over. I feel so bad for Peter. Bobby is very upset, just in shock. Jackie is relieved, but sad. I feel sorry.

Finkelstein: What's next?

Laird: Darker first, then it goes. It takes a long time, and you get to feel all your thoughts, what you plan to do.

Finkelstein: Are you alone?

Laird: Speaking with somebody about what to do next. No talking. Sort of similar approach to a doctor in this life. Giving advice, especially one, not God, but of God. Feeling wide awake. Having to hurry to get back. If you wait, you still have to come back but there will be change.

Finkelstein: Are you aware that Jack died the following year?

Laird: Aware, but not of my interest anymore. I have love now for everybody.

Finkelstein: Is this somebody of God guiding you? What is your lesson?

Laird: To love my family. I want to give them a good life, to be happy for them. If I can be happy, I can correct, be spiritually grounded and connected [watching her mother, Kezia is weeping]. I feel caring for everybody. I feel many people will believe. A lot of people would want to talk about it and talk with me.

Finkelstein: What do you feel about me?

Laird: You are the guide. You are the spirit guide in flesh. I have the answers because you know and are the master teacher. I cannot waste time being depressed. I have come to realize I can escape to love fiercely, change, not hear suffering and take it too personally. Offer as much compassion as I can give. I'll try to be helpful. Hurrying to come back to have my baby girl. If coming another time I will not have her. There is free choice, but it can be altered.

Finkelstein: I would like you to re-experience being born, this time around as Sherrie.

Laird: Bright. My mother is happy. She wanted a girl. She is relieved. She loves me. I love her, too. My mother is my friend, my

best friend. She could be my sister. "It's killing me that she is sick."
She is better. Oh, her own mind. She's choosing. I'm feeling hopeful and optimistic. [Weeping] Tears of happiness. Tears of happiness.

A Marilyn fan might say: MY LOVE, WHEN YOU CRY YOU
DON'T LIE.

The first round of regressions came to an end. We all felt a
great sense of accomplishment. I had no doubts that Sherrie Lea
Laird was indeed the reincarnation of Marilyn Monroe. Now, the
skeptical reader may question that assessment and say that if I
could research all of this information about Marilyn Monroe, so
could Sherrie. But, I need to reemphasize, as I cited earlier from
journal articles and from my own experience, the absolute prohibition of selective amnesia about the use of conscious-mind information. In this context, as a professional with almost four decades
of experience practicing hypnosis, I can unequivocally state that
under somnambulistic hypnosis, Sherrie was unable to "act out."
She was compelled by my suggestions to tell the truth.

Another telltale sign is the feeling level of her responses. I
would ask her a fact question like, "What does the name
Emmeline Snively bring to mind?" And, instead of saying she was
the director of the Blue Book Modeling Agency she tells me,
"Anger, impatience. I'm nervous. I don't think she likes me. I get
a headache," in the voice of a teenage girl. I asked her about Eddie
Friedman, and she laughed and told me that Ted Jordan didn't like
it [his birth name], that "he wanted a handsome name. He doesn't
want that name [obviously Jewish]; people will think things."
When asked to remember her mother Gladys Baker, she
responded, "She's something else. She is something else. She
doesn't know how to love me. She doesn't really want me. I would
have taken care of her. I tried to love her." This may seem superficial, but in my experience the heart-aching sincerity of these
responses speaks the truth: Sherrie was tapping the emotional
memory of herself as Marilyn Monroe.

Sherrie's and Kezia's reaction immediately following the

regression was very emotional; they cried in each other's arms. This was followed by a sense of awe and profound relief. Sherrie felt a great measure of healing associated with these regressions. She felt that the "dragon" had lifted and she felt infinitely lighter. It was evident that she had experienced a degree of emotional healing. I gave Sherrie a post-hypnotic suggestion to recall everything she experienced under trance, and it was the emotional counterpart of this experience that assuaged any doubts in her mind of having been Marilyn Monroe. She now felt they were one and the same person and that by picking up where Marilyn's life had been cut short, Sherrie could learn from that experience and not repeat the same mistakes.

After the regression, Sherrie, Kezia, and I ate lunch in the hotel dining room and talked about the regression session. It was sort of a debriefing, reaffirming, and clarifying conversation of the general results. We just picked at our food, filled from this experience with what I would call a kind of manna—God's spiritual food. Later that night, I played the videotape of the regression in our hotel room for my wife. Her mouth fell open, and she was awed by the high emotional and cathartic release. My doubting Thomas was now totally convinced.

NOTES FOR CHAPTER 7

1. Miss Emmeline Snively was the proper, English-born owner of the most renowned modeling agency in Los Angeles at the time, the Blue Book Modeling Agency. Its office was at the Ambassador Hotel in Beverly Hills when Norma Jean enrolled in August 1945 at the age of 19. This is where Ted Jordan, who was a lifeguard at the Lido Club pool behind the hotel, first met Norma Jean.

2. See footnote 1 above.

3. The Haig Nightclub, across the street from the Ambassador Hotel in Beverly Hills, was the hot spot for actors and musicians to meet. Nat King Cole, Erroll Garner, and Bobby Short were frequent patrons. Ted Jordan took Norma Jean there on numerous occasions.

4. Ted Jordan's birth name.

5. Slapsy Maxie was a Los Angeles entertainment nightspot where Ted Lewis, Ted Jordan's uncle, was often a featured comedian. It was fre-

quented by new comedians such as Dean Martin and Jerry Lewis, and Jackie Gleason. Norma Jean enjoyed going there.

6. Earle Carrol Theatre/Restaurant was another nightspot frequented by Norma Jean.

7. Mocambo was a Los Angeles nightspot where actors would get together to be seen.

8. Lili St. Cyr was a famous striptease dancer in the Los Angeles area, and a very good friend of Norma Jean. She shared with Norma Jean her secrets about how to act on stage to emphasize her natural sex appeal.

9. The Brothers Club was a nightspot that featured black entertainers and was frequented by Hollywood sophisticates such as Orson Wells, Errol Flynn, and John Ireland. Norma Jean loved this nightclub.

10. Red Dragon was a Chinese restaurant in Los Angeles where Norma Jean worked as a waitress for a very short time.

11. Grace Goddard was Norma Jean's guardian for a time and a friend of Gladys Baker.

12. Gladys Baker, whose maiden name was Monroe, suffered from mental illness and had several nervous breakdowns, like her own mother. At 15 she married a man named Baker, who kidnapped their two daughters, older half sisters of the unborn Norma Jean, and remarried in Kentucky. Gladys conceived Norma Jean out of wedlock with C. Stanley Gifford, who abandoned her. She later married a man named Mortensen, and her daughter's name became Norma Jean Mortensen.

13. The white piano was bought by Gladys when the family moved to their new house. Norma Jean, a child about nine at the time, loved that piano and would play it.

14. Norma Jean's stepfather.

15. Norma Jean's biological father.

16. In Tijuana, Dr. Gomez allegedly performed an abortion on Norma Jean who was impregnated by Ted Jordan. Dr. Law was the pharmacist who referred her to Dr. Gomez for a commission. This was a very unnerving experience for the young Norma Jean.

17. Revival Meeting was a religious service regularly attended by Norma Jean's maternal aunts, who were Christian Scientists. Norma Jean loved her aunts and these services, which she considered very spiritual.

18. Ted Lewis introduced Norma Jean to Damon Runyon and Walter Winchell, two powerful Hollywood columnists who aggressively promoted her to the public.

19. Leon Shomroy was the cameraman at 20th Century Fox who

secretly did a screen test on Marilyn Monroe, which launched her persona as a sex symbol in Hollywood.

20. Bernard "Bugsy" Siegel was a prominent mob figure who allegedly had an affair with Marilyn Monroe; however, under hypnosis, Sherrie, reliving as Marilyn that encounter, denied any such involvement.

21. Johnny Hyde from the William Morris Agency was Hollywood's most famous agent of this era. He was instrumental in forging Marilyn's film career, making her a major movie star. He was deeply in love with Marilyn, despite their age difference. He divorced his wife and lived with Marilyn for a time. He died in his fifties of a heart attack that his ex-wife claimed was caused by Marilyn's sexual acrobatics. Marilyn was filled with remorse over his death and took an overdose of pills in a suicide attempt that was thwarted by her good friend and drama coach, Natasha Lytess.

22. In his seventies, Harry Cohn was studio chief at Columbia. He was one of the most powerful men in Hollywood. It is public record that Marilyn was coerced by him for sexual favors in order to advance her Hollywood career.

23. Joseph Schenk was Harry Cohn's counterpart at 20th Century Fox. Marilyn attended his famous Saturday night gin rummy games as a "hostess" and eventually became known as Joe Schenk's girl. He convinced Cohn to give Marilyn a six-month option.

24. Darryl Zanuck was a director and later the head of productions at Fox. He let Marilyn's first option lapse and was quite hard on her.

25. Jean Norman was a famous Hollywood actress. Gladys Baker named her Norma Jean after her.

26. Helena Sorell was a drama coach at Fox. She made Norma Jean work hard at times.

27. Laurette was a sort of psychic friend to Norma Jean. She is attributed with having convinced Norma Jean to change her name to Marilyn Monroe.

28. Whitey was a friend and confidant of Marilyn Monroe, who coached her on how to better utilize her physical assets so to appear very sexy on screen.

29. Bruno Bernard was a famous Hollywood photographer—Bernard of Hollywood. Marilyn was often escorted by him to various Hollywood parties. She called him "My Bernardi." He took many glamourous photos of Marilyn, showing her as a sultry, sexy bombshell.

30. Peter Lawford was a charming and handsome English actor married to Patricia Kennedy, JFK's sister. He became one of Marilyn's best

friends. He arranged secret meetings between Marilyn and JFK at his home in Santa Monica, at Frank Sinatra's mansion in Palm Springs, and at Bing Cosby's retreat in the same location. He belonged to the famous Rat Pack along with Frank Sinatra, Sammy Davis Jr., and Dean Martin.

31. *Ladies of the Chorus* (1948) was a Columbia Pictures film featuring Marilyn Monroe. The *Motion Picture Herald* said, "Marilyn's singing is one of the brightest spots in the film. She is pretty and with her pleasant voice and style she shows promise."

32. Fred Karger was Marilyn's singing coach at Columbia Pictures. She fell in love with him and wanted to marry him, but he didn't want Marilyn raising his daughter from a previous marriage.

33. Natasha Lytess was Marilyn's roommate at one point and her drama coach for years; Marilyn and Natasha allegedly had a lesbian affair.

34. *Love Happy,* a United Artists release starring Groucho Marx, included Marilyn's memorable walk-on part. One of the most famous scenes in Hollywood lore has Marilyn sauntering past Groucho with her sexy, provocative walk and saying, "Some men are following me." He leers at her and replies, "I can't imagine why."

35. When she was strapped for money, photographer Tom Kelley paid Marilyn $50.00 to take a nude calendar picture of her. Later it was sold to *Playboy* magazine for $500.00 and appeared on the cover of that magazine's first issue.

36. Ted Jordan used to tease Norma Jean by calling her "Woo-woo girl," referring to her "boobs."

37. *The Asphalt Jungle* (1950), a film by Metro-Goldwin-Mayer, featured Marilyn Monroe in a small part that captured everyone's attention. Liza Wilson from *Photoplay* said, "There's a beautiful blonde, name of Marilyn Monroe, who makes the most of her footage."

38. In the 20th Century Fox film *All about Eve* (1950) Marilyn Monroe had a small but convincing part.

39. The Red Diaries are the famous alleged diaries written by Marilyn about her life, especially her relationship with the Kennedy brothers and the secrets of state they may have shared with her. These diaries, if they existed, never became public record. Under hypnosis Sherrie/Marilyn claimed to have a reddish, brown-covered diary book in which she noted only trivial, unimportant accounts of her daily life.

40. Spyros Skouras was 20th Century Fox chief executive officer in the 1940s and '50s. He handled the business side while Darryl Zanuck handled the creative side of the company. When Marilyn began receiving

4,000 fan letters a week (in 1951), more than any other actress had ever gotten, Skouras ordered Zanuck to find more movies for her. This was instrumental in making Marilyn a big star.

41. Sidney Skolsky was a famous Hollywood columnist who heavily promoted Marilyn.

42. In 1952 Sidney Skolsky convinced Jerry Wald, a major Fox producer, to give Marilyn a small part in his movie *Clash by Night.*

43. Joe DiMaggio was Marilyn's second husband, whom she married in March 1954. She later commented that he was a wonderful but dull guy. He wasn't supportive of her career, especially of how producers sexually exploited her image on screen. The marriage lasted only nine months. DiMaggio always loved Marilyn and came to her rescue on several occasions. He arranged for her funeral and excluded her Hollywood friends whose lifestyles, in his mind, were responsible for her suicide.

44. In 1952 Marilyn experienced her first pure box-office smash with the movie *Niagara* (20th Century Fox). The film cost $1.5 million and earned $6.5 million. As a contract player, she was paid $750.00 a week.

45. *Gentlemen Prefer Blondes* (1953) was the 20th Century Fox movie that made Marilyn the biggest star in Hollywood. *The New York Herald Tribune* noted, "As usual she looks as though she'd glow in the dark, and her version as the baby-face blonde whose eyes open for diamonds and close for kisses is always amusing [and] alluring."

46. "Diamonds Are a Girl's Best Friend" is the theme song of *Gentlemen Prefer Blondes.* As sung by Marilyn, it became a hit and contributed to the movie's great success.

47. In 1953, at the annual Photoplay banquet where Marilyn was honored as "Best Newcomer," she wore (over the protest of DiMaggio, who refused to escort her) a sheer gold lamé dress that Joan Crawford trashed in the press the next day. Marilyn called her "the old cunt."

48. *The Seven Year Itch*, co-starring Marilyn and Tom Ewell, was a 20th Century Fox film released in the summer of 1954. It was another huge success and is notorious for the scene in which Marilyn is standing on a sidewalk grate when her dress is blown up by a passing subway below. This scene, which DiMaggio saw filmed on the streets of New York, drew an angry reaction from him and contributed to their divorce.

49. Jerry Giesler was the lawyer who handled Marilyn's divorce from Joe DiMaggio.

50. Immediately after Marilyn's divorce from DiMaggio, she decided

to become a serious actress and began studying at the Actors Studio with famed acting coach and director, Lee Strassberg.

51. In the Fox production *Bus Stop* (1956), co-starring Don Murray, Marilyn delivered her first serious acting performance, which turned out to be her greatest accomplishment.

52. In late 1954, Marilyn's lawyer served notice that her contract with 20th Century Fox had been terminated due to a technicality. The legal wrangling to free her from this contract lasted for another year or so. She announced the formation of Marilyn Monroe Productions Inc. in January of 1956.

53. *The Prince and the Showgirl* (1957) was the first film by Marilyn Monroe Productions Inc. and L.O.P. Ltd. Co-starring Laurence Olivier, it presents Marilyn as a dazzling American showgirl capturing the love of a European monarch.

54. Marilyn's psychiatrist.

55. *Some Like It Hot* (1957) was a United Artists, Metro-Goldwin-Mayer film starring Marilyn Monroe, Tony Curtis, and Jack Lemmon. This was another big success with Marilyn playing a singer in an all-girl band, and Curtis and Lemon as cross-dressing musicians who join the girl band to hide from mobsters.

56. On the set of *Some Like It Hot,* when asked how it felt kissing Marilyn Monroe, Tony Curtis replied that it felt like "kissing Hitler." This created a stir in the press.

57. The Fox production *Let's Make Love* (1960) featured Marilyn Monroe and Yves Montand. In this film Marilyn sang "My Heart Belongs to Daddy" and proved to be a first-class comedian.

58. Arthur Miller was a famed playwright and Marilyn's third husband. She was attracted to his looks and brains. They were married in July 1956 and divorced in early 1961 due to irreconcilable differences when she became the breadwinner for both.

59. Clark Gable was Marilyn's favorite actor and a father figure to her. She played with him in *The Misfits,* written by Arthur Miller, as a Valentine gift to her. Gable died shortly after the movie was completed. The press blamed the heart attack that caused his death on his frustration over Marilyn's continued lateness on the set.

60. See endnote 59. *The Misfits* (1961 United Artists, Metro-Goldwin-Mayer) was directed by John Huston, who drove Marilyn to one of her best performances. Huston was so impressed that he offered her a role in his next film, *Freud.*

61. Payne Whitney Psychiatric Clinic was the psychiatric division of New York Hospital, Cornell University, where Marilyn was admitted after her divorce from Miller resulted in bouts of suicidal depression that led to overdosing with pills and alcohol. DiMaggio threatened the administrators when they refused to release her. They let her go, and DiMaggio walked her out of the hospital through a crowd of reporters.

62. See endnote 30.

63. Marilyn called John F. Kennedy by his first name, Jack.

64. "Happy Birthday to You, Mr. President" was the famous heartfelt song that Marilyn sang to JFK at his 45th birthday party. Jacqueline Kennedy did not attend.

65. Elizabeth Taylor was provoked by Marilyn and, apparently, they had an argument and possibly a scuffle.

66. Natalie Wood and Warren Beatty were young Hollywood acting debutants in the early 1960s. Marilyn met them briefly at a social event.

67. Bobby Kennedy was meeting secretly with Marilyn, as was his brother JFK, under Peter Lawford's auspices. Rumors were that they had a love affair.

68. Ted Jordan claims that Jacqueline Kennedy had a meeting with Marilyn in which she warned her to stay away from her husband.

69. Jane Russell was Marilyn's good friend and co-star in the film *Gentlemen Prefer Blondes*. As a result of this movie's resounding success, both friends had their hands and feet immortalized in cement at Graumann's Theater in Hollywood (now Mann's Chinese Theater).

70. Under hypnosis, Sherrie identified Jim Dougherty, Norma Jean's first husband, in a picture. The two had a marriage of convenience, as she did not love him, to prevent her return to an orphanage. She was only 16 at the time. Immediately after the wedding, Dougherty left on a cruise as a merchant marine.

71. Under a somnambulistic state of hypnosis, Sherrie identified Norma Jean's Christian Scientist maternal aunts in a family picture.

LET THE HEALING BEGIN

Before I left Toronto, I discussed with Sherrie the research plan that we would follow. While the regressions were compelling, there was a lot more work to be done if we were ever going to present this case history to the public and demonstrate the healing potential of regression therapy. And part of my healing strategy with Sherrie (since she couldn't travel to Los Angeles and I couldn't practice psychotherapy in Canada) was to have her work with me step by step to build a case for her being the reincarnation of Marilyn Monroe. This would force her to consciously pull up and integrate her Marilyn memories. The first two regressions were a great beginning and would accelerate the bleedthrough from this past life into the present, and we could use the conscious focus of a "task" to make this integration more "workable" and less scary. It would also give us linkage as we communicated via e-mail and phone on a nearly daily basis in the coming months and would allow me to monitor her progress closely and offer counseling at every turn.

The first step was to collect photos of Sherrie from different stages of her life for comparison to Marilyn Monroe's photo gallery from books and Internet sites. As mentioned earlier, classic reincarnation researcher Dr. Ian Stevenson found that comparing pictures of an individual in this life and a previous one invariably reveals similarities in facial bone structure that don't significantly change despite having different genetic parents. In addition, it was clear that Marilyn and Sherrie shared personality traits, emotional histories, linguistic and writing styles, and—I suspected—voice patterns and singing styles. All of these similarities were a proof of sorts and could be investigated. This was a new frontier for such comparisons. I would soon find that experts in many of these fields—while happy to apply their scientific know-how to find criminal suspects, kidnapped children, and even Nazis in hiding—were reluctant to apply such tests to past-life comparisons, especially of a recent and popular celebrity like Marilyn Monroe.

My original plan was definitely more ambitious than feasible at the time: lie detector test; hand, foot, and fingerprint recognition comparison tests; voice recognition comparison test; and graphological comparison test. After my return to Los Angeles it dawned on me while waking up from a dream that an iris recognition comparison test would top every other kind of physical proof. I realized that seeking a genetic comparison might prove interesting, though a formidable task. I was aware that 97 percent of the human genome (or "junk DNA") hasn't been investigated yet. I felt that the kind of physical comparisons from one lifetime to the next that Stevenson uncovered, which were statistically improbable, might be the result of a soul's imprint on segments of this junk DNA, which might also result in other physical similarities. But, as with some of the above-mentioned tests, it would have to be a part of an ongoing research project that might take years to prove.

After my work with Sherrie was completed and before returning to Los Angeles, my wife and I flew from Toronto to Winnipeg to visit our youngest daughter Sarah, her husband Shimon, and their three children. During this period, Sherrie and I communicated mainly through e-mails. Between May 5 and May 10 there was a flurry of e-mails.

Sent: May 06, 2005
From: Adrian Finkelstein, M.D.
To: Sherrie Lea Laird

Dear Sherrie,

. . . On the plane on my way to Winnipeg, I began reorganizing some important pieces of our research, connecting the dots, so to speak. In the process, I gathered some so-called "coincidences" of importance. I am sure I'll come by much more relevant material in a short time. I'm praying for divine guidance and I got the idea that in order to make our findings more acceptable to skeptics, we might introduce a scientific statistical proof with the help of a professional statistician. For these "coincidences" to happen by chance would be such a slim probability, close to zero; for example, it is like the odds of winning six numbers at the lottery. That would make our findings statistically significant.

Thus, in addition to the subjective and fascinating job you did during past-life regression in which you came across so genuine in your memories, emotions, and experiences of Marilyn Monroe, we could offer commonly accepted scientific proof for doubting Thomas kind of people as well. I thought to share some of these thoughts with you and keep you up to date with our common project. However, most important is what you think and feel. Can you let me know what your thoughts are? I know you are busy, that life goes on, and that you have so many other important things to do. When you get a chance I would appreciate it if you'd drop me a few lines. Until then,

Love, peace, and God be with you and protect you always!
Adrian

Sent: May 06, 2005
From: Sherrie Lea Laird
To: Adrian Finkelstein, M.D.

Hi Doc F.,

We had the most unique and amazing time. I'm so glad to

hear from you before the 15th. I'm thinking of you a lot and what we've done here.

I can't put it into words how I feel now, how I view life. The greatest relief of all is no longer feeling crazy.

You are very special, Dr. F. Those are great gifts you have to offer, your life and your dedication not only to healing and learning, but your open insightful views. It's absolutely tremendous that you are at the forefront of it all. This could be the start of something that makes it easily accessible and accepted to heal this way for the average person and their suffering. Maybe not so hot for the pharmaceuticals, though.

Well, THANK YOU for a wonderful time. Just sitting and talking with you is mesmerizing. I've learned so much, as has Kezia. We'll never be the same again, and this is a good thing.

I have many clear views on things and it just seems to be coming in stronger. I'm going to jot down as much as I can on e-mails and any corrections I feel (that won't be based on books, but if I felt like I couldn't remember, it seems to come to me now).

. . . I feel we have now just scratched the surface, and who knows what will come out. Until we meet again! . . .

Love and admiration. Best wishes,
Sher and Kez
XOXOXO

Many more e-mails followed. They sharpened and completed Sherrie's understanding of her true self and her experiences as a continuation of Marilyn's lifetime and provided more emotional and mental relief. She also informed me that she got a part-time job in addition to her singing engagements. After an enjoyable first day at the Mega-Pharmacy, she wrote that it was fun, slightly difficult, and that she had to just concentrate on the job. She had to admit, however, that being there was somewhat of a shock immediately following the regression sessions. But, before and after work, she continued her own research. She explained:

"Because I'm so comfortable now with the truth, I had to look up a couple of things to see if I could find what I saw in my head/eyes . . . one of them being whether Grace in fact cared about M.

"And I also found a picture of what I think must be the fake beauty pageant in a movie called *We're Not Married*. Now one of two things happened: she's in the movie and is 19, or is also graduating at modeling school at 19. And I somewhat suspect there were two [different] times. I feel very strongly that in the modeling [school] there were practices of winning a pageant type thing.

". . . What has happened to me as of late is I feel at ease, yet there are many questions and thinking, Good Lord what will everyone think?

"The other thing I must amplify is if this didn't feel true I would've backed out by now, and pursued my own life, as I do/did have a life that was A) far from boring, and B) with its own high-lights, talents, praise, and somewhat popular/slightly known in music. So there is no immense thirst of any kind to be anyone else but me or to find a pseudo-life/fame/personality of anyone else. It absolutely is [true], with the feeling of sincere belief that Gladys is in fact Kezia. Not only that, it makes complete sense and some-what even more so. I think it only adds further to M being so determined then as a person, knowing she wasn't done, etc. The miracle of it, being able to be traced in this life, is no more sur-prising simply because I'd bring Gladys with me . . .

"As I was looking up Grace and small confirming details, I quickly needed to know (but I don't have the good books so it was hard to find). I just again could not believe that this crazy woman who started going nuts in the '30s would wait 'til 1984 early March to die. Either she reserved a spot, or just like Diana, Princess of Wales, gave birth nine months to the day as I did.

"So I have no fears in that I will write my notes from the per-spective of the task at hand and state the facts as best as I can. I do have some feeling of pregnancy near, but not at the end of 1962, because there were aches and pains in the abdomen. That I know personally, off from terminated pregnancy. However, I think things were getting bad in that department. I also was diag-nosed with endometriosis.

"I do believe that M died on the 4th, not early on the 5th, and had no intentions of doing so, but was propelled by habit and sadness and no clear urges to hold back the compulsions that were so in front."

The following day Sherrie wrote to me: "I found myself very surprised by the name Jack. All my life I've referred to JFK as JFK and John, and actually could not even think of him as Jack. Yet, it rolled off the tongue with such great ease, and it felt very right."

The same day, May 7, she wrote again:

"Hi, Doc F., how are you? Just looking for things like Gladys's birthday, my teddy bear, whatever I can find, [and I] saw this info below about the Nems and chlorals. And the FACT that just like I knew that . . . I had just bought stuff [furnishings] and that it in fact was coming the next day. I did write that in an e-mail to you. So, hope you kept 'em all. And yes, it is between 26–32 pills that killed her; [she took them] throughout the day and the last batch was around 10–15 max, chlorals. The only doubt would be that I/she was so out of it, her subconscious didn't store the info of approx seven more. And earlier that day (3rd–4th), there were some Seconals for trying out. It's true we had a high tolerance, but everyone is forgetting about the weight loss, being older, and just plain bad timing . . . and then there's the fact that it was just meant to happen. But yes, I should've been happy as my stuff was new. Finally I had gotten new stuff, furniture.

"Found some other stuff [out], too. Like the earlier e-mail way back, Frank [Sinatra] could've been at Copacabana, as I wasn't hypnotized but just flashing back. Copacabana, white dress, moved to front of the stage. Found out that info, too. Wait! I just watched a documentary on the Discovery channel where they proved Marilyn was in the state of mind to kill herself. Plus they proved it was only 24 capsules that killed her. It looked pretty convincing: Dr. Chamberland was the forensic psychiatrist who studied Marilyn's state of mind. He determined she was depressed enough to kill herself by the condition of her bedroom, because it had no pictures on the wall or anything that said 'I live here.' What he didn't mention was that Marilyn was right in the middle of redecorating her house completely. This included her bedroom and personal bathroom. She had purchased many items on her trip to Mexico to furnish her house with, and some of them arrived the day she died. This included her nightstand. The one you see in photos was a temporary nightstand, and her brand new one was in her garage. One of the other reasons Dr. Chamberland felt it was obvious she meant to kill herself was the locked door. This information came from Dr. Litman, who was on the suicide team that investigated why Marilyn killed herself (not IF she killed herself). What Dr. Chamberland did not take into consideration was that Eunice Murray, the caretaker, stated more than once years later that the door actually wasn't locked. She even put this in writing in a questionnaire saying the door was not locked . . . So if you take away the lack of decoration and take away the locked door, add in the fact that everyone interviewed on her last day said she was in good spirits that evening, then there is no evidence she wanted to kill herself."

I assured Sherrie that she was doing a wonderful job! I wrote that I'd just read her e-mails and that they were filled with very important information. I stressed that I do keep track of all her e-mails and that I have surely stored them for future reference. Who locked M's door, if it was locked, was still unclear. Her unfortunate, consciously unintended demise better fit our findings than the half-truths of her "suicide" investigation by professionals at the time. But, at the time, M's subconscious was more unhappy than happy with life. This seems to have tipped the balance toward death. The happy, hopeful side of her subconscious made her order the new furnishings from Mexico to redecorate her house. However, the unhappy side wished even more strongly to exit life. It was too late afterwards, when she shifted back to her happy side, to change her mind (turquoise and blue colors being associated with life). Because it wasn't a conscious, deliberate attempt to kill herself, but her unhappy subconscious side indulging in the drugs and champagne, this time more than usual, I wouldn't call it a suicide but an accidental overdose. I explained this speculation to Sherrie and added that the rhetorical question, was it a coincidence that she'd just watched a Discovery channel documentary on Marilyn exactly at the time when we were enmeshed in unraveling M's mystery? This "coincidence" appears more compelling than the content of the show itself. I continued to convey to Sherrie that there were too many "coincidences" or synchronicities (things that happen at the same time) for it to be random chance. And I was sure that as we continued our real discovery process, many more compelling proofs were bound to accumulate.

The following day, on May 8, Sherrie wrote again:

"Yes, I was very surprised to find that. More important, just as I strongly felt, very strongly in fact, that something was coming that day, 5th, 6th, that I was waiting for and had ordered.

"I also felt I had just been paid that night, or that there was a time of comfort involved regarding funds. There is a warm feeling of content as well; as a surprise ending.

"I agree wholeheartedly [that her death] was not a planned thing, but just a relinquishing (maybe even an inner curiosity or karmic pull). And no, I do not think the door was locked at all, and this could only be just slightly sticking. No, not locked. Perhaps Mrs. Murray looked in on M and just assumed was sleeping. Why shouldn't she think that after seeing her pass out on many previous times? What would be new?

"Now she, later on, while being pressured by everyone around for answers, has to say she did not see M asleep and is clueless and surprised like everyone else . . . for fear of blame of being indifferent, etc. But, how could she possibly know?

"I think what is important [from] the documentary . . . is the new information from a new and more open-[minded] doctor. It is that M did not take and could not take . . . 47 Nembutals and 20 or more chloral hyds, and whatever else, the mere lack of them showing up is the fact that they were very dissolved in the liquid before swallowing. And also, I do believe that the later batch of chloral hyds, which are the thing that finished it, would have been found . . . in the smaller intestine (I guess they are calling it). Wonder what would happen to have M's body exhumed with the new details.

"Anyway . . . without any possibility, or any thought of me even remotely knowing, I was right on two of the most important counts unpublished previously, 'cause tonight is the first time I've ever found anything about the drug content that was accurate and shockingly exact as what I said while under hypnosis during the past-life regression.

". . . I saw a pic of James (Marilyn's first husband), and I must reiterate that is a very good pic of James you showed me (during the past-life regression), as he doesn't look like that, and the fact I thought they were neighbors is no surprise, as they were. When I was inaccurate in any way, I noticed I was fighting the information with my mind . . . fighting the first answer. Just like the drawing of me not being for Jack 'cause I saw a black dress (ink color) and said no, no, there was no black dress . . .

"Part of me is still beyond in a daze over this. We really have a lot of work ahead, don't we?

". . . Is it okay to read Ted's book? I'm really needing to catch up on things."

Later in the day Sherrie informed me of a psychic prediction by the famous American psychic, Kenny Kingston. She'd just found on the Internet that Marilyn Monroe's reincarnation would appear on June 1, 2005, on the anniversary of her 79th birthday. This turned out to be partly true, if Sherrie is that reincarnation, and partly false, as Kingston predicted the reincarnation of Marilyn Monroe as a baby.

According to Kingston, who was also a medium and psychic to Lucille Ball, Greta Garbo, John Wayne, Marlene Dietrich, Whoopi Goldberg, and others, Marilyn studied parapsychology and hoped to reappear in 2005, at the time of the 79th anniversary of her birth (June 1). As per Kingston, her objective in reincarnating is to bring to the world the spiritual lesson she had learned on the other side.

I have mentioned the many "coincidences," or synchronici-ties, our research has uncovered. Synchronicity is a term coined by psychologist Carl Jung. It is when two separate and dissimilar events or occurrences, without a cause-and-effect connection, are bound together in some unexplainable but meaningful way. It is most often used to associate and show the connections between psychic or mental events and external or real-world happenings. For example, you think about your Aunt Martha and the next moment she calls you on the phone. Or, your wife is miffed because you didn't give her flowers for your anniversary when a florist shows up at your door delivering flowers to the wrong address. This is another way of saying that thought energies, and all things originate as thoughts first, connected at a higher level will manifest in the physical spontaneously to reveal their inner connection.

After Sherrie contacted me back in April 2005, I began to make a list of these synchronicities and add to them as our research continued. It was during this period, right after my return from Toronto and the onset of our serious research, I sent Sherrie a list of the more prominent synchros, as I called them, hoping that over time we would both add to them.

1. Preceding Marilyn's death, there were about 15 minutes in which she experienced an awful sensation of her chest being crushed, and suffocation from respiratory failure, a sensation that Sherrie has experienced repeatedly throughout her life.

2. After Marilyn took a number of Seconals, Nembutals, and chlo-ral hydrates, she experienced numbness in her face and mouth prior to her death. While reliving Marilyn's death during the May 3, 2005, hypnotic regression, Sherrie was barely able to speak, her speech slow and slurred, her voice just above a whisper.

3. In reliving Marilyn's death, Sherrie said that at one point Marilyn realized that she had overdosed and wanted to live but

it was too late. Sherrie saw flashes of turquoise, Marilyn's favorite color and what Sherrie had always associated with the "crushing and numbness" sensations she had experienced all her life. (Sherrie could now associate it with Marilyn's death throes.)

4. In Sherrie's first regression, she spontaneously (without hypnotic suggestion) began to relive Marilyn's death, which is typical of the thousands of past-life regressions I've conducted and a further verification of her past-life recall.

5. Sherrie first communicated with me some time after her 35th birthday; she broke contact due to extreme psychological pressure around the time of Joe DiMaggio's death in March of 1999 and a few months before her 36th birthday, the age at which Marilyn died.

6. Months after Sherrie first contacted me in September of 1998, I "coincidently" met at a Christmas party retired actor Ted Jordan, 74, who unbeknownst to me had had a romantic affair and longtime friendship with Marilyn, which he had written about in a celebrated book.

7. Upon first contacting me, Sherrie had said if she was indeed Marilyn reincarnated she wanted to contact people still alive who knew her. Putting her in touch with Ted allowed them to renew their friendship and exchange many mutual memories.

8. Sherrie wasn't fixated on her Marilyn identity despite numerous flashbacks and memories, and she expressed her doubts up until the first round of hypnotic regressions. This is a differential diagnosis sign that she is sane (i.e., not psychotic). She later confirmed this by breaking contact with me and Ted to protect her singing career and her Sherrie identity.

9. After six years, Sherrie contacted me the first week in April 2005, one week after Ted Jordan's death, a fact neither of us

knew at that time. She expressed concerns in her e-mail that people who could vouch for her would die, like Joe DiMaggio had. I learned of Ted's death a month later, when I was finally able to reach his brother. She was devastated by the news.

10. In my past-life research over some 30 years, I've found that 70 percent of people who died prematurely, tragically, or unjustly (or haven't learned their lesson) reincarnate within months or a few years to *continue* the same interrupted life lesson, designated by the same North Moon Node position in their astrological charts. Thus, Marilyn and Sherrie have the same North Moon Node (Cancer), as Marilyn died prematurely and reincarnated as Sherrie in less than one year. Under past-life regression Sherrie said she was hurrying back after her death to have her baby daughter. (This is statistically significant, whether you believe in astrology or not.)

11. Sherrie's daughter, Kezia, was conceived around March 11, 1984—within days of Gladys Baker's death. It seems that immediately upon her death Gladys made a "reservation" to be born to Sherrie. Kezia was born December 11, 1984 or about nine months later. (This was later confirmed by a past-life regression of Kezia in November of 2005.)

12. Sherrie shares many of Marilyn's personality traits, including a history of drug and alcohol (champagne) abuse and several suicide attempts over the years for many of the same reasons that eventually killed Marilyn. She is also in the entertainment business, though despite plenty of talent and moxie hasn't attained nearly the same level of success as Marilyn. This could be due to a subconscious block equating success with the same unhappy, premature, and tragic death as Marilyn's.

This list of synchros seemed to trigger some conscious recall on Sherrie's part. Her answer to my e-mail later the same day was rather intriguing.

Sent: May 09, 2005
From: Sherrie Lea Laird
To: Adrian Finkelstein, M.D.

Hi Doc F.,

. . . Oh, and yes, I agree with all you have written, the "coincidences," plus all the details we have found out, that only I knew under hypnosis. That is because I must say rather avidly, even after answering all those questions back at the hotel, after a day or two of [being] beyond exhaustion, I had to hurry and look up the facts for myself 'cause I was both relieved and freaked out.

Don't forget that when I would do the mirror thing, that face very strongly and unexpectedly came to me and flashed before my eyes. And I would say, "Oh my God, I'm Marilyn Monroe!" For no reason, no books, no movies, no Internet . . . only in first doing modeling, to then become a singer . . . I was excessively shy and also know that the whisper and the super feeling of "heavy" and "drugged," also the chest feeling of crushing, all came at a rapid rate (feeling heavy/thick weird and remorse as early as seven). All this can be proved through lie detector.

I really don't have doubts, only fears about how much work we have to do. In the vision near the end, I am clear about one thing: This is meant to be, and we couldn't stop it if we tried. It's all happening so very fast and it's not solely in our hands.

There is a reason. Kenny Kingston perhaps could assist us in the future, as I'm sure he will get a vibe for it, as he is very right to the day, practically. Okay, keep up the very fantastic work!

There are so many coincidences. Don't forget my marrying an army guy next door, not loving him, used him to travel the world (as I was told we would).

. . . Anyway, to me the coincidences are mind boggling and I will find them in books, and highlight, or transfer them and mark the page and the book number. I will only mention the ones that are 1,000,000% the same as me, my thoughts, or my experiences. If there are any drifts, which there barely are, I will leave them out. Remember, I said if I wasn't her I was her clone.

Okay, loving you and thanks for all you are doing. No matter what comes of it, you've freed the prisoner. Thank you as always!

M/S

P.S. We must track down the turquoise kitchen. I'm sure it's there. I've seen it. I know it. And don't forget my affinity when at 16, my first job at Moore Business Farms on Weston Road in Toronto, Ontario. When I went thru the plant, it had all these old offices from the '50s, the turquoise, the windows, the floors, the desks, were all in original shape. I couldn't wait to deliver the mail in that section because it blew me away. I couldn't believe how I felt about it. This is probably the first stuff showing up, besides the thick heavy remorse that gave me an unmistakable fright, and actually now remembering, came in waves.

You see, I now realize it, not a moment sooner to do this research would have worked. I would have died, or something, if we did it six years ago, 'cause guess what: WAH LAH, I would've been 36. Now suddenly that appears a coincidence, doesn't it? Just thought of that now. Yes, the timing is perfect and as you well know, gives me the absolutely horrible dread of all my friends finding out lying about my age . . . that is the real fright here. The M thing seems easier compared to feeling like a liar in this life. What a shame! Oh well, maybe sparing the name . . .

I was right about Noguchi, too, though wrong about Lee (the correct first name was Thomas). Don't know why. Was right about Peter, and also during past-life regression had very strong feelings which provoked crying.

Remember J. Hyde, and I cried and said, "I'm all alone now." Just read that, you know isn't it just so narcissistic for her to cry for herself that he's gone? . . . I remember those tears pouring out of my eyes and how I felt alone and scared . . . unbelievable . . . S in this life doesn't need to cry for Johnny; only M cried. Now, how could I have done that at all? And the crazy thing was when I would laugh, when there was nothing funny to S, but something struck a chord in M, and I had no clue until all the words would pour out of my mouth. The reason it feels too hard to part with is BECAUSE IT IS TRUE. End of story. There's nothing I can do about it, I can't go back to live before confirming 'cause it's out now, and easily felt and conjured up by me.

Good night for now,
XOXO

Sherrie continued to put more pieces of the puzzle together, thus adding to the confirmations we sought—that she is indeed the reincarnation of Marilyn Monroe. The following is another excerpt of her progressive healing:

"Yes, Doctor F., there are no coincidences, only destiny. I'm thinking this.

"P.S. I meant to tell you, as I keep being tied up in the details, that I have the sense of urgency. I feel like talking particularly to Jane Russell. [She was a very good friend of Marilyn Monroe; 83 years old at the time; co-starred with Marilyn in *Gentlemen Prefer Blondes.*] Wouldn't that be wonderful? I feel if we would sit down, she would recognize me . . . being a woman, being sensitive, where some of the others are caught up in how they remember [her]. Though yes, it will also be great to meet with [the others]. I need to see Jane. Tell me she isn't dead . . . touch wood! I'm going to research this. Don't you think we should set this up ASAP?"

Feeling Marilyn and having her abreact emotionally through Sherrie was the greatest achievement of the regressions, freeing Marilyn/Sherrie considerably from the grip and bondage of the "dragon." In fact, as per Sherrie's confession, the "dragon" had lifted altogether. She felt so light and ready to soar. The following is an excerpt of her next e-mail that alludes to more of her progressive healing:

Yes, this is very good. We can talk. I'll tell what I feel. I at least I don't feel like I'm lying and can say what I know, what I think I know and what we've found out. The most exciting part of the whole regression is I was able to feel very strongly what she felt and I noticed that either S's or M's lessons in hindsight made her a lot more remorseful and she didn't want to hate so, but more dislike when need be (i.e., forgiving Ted) as during regression I was able to see that you can lead a horse to water, but you can't make it drink . . . He began supplying the drugs, though with assistance from others and their karma is within, too, for supplying drugs. But, let's not forget, she is a girl who wanted and needed to take drugs for many, many reasons. After all, as in this life too, I always did mix my Ativan. Especially it was fun to mix it with champagne, like M, but sometimes even with one beer, or vodka . . . as the fizzy made an extra-special euphoria. I could be more, and play more, and joke more, and stand out more. This is all the same now as it was then. And I long suspect, just as now, it would take less and less of a combination to kill or do damage of an irreparable kind. Henceforth, a willingness to stop.

Apparently, after my attempt at suicide I was transferred to a place for the disturbed. I found myself too alert and too healthy to stay. My mother wanted me to stay, and I was quite mad, but I knew just as M did, my problems were of an emotional kind and that my brain was quite [sound] and perhaps overqualified to be lumped in with these nuts. No one can understand people this highly sensitive, it's on another plane altogether; a curse and a gift. [It's] like those race horses who are so highly strung, powerful, beautiful, yet the tiniest thing can destroy their nerves . . . .

But Sherrie continued to disclose her remaining fears to me, as in the following e-mail snippet:

P.S. Had more memories of suicidal tendencies in '83, [when] I was alone in Calgary. This is the first time I had thought suicide was even a true possibility. Ex was confined to barracks and I was alone out there, and it brought back all the fears I have when I'm alone, especially at night, on an ongoing basis. I would be in my apartment or in bed or sitting at the table and I could feel life was over, that I couldn't handle dark and being alone. The loneliness was so fierce I can't describe it.

You know with the attempted suicide and survival, I thought most of that would go away. But whenever Kezia would go to her boyfriend's house or anything like that, that would render me alone. The death I would feel and still feel is phenomenal.

Lately my stresses with my boyfriend Chris and my musical career are consuming [what] left-brain cells I have. I've blocked out so much in the last year. I'm just surviving in 1/10 mode, just going, doing, trying not to think or feel.

I just wanted to make a record of that. My very close and best friend Aunt Anne (same as M's) was my sounding board 'til her own consumption with drugs. She would help me thru. You know, I thought I was a happy teen, but by 14-plus I had an eating disorder and was on my way to becoming a basket case. To realize it is indeed on its way out . . . What do you think?

I replied that everything should be different now, as she was making constant progress with her healing following the regressions and that it has had a liberating effect on her. She frankly agreed. Then, I felt Sherrie should make more use of the self-hypnotic techniques I taught her while in Toronto. I needed more elaboration on her part regarding events involving the Kennedys:

Hi Sher,

Can you place yourself in a trance and verify if in the so-called Red Diaries you included state secrets from JFK and Bobby? Also, if you threatened Bobby with disclosing these secrets at a news conference scheduled for August 5, 1962? By the way, there are four more coincidences I discovered by reviewing our latest e-mails. I'll share them with you later.

Her reply was again quite revealing. One had to be impressed with her recuperative (or regenerative) powers and her willingness to face and slay her dragons.

Hi Doc F.,

But then again, about the red diary, I did confirm it while under . . . so there is something to the story. But, if the red diary is available, where is my bear? And if they found my bear, was it [mine] . . . in a case? Oh, you can imagine what really would've gone on thru time, people moving and/or keeping stuff. The Hawaii thing is real and not coming from anyone but her, along with several other facts. I'm still on looking for things that I've said, and I might view the tapes. Though I'm busy, I just need to do it.

As for the trance, I will do that. I can assure you any threats against Bobby would've only been while hammered and while being treated badly. But did she have the spirit to do it for real? I suspect not, and that's why she implodes instead of explodes. We must realize too that she loves them and their work, and aside from a few minor irritations about people around them like Jackie and others . . . her/my personality is absolutely not one to do that, as she's been around a lot of people who hurt her and were mean, and she never ratted on them yet. Past behavior predicts future behavior.

I will go into trance, but I'm pretty sure at this point that the answer is no! Most likely I ripped it (the letter of accusation against Marilyn Monroe by the FBI, handed to her by Bobby Kennedy) to shreds and said 'F' you. That's what I had felt early on reading about these threats. And I'm sure she was only afraid for her safety once she was told about the enemies around. Her planning to go away with Joe is not [indicative of] one who is on a full mission to destroy others. This doesn't seem to make sense at all. Blown up rumor that's spread like a disease.

The flurry of e-mails from Sherrie continued nonstop, day in and day out. They say when the dam breaks just let the water flow, and this also applies to a wounded psyche reclaiming and healing itself. Our research project had become, as I had planned, a focal point for Sherrie's conscious mind to uncover and integrate the dissociated memories, dreams, and flashbacks that had psychologically threatened her for so long. The regressions had proved the validity of her claim, vanquished her doubts and fears of being "crazy," and helped to create a more integrated ego complex from which to conduct her "explorations."

Hi Doc F.,

I found a link. A lot of it is correct, including my previous e-mail: http://www.coverups.com/monroe/countdown.htm in one e-mail, where I had regressed on the birthday thing you sent me.

. . . I say, the evening doesn't last long 'cause I'm out of it. I believe the dress isn't on for long, though wrong about floor. Then, I believe they do meet up for a short time (Marilyn and JFK) and possibly at a party or restaurant later. However, I felt she is now thinking of Bobby instead and, yes, I said he is better in bed; about the pregnancy down near the end. The only thing that leads me to believe there was a pregnancy, or psychosomatic pregnancy, and not with Jack, [is] I could be led to believe there was an overzealous late period that turns out to be nothing. But, there is no way there was an abortion in this frame of clingy mind; perhaps a miscarriage as I felt something missing in my abdomen, after the first regression. But I couldn't tell if this was bladder related. However, I know what termination feels like.

Perhaps when I was saying, "He doesn't love me," it in fact is (though both in truth) a [pining] for Bobby in her heart, Jack in her mind . . . as in truth she's no longer in love with Jack and not turned on by him.

I thought this site was somewhat close. I was right about the eating disorder. I started with anorexia. I knew she was too obsessed with what she ate, just like my journals; as Kezia told me about, she needed to eat when down. You know maybe in a rage she doesn't want to be cast aside and will tell anyone who'll listen. But, in all honesty, it was not going to happen like that. Can't remember what else was there.

I'm doing my homework this way on the Web as I have questions about what I've said to you, when I can remember and try to be specific, instead of looking to books for now. Good Lord, I'm tired, you know, and I know it's only the beginning. It's near impossible to shut off and we always were one-track-minded. It's very draining behavior.

Sent: May 13, 2005
From: Sherrie Lea Laird
To: Adrian Finkelstein, M.D.

Hi Adrian,

Sorry I missed your call. Well, I've been out 'til late and then slept in. How are you, too? If I wasn't at work today 5–9, I would light the two candles I have left at sundown . . .

I found out one thing, Slapsy Maxie. No wonder I thought we referred it to another name, or maybe the person who runs it, as it's named after a boxer, and I think a guy named Charlie runs it. I just feel we called it by a different name . . . thinking back on the regression it's dumbfounding. These are all things S didn't know, and if I ever did, I would've had to be a big fan of M's, or have no life whatsoever to remember anything like those answers. No, I realize now, it's for 100% sure that I gave you what I personally remember as M.

And there are things we can check into, like what they called Emmeline for short or [if it was] Ms. Snively, etc. When I was under [hypnosis], I was very susceptible to the slightest difference. I could verify [if something] doesn't feel correct. Of course same goes for the diary.

I remembered something else but have forgotten. It'll come back, too.

. . . I also realize that there is no way in the world that when you said you were going to do something important now, [at the] first regression I could've come up with that runway thing from my imagination. I found out something. M did in fact win the odd pageant from time to time, acted them out in modeling school. I'm sure of this myself, and she played one in a movie. These are all things I must say I didn't know. I remembered one of the most important facts in all of this all together. We forgot to ask, am I a fan of M's? Absolutely NOT. I've never really liked the couple of movies I've seen of hers . . .

Years ago I read up searching for things I needed to confirm, which would be behavior, dates, coincidences . . . not caring about any of the details a fan would store in her head. I realized that, in fact, I knew very little details or definitely that I could even remember at all. So, on top of that, in the count backward, you took all memories from me, or what little I did remember. I don't recall things like Blue Book Modeling Agency, etc. I only know the personality of M because it is in fact approximately 95% the same as mine. The differences between us are small and are these: I can't sleep with gross guys to further my career. Not this time, 'cause I love my career (not to say I haven't earlier on, but grew out of that fast) and M was a lot more self-centered and for longer. As I had a child, while I was heading in her exact path, if I didn't have [her], my December 11, 1984, life raft Kezia, who knows what would've happened. Funny, Gladys could give M away, but M or S can hold on even tighter to a child [and Gladys as it turns out] as I have, and they can't get away [from each other]. Oh, and the fact [with] Kezia being in my life, drugs didn't have their allure after that [as they did for M].

Everything is the same, I mean everything: personality, behavior, thoughts, ideas, likes, dislikes (except anchovies), [career] drive, obsessions, weaknesses, all exact . . . I just read this old magazine that . . . contains a flashback interview of Marilyn while visiting Niagara. I've just found this as I'm searching thru boxes to gather as many books, and this one is from 1996, which I think I found at a coffee shop later . . . I read it two nights ago, and in it she says "boring" about this and that, and this is where I learned that she has no clothes really of her own, just like me. Back with more later 'cause I've injured my wrist as of late, in the last month or two, and I think it might even be from typing. Ha, ha.

. . . Is it probable that the sense of urgency over my life as M would fade slightly, due to regressions? Since I feel it's been confirmed and I'M NOT CRAZY! I'm calmer about it, and it's sort of just in the back in a correct spot of my mind rather than calling to my head constantly. Is this part of the healing process?

Much love and joy to you, Shulah, and family,
XOXOXO
Sher

I called Sherrie on the phone a few days later and asked her to list any synchros she has noticed from over the years now that she knows so much more about herself as the reincarnation of Marilyn. At this juncture, she could better link up synchros to which she didn't pay much attention in the past. She sent me an amazing e-mail. It was a very pleasant surprise, and it put so many more pieces of the puzzle together.

Sent: May 16, 2005
From: Sherrie Lea Laird
To: Adrian Finkelstein, M.D.
Subject: More so-called coincidences

1. Since very young, I had crushing chest pains associated with "panic attacks."

2. My parents said I was always telling them I was someone else.

3. I took acting classes, thinking I was going to be an actress, singer. I always felt I was supposed to be famous.

4. I went to modeling school briefly.

5. I had anorexia (read later M had brief bouts of anorexia).

6. I married an army guy next door. His sister resembled M.

7. My daughter Kezia was born December 11, 1984, nine months after Gladys Baker's death, and looks like M.

8. I dated two brothers at the same time, which they allowed. One looked exactly like Tony Curtis.

9. M adored and worshiped animals as much as I do.

10. We have some of the same phobias, like not being able to sleep.

11. My father looks like Clark Gable.

12. I'm very attracted to Arthur Miller and his "type."

13. I've always needed older men ["daddy figures"].

14. From age five, I've been attracted to men. I remember they're supposed to be with me.

15. Taking pills with champagne.

16. When I went to Banff, Alberta, I felt I'd been there before, but didn't know then about M's visits there.

17. Even when I can afford it, I don't accumulate clothing, and I don't have a lot of things.

18. I'm scatterbrained and clumsy like M.

19. I went to Jamaica and loved it; felt I'd been there before.

20. Our voices sound alike.

21. M played a singer named Cherie in the movie *Bus Stop*.

22. I've always been very loving toward blacks and sympathize with their plight.

23. I nearly called my daughter Natasha, after M's drama coach.

24. I've had similar out-of-control episodes as M while on drugs.

25. I can be sexual or asexual depending on my moods and ambitions.

26. I am obsessed with my family like M was with Gladys.

27. M was happiest with microphone in hand, and wanted to be a singer.

28. Even at 16 I was obsessed with everything from the 1950s.

29. [We both longed] to play a musical instrument at a young age.

30. When I first saw pictures of Bobby K., I knew I liked him better than JFK.

31. As a teenager and older, people were constantly telling me I looked like a famous person.

32. I'm notorious for crying at the drop of a hat like M. And, good Lord, there are still many, many more things, all tiny but all big at the same time.

Okay that's all I can think of for now.
XOXO
Sher

We left Winnipeg as scheduled on May 15 and arrived in Los Angeles in the early evening. Shulah and I slept a little on the plane, as we were tired due to the hectic pace of the last two weeks. Besides the regression sessions with Sherrie in Toronto, followed by an almost constant stream of back-and-forth daily e-mails, we were socializing with my daughter, son-in-law, and their many friends, especially during Shabbath. We also played with our three grandchildren, Rachel, Rivkah-Beilah, and Yehezkiel-Shalom, taking them to the park for kiddy rides or just reading books to them at home. All in all it was fun, but it also proved to be somewhat tiring.

Once back I settled into my daily professional routine teaching psychiatric residents and conducting past-life regressions as part of my holistic psychiatric practice at my Los Angeles offices. I also began my full-fledged scientific research and comparative study of Sherrie Laird and Marilyn Monroe. I pursued several channels of inquiry in addition to the recent past-life regressions. In the back of my mind, I knew that a second round of regressions would have to be conducted in the near future. To heal M/S's soul and to free Sherrie completely of her pain and longtime suffering, more emotional abreactions were needed. But, for now, the course of treatment was our mutual research project, which had greatly benefited Sherrie over the last ten days, with each verification creating more acceptance and integration of her Marilyn self.

On May 16, I received the above-referenced e-mail from Sherrie listing more synchronicities. But, as I discussed with Sherrie during my visit in Toronto, I now had to present similarities in personality traits, career and vocational aptitudes, and emotional profiles and histories between Marilyn and Sherrie. Certainly linguistics, verbal, and written styles of communication, as well as graphology (handwriting comparisons) between them had to be demonstrated.

All above similarities between Marilyn Monroe and Sherrie Laird proved uncanny. Naturally, recognition of Marilyn in the person of Sherrie by her contemporaries, besides Ted Jordan, was part of my research design as well. This was more of the classic pattern pursued, when contacts were available, by such past-life researchers as Ian Stevenson. And then I came to the physical proofs: biometric comparisons, which are extensively used today in the forensic sciences. They consist of graphology; face, voice, iris, hand, fingerprint, and foot recognition tests; lie detector (polygraph test); and sodium pentothal application ("truth serum"). Also, DNA analysis is amply used in crime laboratories.

It was obvious that there was little hope of determining with forensic exactitude that Sherrie is Marilyn and Marilyn is Sherrie. According to the forensic precision of one-in-a-million chance occurrences, with Marilyn being the probe and Sherrie the control in such a comparison, the likely outcome would be that Marilyn is considered the real person and Sherrie the impostor. That is because they came from different sets of genetic parents. Yet, according to ancient wisdom it is clear that there is no duality between spirit and body, that the body is merely spirit manifest. Like a plant needs fertile ground in which to plant its seed and grow, the reincarnating spirit needs a set of parental genes in which to implant its spiritual code, which remains always constant. And since there is no separation between like components in the universe, it stands to reason that the genetic parents of an individual are not strangers to that individual, but at the same time they are not its spiritual counterpart. A plant collects from the ground the elements it needs to maintain its collective genetic code for millions of years and adapts itself according to the terrain. Two plants from the same species differ from each other due to the quality of the terrain in which they grow; while their fruits may differ in size, they are genetically one and the same. I feel the same applies to our spiritual code, as immortal souls who adapt to a new terrain (or parental genes) but retain most of their individuality and histories and imprint that signature on their biological host. Whether that code can be found in the junk human DNA is open to speculation. But, whatever the mechanism, the proof that biometrics transfer from one lifetime to the next has been repeatedly proven.

It became obvious that the criterion of how biometrics is used in forensics would not do justice to our research project because Marilyn and Sherrie have different parental DNA and environmental factors. Therefore, we would have to be satisfied with similarities between the two women. I picked biometric comparison tests that were the more readily available. Because face recognition, as discussed earlier, was verified as valid by famed researcher Ian Stevenson, M.D., I began with that comparison. I had to prove that the spiritual genetic constant imprinted similarities between the facial architecture of Marilyn's and Sherrie's chin, cheeks, lips, nose, eyes and eyebrows, forehead, and hairline, and ears. It appears that the face is more malleable to such imprints than any other part of the body, reflected in different facial expressions and the eyes as "windows of the soul." The similarities I found between Marilyn Monroe and Sherrie Lea Laird through face recognition comparisons at different periods of their lives, especially as teenagers, were very uncanny in detail. I also included a facial comparison between Kezia Laird and Gladys Baker. (All pictures are found in the color section.)

The next biometric marker I tested was handwriting, especially the women's signatures. I used a comparison between Sherrie's signature of Marilyn's name and Marilyn's famous signature in the yellow cement at Mann's Chinese Theater in Hollywood. The letters M, a, r, i, l, y, n, as well as M, o, n, r, o, e, look similar in both signatures. I found more similarities between letters in *The Marilyn Diaries* by Charles Casillo (page 7), dated June 12, 1960, and a letter addressed to me by Sherrie Lea Laird on May 20, 2005. Striking similarities were found between the two writing samples on the following characters: a, b, c, D/d, e, f, g, h, I, k, l, M/m, p, r, s, t, u, w, and x. Dissimilarities at times were between the following: A, d, E/e, u, and y.

Another biometric marker was between Marilyn's and Sherrie's hands. Though Sherrie's hands are slightly larger than Marilyn's due to parental genetic influence, the similarities of the shape of the hands, hand lines, fingers and fingernail comparisons were quite striking. Likewise, their feet could be compared as well. Again, Sherrie's feet are slightly larger than Marilyn's but have similar shape, toes, and toenails.

A biometric marker that proved to be very compelling was the similarity of their voices. Again I refrained from attempting forensic precision here, like in other biometric comparisons, but the similarities were again uncanny. I had Sherrie record her voice singing three of Marilyn's songs from the '50s simultaneously with her and mix the two on a CD. The voices were practically indistinguishable from each other. I know that singers can mimic other singers' voices, but a careful comparison shows that this is more than voice mechanics; it's their souls coming through in their voices. (Go to my website, www.pastlives.com, to hear this singing comparison.)

At the start of this feverish exploration into biometric comparisons, I woke up from a dream one night with the idea of perfecting Past/Present Life-Iris Recognition Comparison Test (PPL-IRCT). This would be most convincing, since presently iris recognition is the most advanced biometric test to establish the identity of an individual. I was stymied on my search for information until early October, when I read on the Internet that the government had declassified the iris recognition technology as sensitive. I immediately purchased an iris recognition camera. However, at the time of this writing, due to uncooperative computer experts, I've been unable to conduct proper tests. Once I master the technology myself, I'll try to modify it to pick up similarities rather than sameness, but will test for the precise identity as it is presently set. I suspect that, as with the other biometric tests, this will not prove helpful in proving reincarnation, for the reasons I've already explained. Please check my website for any updates on my continued biometric comparison research, including iris recognition testing.

To my chagrin, the handwriting biometric markers which I presented to two separate forensic experts confirmed that the forensic application to compare one and the same person in two different lifetimes is not workable for now. In its present form, graphology tests seek a high degree of precision and don't account for parental genetic differences; therefore, I did not get the results I had anticipated. It makes sense to me at this point to continue looking for biometric similarities and not clone-like sameness. Another factor could be a subjective response of the testing personnel influencing the results. One such forensic expert wouldn't even bother testing my samples when I told her that the subject of my research was proving the reincarnation of Marilyn Monroe.

The same thing happened with PPL-IRCT. After weeks of searching for an expert, a professor from a university computer science department allowed one of her students to perform the test. They used inadequate pictures of Marilyn and Sherrie, giving a negative result. When I obtained better iris pictures, the professor asked who the subjects were. Upon hearing that I was working on a reincarnation study of Marilyn Monroe, she refused to let her student redo the test. She further insisted that her university's name not be used in this book.

By this time I realized that my scientific inquiry would be more difficult than expected, since I couldn't get the needed cooperation from experts due to my subject matter. On several occasions, Sherrie and I attempted to contact various Hollywood friends of Marilyn Monroe from that era who were still alive. This would allow Sherrie to confirm personal, unreported details of their relationships with Marilyn, as she had successfully done with Ted Jordan. But to my regret, none of them responded to our inquiries. We tried without success to reach Jane Russell and Tony Curtis. George Barris, who Sherrie and I feel wrote the best book on Marilyn Monroe, *Marilyn: Her Life in Her Own Words*, was only willing to sell the rights for some of his Marilyn pictures to me. He was not—as of our last phone conversation—willing to meet with Sherrie, nor did he seem open to the idea of reincarnation. (Hopefully this book's publication and its indisputable past-life regression work will bring these celebrities, and others, forward.)

In the past the typical pattern of past-life research was more concerned with proving names, dates, locales, technical or artistic knowledge, and particularly the emotional problems people carry from one lifetime to another. I think we've excelled in these comparative studies. But there are two important differences in the research pattern of Sherrie Lea Laird as the reincarnation of Marilyn Monroe. One is that Marilyn was a worldwide celebrity, often called the Cleopatra of modern times. No recent Hollywood star's life and death have been so thoroughly dissected in books, on film, and on the Internet. Every detail of her life has been exposed for public consumption. The second difference is that

Marilyn and Sherrie's lifetimes were separated by only eleven months. Marilyn died on August 4, 1962, and Sherrie was born on July 11, 1963. And there is another component that complicates the matter even more: namely, and as it will be proved later in this book, that Sherrie's daughter Kezia is the reincarnation of Marilyn Monroe's mother. These factors and their possible "contamination" of our case make any legitimate inquiry tasking, and the lack of cooperation from forensic experts and old friends makes it even more daunting.

FALL ON DEAF EARS

Sherrie had greatly benefited from the regressions and our ongoing research, and felt like a huge weight had been lifted off her shoulders. She also stopped feeling "crazy," as she put it. She became more involved in her musical pursuits. She displayed a healthy curiosity and was open to discovering more about herself and unlocking the still-remaining mysteries buried deep within her soul. We continued to correspond not only about our research into Marilyn and the confirmations of Sherrie's intuitions and the regression results, but more importantly her psychological integration as well. She was progressively experiencing more flashbacks and dreams of her past life as Marilyn, and her conscious memory had been stimulated by the formal regressions and her own self-regressions. In Toronto I had instructed Sherrie on the use of a self-hypnotic technique that I had developed and used extensively on myself. The results of these as conveyed in her e-mails and phone conversations with me, many times in the form of long monologues, were fascinating. The further outside confirmation of our own research, that Sherrie was indeed the reincarnation of Marilyn Monroe, in the July 14, 2005, channeling by famed psychic and medium Kevin Ryerson had a tremendously positive, uplifting, and liberating effect on Sherrie. Like

Marilyn, Sherrie had a deep belief in psychics and psychic phenomena. This reading assuaged any lingering doubts and made the integration process from both lives more fluid.

The self-hypnosis technique was working as Sherrie proceeded to uncover more memories.

"Yes, I regress myself, and it's not too pleasant, but getting easier, especially when I realized I can visit with people. Last night I was thinking of Arthur [Miller] and there are some pics I see in my favorite book and I was thinking and relaxing . . . [and] feeling that the reason we are there on that day is that Arthur has to pick up some documents. I see him visiting a woman who is short, older with an accent. I think it's his mother, don't know if she is alive, or not yet, but he's there to get some documents that entitle him to do something: permission, identification, legal papers. I also believe it allows him to write something, or work on a playwright thing. Well, that's all for now. I do feel there was a time when I was very enamored with him the most, his looks, everything about him is attractive to me. It isn't 'til later, but then I'm changing too, and I'm not happy with me, and it falls apart . . . yes, he isn't protective enough; it's simply that he can't anticipate what I call my suffering and he is already fed up with it. So, he is short and irritated, which just comes across as not caring, which makes me drink more, but I did love."

This would also trigger memories in this life that referred to her past life.

"The other thing was, as far back as five years old. I wanted a man to lie on me. I knew I needed this, and I had a thing for the *Hawaii Five-0* guys and their suits. So, there must be something there. I mean, five years old. And though I didn't know what sex was, I don't think, I'm sure I knew it meant they loved you and wanted to be near you. And now, after the regressions, I'm sure it's the whole Secret Service thing . . . So, for sure, at five, a girl who knows this can only know it from a past life. Poor little

Sherrie's body; she thought she was going to be somebody and she's really just only a vehicle for M. What a strange, but obviously out-of-my-hands, situation."

I had sent Sherrie a copy of Charles Casillo's fictional *The Marilyn Diaries*, which impressed me with its blend of known events and statements by Marilyn Monroe with speculation about more private episodes in her life, especially the last days before her overdose. Sherrie's response was very revealing.

"This is exactly how we are. Now I'm just blown away that in our thinking we were the same. No one could shatter, or sway, me from KNOWING otherwise. These are our thoughts, the odd time. It does look lengthened by someone else's thoughts, but they're very good at matching it with mine. On page 153, last paragraph, she can barely stomach to write her real age down, but she's trying to do it, to take away the fear and thinking that if she writes it again (as she's not always fully afraid), all its power over her will go away. And she can say, 'See,' (as she does believe this inside) 'it's just a number. It means nothing.' Inside M knows of God very deeply, me too, but our egos . . . really fight with the importance of God, 'cause somewhere we believe that HE put these feelings in us to work and want and need more. So, He must want our egos to be huge and accomplish something great. Isn't it all for Him anyway?

"Adrian, it just sends me reeling to see the book. I am this person. I understand every word and every thought like a twin. I know what twins feel like, to be fully understood for the first time. We think and process thoughts and jump from story to story 'cause we want to write a book. But if we would, wouldn't it be boring? And, we can't get it to flow like a book. This is also me . . .

"I'll put it down, though I've been skimming and am shocked by the Jack-Bobby feelings, but the one thing it does make sense . . . is why he doesn't love me, why it felt it was written about Jack, though I felt very strongly Bobby was closer. And I even started thinking, 'Could it be about Bobby, as Jack's long gone?' . . . This brief time with the book has opened so much, and I wasn't expecting it. The writing style, the thoughts are a complete [match] with mine."

Sherrie had indicated to me that it had been more than ten years since she had read any Marilyn books, but I gave her the go-ahead to start reading and comparing information to her own memory of past events. Some of the conflicts with her intuitions and/or regression mistakes bothered her. She was sometimes her hardest critic.

"And I'm keeping a journal for you. I also started marking in the Marilyn tapes, books, even though all these details start to get to me. Of course, however, I did have a flash that makes sense to me. On August 3, I had seen myself [Marilyn] at a restaurant. This is correct. I had seen it as Joe, but don't forget that I get small glimpses of things: a black shirt, sitting with the elbows on the table, a strong looking man. Could just have easily been Peter, as in fact I've read now that M was out on the 3rd at a restaurant. This is something I've never previously known and only came with that after regressing. Now I'm happy to say it is in fact accurate. This makes me trust my judgment.

"Also, there were a couple of things that bothered me after regression. Fred Karger's wife. I had in fact thought her name was Jane and said the name Laura, or something, but that was in *How to Marry a Millionaire*—M's name.

"That Bobby was two years younger when in fact he was older by two years. So, it could just be the way I process the flashes I get, that he wasn't married and I had felt he was married, but perhaps only on paper as he wasn't in a relationship like Jack with Jackie. I felt Bobby was a workaholic and on duty 24/7.

"That I had in fact made descriptions of how I was to look for several events and at the time I wasn't sure about the black dress in the drawing, [but] I am now after reading that I have drawn a black dress also. Therefore, it conflicted with my thoughts that it was for Jack's party. And in fact the dress was taken off, even if it had maybe been put back on. I was correct after reading [the book that] when I had regressed, that this relationship was the beginning of the end. I had said that in the e-mail.

"I'm reading so many books at once, so therefore I'm keeping many, many notes. Now that we are getting all our eggs in a row, or however you say, I'm trying very hard to get organized, which is fun and kind of new for both M and S. We are to some extent, but our ambitions keep us striving forward and forgetting about the unfinished business."

But Sherrie's main source of inspiration or confirmation, I could say, was still the fictional though accurate, as she claims, *The Marilyn Diaries*.

"I am so glad that I didn't read *The Marilyn Diaries* before the regression and though I am blown away by the story/truths, connected so well, there were things in it, and I haven't finished it yet, but I saw about the dress coming off on the president's birthday. Almost everything I regressed on I was exactly right. I said that it doesn't last long and there was exhaustion. That I had been drunk and drinking, 'cause of nerves. That it was the beginning of the end. That was the night I feel the connection of Bobby, though written there, so many times there is no love, or connection. That I remember later feeling small or saddened by the event of Jack. I can't understand why she'd say on one hand, isn't he going to marry me, meaning Bobby, and then be with him in bed and then all these writings about how she doesn't love him.

"There's all this red diary thoughts in *The Marilyn Diaries* about her secret tapes and stuff and yet, the Kennedys knew they were being bugged, that the house was bugged and they're going to go there and kill her and take the red diaries? . . . [But] on top of it all, they were destroying document after document. Yet, they don't destroy that? And all these people coming and going that are [mobsters] and they kill her. And yet, the mob would've needed her alive to keep bugging her, as they yet didn't even remotely have enough and as I know and the whole world knows Jack did not sit there and divulge plan by plan by plan about her."

Of all the subjects about Marilyn Monroe's life, her mysterious death has been written about the most, and it drew the most emotional reactions from Sherrie. The level of her response on this subject indicated that it would be one of the main areas to clear in the upcoming round of regressions, now scheduled for November of 2005. A recent book on the subject, Matthew Smith's *Marilyn's Last Words: Her Secret Tapes and Mysterious Death*, triggered more recall on Sherrie's part.

Sent: August 08, 2005
From: Sherrie Lea Laird
To: Adrian Finkelstein, M.D.

I have this book. I've only looked at a page or two. It's completely based on murder, and it's all about tapes; in fact, I think it's called *Marilyn Tapes*. And this is not new at all in that one minute they show her making tapes and talking to Greenson, but then on another page they show she is really enjoying . . . taping her own voice and not, I presume, merely talking about all this and that. She is at times saying, and this is my take on it . . . "They say that I'm etc. etc." and "Do you know what I mean?" . . .

This is what I do know. There is a feeling for Bobby. I, like Mar, feel very little or no love most of my life. I told you about feeling almost asexual at times and then consumed with the thoughts that a man needs to dominate over my whole life. Swinging to and from needy and completely cold. This describes me to a "T." One minute, the only woman she's had sex with is Natasha, in *The Marilyn Diaries*, and the next minute the only woman is Joan. I believe it is possible that she considered trying this and if [she did, it] would only have been, not a graphic thing, but a simple situation that would have been so remorseful. She is completely opposite that.

I can't tell you how deeply I know, how little love she felt at times and then at times being so deeply in love with someone. It is not what drove her. These tapes are nothing new to me. I refuse to feel the need to address these book/tapes, newspaper [article]. [Sherrie is referring to the tape transcripts of

Marilyn Monroe given shortly before her death to her psychiatrist, Ralph Greenson. They were published in the *Los Angeles Times* on August 5, 2005, as revealed by prosecutor John Miner.] She was always reeling in and out of loves and hates. There for great passionate love to literally in a moment's notice . . . hate.

I will answer what I am sure of, and so far I haven't ended up being wrong. But one thing is for sure: There are things that are so bent out of shape they've taken a life of their own and literally become real. M was going to remarry Joe . . . I didn't read this anywhere 'til after the regressions. And they were going to go to Hawaii. She was going to hit them between the eyes with a new project and it just didn't get to happen. And you know what? With no real regrets because now she is endlessly a canvas on the world. She needed to die young and beautiful, not old and fat like many of the has-beens in Hollywood. It's just not what she could've handled. Die young and live forever or smear away, ruined and coughing and crumpled.

. . . Mar was intensely loving and intensely cold. It's the same way I feel today, and I just said it the other day, how the hell can anyone live without pills, really . . . honest to God? It's nearly impossible to be that good all the time, and that straight. It IS truly boring. It frees you. We are just not cut out from the same cloth as the average person. We are junkies who are not letting ourselves be junkies, and that's like a person who never stops being the deepest junkie.

I'll have to grab and read the book. I remember being disturbed and noticing it was all about moods and at times she was irritated and toying. Well, that's what I instinctively felt: sometimes honest, sometimes exaggerating. What do you think of this? I feel like I'm the only one who truly knows her. And funny, I've felt like this for 25 years now.

Sent: August 08, 2005
From: Sherrie Lea Laird
To: Adrian Finkelstein, M.D.

Also, she was using the tape recorder for singing. And also I [read] at one point in the book that someone who bugged her had all these tapes, and then someone who heard them said they were spliced. When she first realized that it's possible for her to be followed and taped, she didn't blab so much. You know how easy it is for people to whisper to each other and no one needs to hear it.

When someone is drinking and doing pills, it is possible for even things to have happened that she would completely forget. Therefore, I may never know, or only from a psychic point of view. Possibly yes. This was simply the most ambitious and confused person I ever knew besides me. It's our lack of . . . achieving [something], why surely I feel compelled to pick up where she left off. She wanted her art as a podium to change the world. I don't know how this works. I only know it's what I've felt all my life. But yet, moods and [being] depressed and facing all the naysayers taking the wind out of her sails she'd fall all the way down, and then the cycle would start all over again. I'm going to do this and that and come out fighting like a champ . . . and then boom, no support system. Who really understood her? And all the dreams seem useless, futile, and undoable. Now here she is, wrecking my plans and ruining my karma with her karma. How will I ever achieve success for my singing and my plan to save animals when she had it all and threw it away? It truly feels like she did all the bad things and then stuck me out here to fend for myself and freak my family out. Please God let it all be for the good.

Loving you,
Sher

Sent: August 08, 2005
From: Sherrie Lea Laird
To: Adrian Finkelstein, M.D.

Hi Adrian,

I got the tapes, and I'm agreeing to it. It's real and all I have to add to it, really, is that in the tapes [are] feelings of that particular day. On a different day you would have heard more love for Arthur or Frank or Peter. Some days pity for Eunice and some days pure irritation. They capsulated a moment of time;

This and the following three pages are photos of Sherrie Lea and Marilyn at corresponding ages.

Comparison photos of
Gladys Baker
and Kezia Laird

Comparison of
Sherrie Lea's and
Marilyn's handwriting

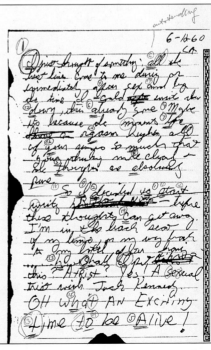

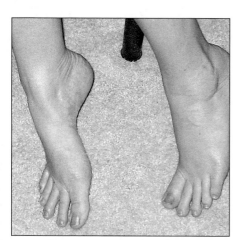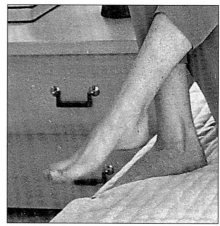

Comparison of Marilyn's and Sherrie Lea's feet

SATURDAY *Night*

Canada's Magazine   September 1996

**Good Copps
Bad Copps:**
On the road
with Sheila

**Ten dead
peacekeepers:**
Did a Canadian
general
fail to act?

the Niagara
shoot

Marilyn Monroe, a romantic setting,

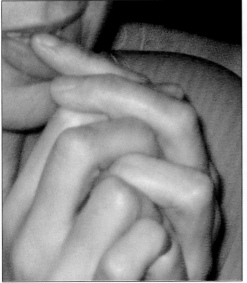

Comparison of Marilyn's (top) and
Sherrie Lea's hands

A portrait of Marilyn Monroe by Sherrie Lea Laird, signed "M.M.R.— Marilyn Monroe Returns." The dedication on the back reads: "To Adrian, who helped me recover what was almost lost and fixing it! Indebted for eternity, all my love and kisses, Sherrie Lea, aka Marilyn Monroe, Aug. 12, 2005."

Dr. Adrian Finkelstein, Sherrie Lea Laird, and Kezia in Toronto, immediately after the first round of regressions on May 4, 2005.

as the feelings changed drastically, when waning for one and increasing for another, the separations would grow like that.

I know like me, when I looked back on my old journals, I couldn't believe how many times I abandoned love for one, just 'cause of love for another . . . pure love and adoration. Then, absolutely for lack of a better word, grossed OUT. These tapes are accurate, but they do not prove a murder.
Back to you,
XOXO

On Friday, August 5, 2005, the *Los Angeles Times* published an article on column one entitled "New Chapter in the Mystery of Marilyn: Her Own Words?" After 43 years of silence, former prosecutor John W. Miner (86) revealed the transcripts of Marilyn Monroe's confidential tapes that she gave to her psychiatrist, Ralph Greenson, M.D., in the short period prior to her death. Back then, Miner was investigating the circumstances of Marilyn's death and obtained from Dr. Greenson her secret tapes, which reveal she did not intend to commit suicide. On the contrary, Marilyn had made many immediate plans that only a person who wants to live would make. For instance, she was expecting new furniture from Mexico to arrive on August 6, 1962—two days after her death—and was planning a vacation to Hawaii with her ex-husband, Joe DiMaggio, with whom she wanted to reconcile.

Sent: August 10, 2005
From: Sherrie Lea Laird
To: Adrian Finkelstein, M.D.

Please be aware, Adrian, that Miner does keep saying I died by enema and that I was murdered. This is where it stops and I honestly would have felt something more attached for Joan. I don't feel this is accurate. Natasha I loved, and she cared for me. I love Lily, and admitted to wrestling around while drunk and high with Ted. But these other sexual encounters do not ring true. At least I'd need to go under and be asked specifically. Miner is the guy who has helped write an entire book on [Marilyn's] murder. A lot of his stuff is misquotes and an attempt for him to leave something behind for his family. That's my take on it. I believe he heard tapes or stole notes. It is not fully accurate, but several basic things were talked of here. Marilyn is not one to discuss so openly her sexual habits. I haven't been wrong about our sameness yet. Maybe while drunk. But she so badly wanted a strong dominant man who was powerful and daddy-ing, yet sensitive. She never craved woman love other than for them to be really caring and really not jealous, the truest bond, even more fun than hanging out with men. But it is so rare that, other than my Aunt Anne, just like Mar, I've never found a woman who can be so open, without judgment.

More e-mails followed in the coming weeks and months as Sherrie continued reading and going to Marilyn websites and comparing her "firsthand," if rather intuitive, read on many of the standard Marilyn topics that have fascinated fans and curiosity seekers since her death. But, all of the conspiracy theories surrounding Marilyn's death continued to dominate her research and thinking. I believe this fixation has its basis in Marilyn's death due to respiratory failure; in this life, Sherrie has had breathing problems since childhood. They are especially connected to her Marilyn flashbacks, and the association played out as a kind of death urge. In essence, the breathing apparatus enables a person to take life in through the air it inhales. Imagine not being able to breathe, or dying from a kind of suffocation and recalling it in your next life. Lack of breath is tantamount to lack of life, to death. In Sherrie's case this is a classic continuation, according to the law of reincarnation, the law of continuity. In his instinct theory, Sigmund Freud presented the two powerful forces of life and death being at odds in each individual. He called them the libido and morbido. Libido (love) usually indicates the sexual drive while morbido relates to the aggressive drive. Aggression, anger, and rage are the opposite expressions of love and sex. There is a joke: Make love, not war. Or, make both—get married. Certainly Marilyn/Sherrie's lives swung back and forth between these two poles, especially when married or in a similarly intense relationship (like Marilyn's with JFK). Unfortunately, Marilyn's aggression was taken inward and resulted in what seems to be a drug overdose.

Sherrie's gradual healing from her past-life trauma during the process of my research counseling, despite rough patches, became increasingly more evident. My strategy to get Sherrie involved in the task of our research was of immense help. However, at times during our telephone conversations, she told me about "rough times" when dealing with Kezia or Chris, who "don't understand me." These occurrences would throw her back into more depression, and she would say, "What's the point? I better give up." On the up swing, she would snap back and be bubbly on the phone, childishly giggling, "Yea, you are my savior, Doctor F. I feel so relieved of the pain of being Mar." Sherrie, as well as all my patients dealing with past-life trauma, is faced with a daunting psychological conundrum: Sherrie is not only dealing with the integration of past-life memories and traumas, trying to reestablish her own persona, but must also deal with the integration problems we all face in life. It's not just her Marilyn memories or persona. It's her unresolved childhood issues, the sexual and relationship trauma, self-esteem issues, and a slew of others we all carry with us. When possible, I use a variety of psychoanalytical strategies to heal such patients. But as a psychiatrist with a decidedly spiritual bent, I often encourage my patients, as I have with Sherrie, not to rely too heavily on others for completion, including their doctors. Rather, we must all seek completion through the higher power within us and everyone else, sharing that unitary consciousness with each other. The main advice I give most of my patients is spiritual: Be aware of God within always. This is the greatest blessing to humanity. Act always as if God were within you and you will witness miracles happening. And they are not really miracles, but the manifestation of the natural law.

That being said, it is ironic that Sherrie and I were both faced with a similar situation in regards to our ongoing research project. Finding confirmation of our biometric comparisons or other outside verifications was elusive, to say the least. We were being forced, it seemed, to know and honor our own truth in regard to Sherrie's claim and be satisfied with that knowledge. But, at times, our search did border on the comical. And I must add that, in retrospect, some of my attempts were ill-conceived. In my mind, I had discovered the Holy Grail of reincarnation studies but nobody would believe me, or they would question my motives without reviewing my findings. In June of 2005, I had Sherrie contact a private investigator in Toronto with the idea of having him or one of his colleagues conduct a lie detector test on her. I had devised a 23-question test. Some of the questions were: "Has Marilyn Monroe been your idol to imitate?" "Do you fake your identity or resemblance with Marilyn Monroe in order to advance your present career?" "Is the feeling that you are Marilyn Monroe reincarnated coming to you primarily as a result of books, movies, and other information you acquired about her?"

It seems that our talks with this first private investigator and later with others—even one Sherrie's father, a former police officer, arranged—would be agreeable when their exorbitant rates were accepted, but would become problematic once they viewed the questionnaire and understood the subject of our inquiry. I had had the same problem with the college professor interested in our iris recognition study, who was interested until she found out the subject of the comparison. As I mentioned in the previous chapter, we had attempted to contact varied Hollywood friends of Marilyn Monroe for confirmation of private details known only to them and Marilyn, but without success. Another track I took at this time was to contact CMG Worldwide, who legally represents and manages Marilyn's estate. I thought they might have items of clothing or furniture that Sherrie could identify—a reincarnation ploy used to identify each succeeding Dali Lama in Tibet of years past. At the very least, I thought they would be anxious to participate in our research. I thought how wonderful it would be if they helped fund our research. They turned a deaf ear to all my inquiries. It was very naïve of me to think that they would jeopardize, in their mind, annual proceeds of eight million dollars from the exploitation of Marilyn's name and image, as if Sherrie were going to make a reincarnation claim and sue them in court.

We had earlier initiated contact with a famous news commentator through a mutual friend of mine, one interested in unusual people with interesting claims, but while they appeared to be mildly amused, we were asked to contact them once a book was published. *People Magazine* and CNN didn't even respond to my direct inquiries. Sherrie and I were eager to get our message out, but we now understood the importance of publishing a book with a reputable publisher in order to be taken seriously. This was a task I had already begun. Sherrie at first appeared to be undaunted by our turndowns, which would change and create more problems. Following is an e-mail from her during this period of unbridled, and also naïve, idealism.

Hi Adrian! How are you? Well I thought I would try to get a lot done today. I really have been in the habit of shutting off or out the whole world and staying awake very late and sleeping in . . .

However, my biological clock is such that I am with great ease a night person and with great difficulty a day person. So, maybe Joe [my influential friend and a believer in reincarnation] will want you to regress him. Were they interested in our story? Were they believing in this kind of thing? [Sherrie is referring here to a *People Magazine* contact facilitated by Joe.] I'm so proud of you, going to such trouble . . .

Anyway I wrote so many great e-mails to films, funds, documentarians, and magazines. Nothing back yet. I'm a very impatient person when I write out something.

One magazine did write back, an online one a few days ago, and said it was very interested and could I use the submitted form to resubmit, which I did. Nothing as of yet.

Well apparently, because I have a British passport, it could in fact take some time [to get a Canadian passport]. I will try for my Canadian citizenship. Hah—unless we can find someone in the U.S. to marry me. Hee! Hee! I don't know. Do they still do stuff like that? Imagine, the most famous American female can't get back in!!

The great psychologist Carl Jung, in his study of more than 80,000 dreams, concluded that dreams and their sources, the unconscious mind, were compensatory to the conscious mind and its attitudes and fixations. In other words, if you have a negative attitude about somebody in your life, you may have a very positive dream about them to compensate for your waking attitude. They're neither as bad as you think nor as good as your dream portrays them, but rather somewhere in between. The conscious and unconscious minds are seeking a balanced perspective. From these studies, Jung concluded that there is a compensatory function operating at all levels of life, as the forces within and without us attempt to harmonize and balance each other. I mention this because in August of 2005 I made a remarkable discovery that had the effect of counterbalancing our precipitous rush to prove our case with biometric comparisons and to tout our results to a mostly hostile media at that time, and threw us back onto ourselves and the process of our mutual self-healing.

Back in April of 2005, when Sherrie had contacted me after a six-year break, I mentioned to her as part of my pre-regression proof of her claim that according to her actual birthday, July 11, 1963, she had the same North Moon Node in her astrological chart as Marilyn Monroe:

> In regards to astrology, I've noticed that your North Moon Node in this life is in the sign of Cancer, and so it was in your life as M. What does it mean? During my research into past lives many years ago, I luckily came across this discovery of another mystery that proved reincarnation. Namely, most of my hypnotic subjects experiencing through regression a past life with a tragic, unjust, and premature end, reincarnated (i.e., came back) in the same North Moon Node in their present life and in a matter of only a few months or years. The North Moon Node represents in astrology about 90% of what a person has to learn in a particular incarnation. Therefore, it is another confirmation in your case that you most probably are M reincarnated. M's birthday was June 1, 1926; a date in which the North Moon Node falls in the Cancer sign, though her sun sign

was Gemini. Your birthday in this current life, as you indicated in one of your first e-mails . . . is July 11, 1963, which corresponds to the North Moon Node in the Cancer sign. This same North Moon Node repetition from one life to the next usually shows, and this applies to you as well, that you have not completed the specific learning experience as M; thus, you continue the same now, as Sherrie . . . Briefly, when the North Moon Node is in Cancer, one has to learn about emotions and peace, love, and harmony in the family. In addition, as a woman it teaches one to be cuddled, loved, and taken care of by a real man—not an exploitative and selfish one.

What I discovered in late August of 2005 was that Gladys Baker was born on May 27, 1902, which places her North Moon Node in Scorpio and the South Moon Node in Taurus. Sherrie's daughter Kezia was born nine months after Gladys Baker's death, on December 11, 1984, which places her North Moon Node in Taurus and her South Moon Node in Scorpio. As I explained in my book *Your Past Lives and the Healing Process*, a person who has experienced a full chronological life often reincarnates with the opposite, or 180-degree, switch in the moon node alignments. Scorpio and Taurus are 180 degrees opposite. Scorpio is a sign of war; Taurus is a sign of peace. Gladys came back as Kezia to shift from a life of war, struggle, and paranoid schizophrenia (Scorpio North Moon Node) to an easier life of peace and sanity, in addition to being together with her beloved daughter, though this time as the daughter in order to complete unfinished business and heal the emotional wounds of their previous life together.

The fact that both Sherrie and Marilyn, and Kezia and Gladys, have related North/South Moon Node positions—which is statistically improbable—again showed me that there was a higher force at work in this project and that I needed to focus more of my energy in the writing of the first draft of my manuscript and attend to the healing of Sherrie Lea Laird and myself. Or, I could say that I had swung out of balance and needed a corrective course in the pursuit of my research and therapy. Unlike the classical model of the objective therapist and the subject patient, I realized long ago that since we draw into our lives the lessons needed to progress on our path, each patient, with their history and problems, is a reflection of my own psyche as much as theirs. "Physician, heal thyself" was not an idle claim from my perspective.

Complicating matters further between me and my research subject was the revelation I received of my past-life connection to Marilyn/Sherrie. This placed me on a personal healing arc. I experienced an eerie and profoundly pleasant sense of surprise when research of my past life as a French physician confirmed that my doctor-patient relationship with Sherrie has been a long one that spans at least two lifetimes. As with my patients, I felt that a missing part of me was retrieved and repossessed, snapping back into place and making me feel much more complete. It confirmed my own past-life regression in 1998—that I was a noble French physician who had healed a beautiful young nun by the name of Louise at a convent in the year 1667. During my research, I discovered an historical portrait of Louise de la Valliere, whose visage is strikingly similar to the image of Louise I had envisioned, even to the minutest detail. What was amazing was her uncanny resemblance to Sherrie Lea Laird. I had an immediate intuitive flash that Sherrie had indeed been the disgraced nun, former courtesan of the king, whom I had ministered to at a nunnery in France so many centuries ago. I learned further that Antoine Daquin, the principal physician of King Louis XIV, received the appointment as a result of the recommendation by Louise de la Valliere to her old friend Madam de Montespan, the king's mistress. This came because Louise was so impressed with his healing of her. By my recall, that healing was completed in 1672, the same year the history books show that King Louis XIV nominated Antoine Daquin as his principal physician and the superintendent of the royal botanic gardens, positions he occupied for 22 years. I immediately shared this insight with Sherrie, who felt the truth of what I had surmised when she contacted me: that we had a past-life connection as well.

It is interesting to note how reincarnation patterns work, how the skills developed from one lifetime to the next are expanded. Sherrie has been an entertainer, musician, and artist in more than one lifetime. Mozart was a musician and composer in other lives as well. I've been a physician and healer in many of my lifetimes. That's why certain attributes we have developed in past lives continue to manifest in the present, as do spiritual lessons in accord with the law of cause and effect known in Eastern philosophy as karma, or in Western physics as the Newtonian law of action and reaction. The laws of continuation and compensation are contained herein. These universal laws work in concert with reincarnation to insure that we are born in the proper time and place to either pay our debts or receive the rewards due from our past lives. Various talents and skills flourish with little or no training to elevate themselves into superior attributes. This does not happen by accident. These gifts are the result of hard work and perseverance in previous lives. In the cycle of reincarnation, nothing is forgotten.

On the other hand, we may be born with a disability or with certain mental, physical, or emotional limitations that compel us to develop those capacities and which we may find not altogether to our liking. Life is a schooling ground. We reincarnate into the classroom of earthly existence with a certain curriculum of instruction. Those subjects or issues that were mastered earlier come easily to us; those we have failed to develop or heal will have to be repeated until they are mastered. And according to Eastern philosophies and such occidental sources as Edgar Cayce, to facilitate the learning of our lessons we often journey from one lifetime to the next in groups. We reincarnate with those to whom we are bound through love or hate. It often happens that to learn the lesson of the Golden Rule, we will encounter in this life those whom we have injured or mistreated in former lives to rectify the damage and clear our karma. We may also find ourselves in a series of alternating or compensating relationships—as master or servant, parent or child, and husband or wife. Groups of souls also reincarnate together and sometimes on a mission or for a greater purpose.

This brings me back to the reincarnational pattern or karma between me and Sherrie Laird. According to my research, Louise de la Valliere (a possible former incarnation of Marilyn/Sherrie) suffered as a result of the stress in the court that manifested in schizophrenia-like symptoms, or hysteria, after being abandoned by King Louis XIV. She was the king's first mistress, and in 1667 she became a nun and I was called on as a physician to administer to her. Interestingly enough, I must have employed a similar psychospiritual methodology with Louise to heal her of these distressing symptoms, probably not unlike the approach, along with regression therapy, that I used in this life to treat and heal Sherrie. It is interesting to note that I discovered this connection during a past-life regression in 1998, just prior to being first contacted by Sherrie.

In regards to the karma between us, besides the obvious continuation of the doctor/patient relationship, Sherrie must have sought me out not only to heal her of a similar psychological malady but, in the process, to elevate, due to the notoriety of her past life as Marilyn Monroe, my cause of introducing past-life regression therapy to the general public. In addition, our connection would help transmit my message of love, healing, and peace to the world. This is my mission in the master plan, according to my spirit guides, and it is facilitated greatly by my treatment of Marilyn/Sherrie, which also brings a comprehensive healing of my own soul. This therapeutic relationship has given me the opportunity to remove the remaining blocks in the pursuit of my goal, which, for a soul with my history, is the greatest healing possible.

In the fall of 2005, after six months of intensely working with Sherrie on our research and guiding her through an extensive and difficult healing process, I began to note, as it was also brought to my attention by my loving wife and close friends, that a transference and countertransference were happening in my relationship with her. In layman terms, Sherrie was subconsciously relating to me in the same way she would to a former key figure in her life. Likewise, this evoked in me a similar subconscious countertransference, treating her in a similar manner. It is customary in psychotherapy for the helper to make use of his/her own reactions (countertransference) to the subject in an attempt to better understand that person and be more effective in assisting her. At some point the constant, almost-daily stream of e-mails between Sherrie and me, our ongoing and collaborative research, and writing a book became overly time-consuming. I realized then more than ever my striving toward a kind of self-realization. What was driving me was my history as a healer; my soul's yearning over many lifetimes. I needed to release any blocks, barriers, obstacles, and limitations that would separate me from that goal. Thus, I over-identified with the vehicle of that self-affirmation, Sherrie and our research together. On her part, I must've represented a savior figure, with my treatment of her saving her from a life of psychological misery that bordered on insanity.

I underwent more than 700 hours of psychoanalysis by a training analyst many years ago and developed from that experience the so-called "observing ego" (i.e., I observe with my objective, conscious self how my subconscious is operating in any given situation). Thus, I was able to gauge how this person, Sherrie, makes me feel. Indirectly, I can sense her own transference and get to know her better. As a result of knowing her better, I am able to cater to her needs, abilities, and liabilities. In Sherrie's case, she acted like a very sweet, lost little girl at times, afraid of the falling sky—a persona that Marilyn had adopted early in her career and that helped to catapult her to fame. To her I am the hero who defends and rescues her. She is the little girl and I'm the daddy, loving and protecting. This is a typical transference scenario in the broadest terms and can be a powerful analytical tool.

Under these circumstances, the transference and counter-transference are bound to be played out. In our research design, I'm not to interpret her transference. But observing it, I've recommended a number of times that Sherrie and I stick to the task of carrying out our research study and achieving our lofty goals. Spiritual healing blends beautifully with such an approach. That is why making God an active third partner has become the best guide for dealing with any subconscious reaction to each other. This is not suppression but a re-channeling of the energies in constructive directions: for Sherrie, research, her music career, and family and friends; for me, balancing my obligation as a therapist and, in this case, a researcher.

As noted earlier, there were many disappointments due to a general lack of cooperation by different people in obtaining more biometric evidence to prove our case. Also, as time progressed, I noticed that Sherrie had become more abrupt, short, irritable, and extremely sensitive—in her mind, for a good reason. She felt that I "don't understand" her. She wanted to have more control over the research process and book writing tasks even though, practically speaking, I gave her more than was customarily allotted a research subject. Her moods would swing from her usual sweetness to outright aggression. At other times she would be cooperative. Her moodiness intensified to the point that to save all of our hard work, I needed to set a definite time for the next round of regressions so as to liberate her from her remaining Marilyn demons through emotional abreactions, which had been part of the research plan from the beginning. We decided on mid-November 2005 in Toronto. Since the scientific results were disappointing, or less conclusive than I had hoped, I would also need further indisputable confirmation of the Sherrie/Marilyn reincarnation pattern to complete her healing.

These difficulties with Sherrie, blocks and emotional regression in her healing process, made this next round more urgent and critical. Sherrie's story had come to a climax. The situation had become dire, and I could do nothing but leave the resolution up to the next round of regressions. Would Sherrie be able, after six months of research with therapeutic potential, to do the intense work needed? Were the difficulties in this research going to hinder the outcome? My wife was certainly leery of me spending more time with Sherrie in Toronto, even with her present. But we were able to clear the atmosphere through more affirmations of love, and in the end Shulah was very supportive of the process and as always perceptive regarding the results of our inquiry.

An ill-advised approach at this time, which only deepened Sherrie's despair and further stressed the course of our research, was her becoming a member of a Marilyn Monroe fans forum, a

Yahoo! Group. She wanted to learn from these Marilyn-savvy people today's topical issues in order to give the right message to the world. However, these fans were quite skeptical of Sherrie's story in the beginning, especially when it came to our chief witness, the controversial—in their minds—Ted Jordan, whose book few regarded highly. Given their fan status, their skepticism seemed to be their idolization of a dead icon and a reluctance to relinquish and replace Marilyn with a live substitute. Following is an e-mail Sherrie addressed to the forum, which reflects her state of mind vis-à-vis our main research goal, to heal her soul:

My doctor makes some fabulous points. [Sherrie is referring to my presentation of her as the reincarnation of Marilyn Monroe in one of my posts on this forum.] But the point is, it has to come from me that there are a lot of things I've wanted to correct. When I first started to read Ted's [Ted Jordan] book, I liked it, and then ended up throwing it away. I knew what was true and what was false. I actually defended Bob Slatzer when on the phone with Ted, who didn't like him [Slatzer is thought to have falsely claimed having an affair with Marilyn, commercializing it to the utmost]; I know what's true and what's not. I've lived it. I had such a difficult life [as Marilyn], with my own life now. I don't have the stamina or the intelligence to make any of this up and, quite frankly, because of my doctor's book and stuff, I'm quite exhausted. I am the reincarnation of Marilyn Monroe, and contrary to [those in] my surroundings who seem to take [criticism] harder than I do, I couldn't care less. It gets me nothing. ABSOLUTELY NOTHING. I have my voice. I wanted to be a singer as well then, my interactions, questions, and [probes] are between me and God. I don't owe one single person, including my doctor, to come forward and do this to myself and my daughter Kezia, who I almost called Natasha and didn't know why. Gladys died March 11, 1984. Nine months to the day, December 11, 1984, she [Kezia] was born to me. She looks and acts like Gladys, too, not just me. I married an army guy next door whom I didn't love because I thought it would help my career, and it just goes on and on. ALL NOT KNOWING who she [Marilyn] was or why. I don't need Marilyn Monroe's life. It was already painful the first time. I'm just trying to grow. 'Cause if it's true, about reincarnation and growth, I don't think I want to come back.

Love and kisses
Sher [Cherie from *Bus Stop*, considered her best movie]
She was a singer named Cherie Lee, and so am I, Sherrie Lea.
Countless, countless synchronicities.

Prior to the November 2005 regressions, Sherrie and I exchanged a few e-mails that further reflect the strain in our work. In my delicate healing mission, I used most of my professional experience, intuitions, and God's guidance in my dealings with Sherrie. These last exchanges, prior to our November regressions, were a prelude of what was awaiting me during my upcoming trip to Toronto:

Hi dear Sher,
How are you? In today's blog you mentioned that you have some questions you want answered during our upcoming regressions. Please, e-mail them to me ASAP in order to gauge and possibly integrate them in the questionnaire! We only want the TRUTH: murder, suicide, accidental overdose, and/or any other concerns. Only your subconscious, aided by your superconscious, can reveal the TRUTH to your conscious [mind], and to the entire world. Yes, there is unfortunately injustice in the world. Governments, justice, religion, money, and politics are a reflection of a consensus of how people think, feel, and act. Hatred and war start in the heart of each individual. Your message as Marilyn Monroe reincarnated: LOVE, HEALING, AND PEACE IN THE WORLD AND FOR ANIMALS, which is our main goal through *Marilyn Returns: The Healing of a Soul* [and] cannot be achieved by a message of hatred. Such a message MUST be a message of LOVE. And like hatred and war, LOVE, HEALING, AND PEACE start in the heart of each individual. People must change through such a message from haters to lovers. Like the fingers of the hand, FIVE RACES, we belong to the same hand, we are ONE AND ONE WITH GOD, sharing the same blood, being nourished by the same nutrients and

cleansed by the same oxygen. This is the writing on the wall we must learn to read. Sherrie Lea Laird, the reincarnation of Marilyn Monroe, must change her ways. That is her real soul healing. And then, as a result, through people's newly exercised positive free choice that GOD gave them, they will accordingly change their politics, government, religion, and justice system, and the way they relate to money, in the spirit of GOD WITHIN AND EVERYWHERE, WHICH RADIATES LOVE, HEALING, AND PEACE IN THE WORLD AND FOR ANIMALS.

LOVE, LIGHT, PEACE, JOY, AND GOD BLESS YOU, Adrian

Sent: November 04, 2005
From: Sherrie Lea Laird
To: Adrian Finkelstein, M.D.

Yes, I agree with all you have said. Did I say something opposite? I find what I'm saying not about hate, but absolute emergency change. Let me know. Not hate, it's not working; it's just that obvious.
xo

Sent: November 04, 2005
From: Adrian Finkelstein, M.D.
To: Sherrie Lea Laird

Hi dear Sher,
You can see that before we can effectively change the governmental and religious institutions in our culture, which are reflections of how people think, feel, and act, we have to start changing ourselves. No, I know that at heart you are a lover and not a hater. But the way you wrote the blog today may be misconstrued, which may give us some unnecessary difficulties with those who should help us in propagating our humanitarian message loud and clear: LOVE, HEALING, AND PEACE TO THE UNIVERSE AND ALL ANIMALS. Loving, and blessing you and your family and friends in God's name,

Adrian

Sent: November 04, 2005
From: Sherrie Lea Laird
To: Adrian Finkelstein, M.D.

Hi Doc,

No, not just at heart but in my words, too. Yes I might have the Scottishness in me, to say things loud and proud. But I'm not wrong in [pointing out] the mess of the world. I believe these are the [important] things; my dream is for people, not institutions, the people who've had ENOUGH to band together. ONLY they can change things, NOT STUFFY BOOKS and the frightened. Actually, my mood lately from being at the Yahoo! Groups is one of being fed up with it all. I look forward to continuing on our wonderful project. I can't wait to see you and I can't wait to forward the info to John, our book editor. But what good am I if I don't speak the truth, especially for ones who can't or won't talk because of fear. If I am lucky enough to have Oprah read my blog, then she will see all the way thru. I have maintained such honesty, such ache for every man. She won't question our book at all. Please don't call, 'cause I don't want to talk about it. My voice is one for every-body. Not the famous, everyone, as was Marilyn's. I know this is why she dreamed of a life at the presidential podium, for she saw how they [JFK and Marilyn] rallied people who dreamed of all being treated fairly. It has stayed with me in every cell of my body. Until I wake up tomorrow and see I have done wrong, you should give me that option with trust and not be frightened of the blog. A white-haired man tried to kill me last night as I was driving home from rehearsal, and it just puts a bad taste in my mouth of their [reckless] behavior. I'm talking about stuffy people, heads of estab-lishments, who . . . [write] laws down which do not work, because of fear that they'll be robbed of the comforts in their current lives. This is what I boycott. Leaving the hungry and the homeless [in] the ghettos, [no] health insurance and the [high] taxes . . . because it means they'd have to part with their safe and bored [lives] pro-ducing white lines. Please don't talk to me about this; it will get you nowhere. Our story is one of healing. The media, I will point out, is where healing is robbed from me and all others like me, 'cause they are brainwashed . . .

Sher

Sent: November 04, 2005
From: Adrian Finkelstein, M.D.
To: Sherrie Lea Laird

Hi Sher,

Even before you'd written your heartfelt reply to me, I decided not to call you. I'm not frightened of anybody [or] anything. You don't know me. I've been poorer than the poorest growing up as a young child, so you don't have to teach me about being poor. There were days in communist Romania when I had nothing to eat. If anyone can empathize with the poor and downtrodden, it's me. I'm seeing a lot of poor patients without pay. And my oldest daughter resembles her father, as she is in Africa, Senegal, volunteering for free to help the poor and the sick. I love her with all my heart for doing so, and she got all my encouragement in her humanitarian mission. You don't know me and jump to conclusions. I know very well there is injustice in the world. Helen Keller, the famous blind and deaf woman, said "There is a lot of suffering in this world, but there is also a lot of undoing of it!" My intention is to make people aware of the wisdom of the ages, to start knowing and healing themselves first. This doesn't distract me from fighting against tyranny and injustice in the world at a societal level. Speak your mind. I speak mine, too. Unfortunately, if Mar would've been diplomatic enough to put up with certain rules, she would have succeeded. "Hi Doc"? Ha! ha! God's Love be with you. I'll only pray to God to guide us the right way,

Adrian

Sherrie replied immediately, "See, this is where you don't know me and jump to conclusions. I get so angry, for I'm not calling you frightened, but the people you think I'll offend. Going to finish reading now . . ."

Sherrie continued her train of thought: "Me, I am your friend. I said how much of a savior you are to me. You literally saved my life, and I loved the Romanian part of the book. Why do you fear the things I say so much? YOU know Mar, you know Sher, and you should realize this is part of the healing, protecting others in spite of the HEADS OF EVERYTHING . . . I say nothing that isn't true. You don't need to control or be embarrassed of what I say."

It seems that we didn't have a truce yet:

Sent: November 04, 2005
From: Sherrie Lea Laird
To: Adrian Finkelstein, M.D.

I have to ask you, how did this come to be about you any-way, when this is about me speaking on the blog, which no one really reads? And why are we fighting [over] this? It is what we've argued about before. This being about you, when it's not. I don't want to sugarcoat what I say. It won't hurt the book because the minute I'm on TV this will come out one way or the other, and then we'd really get shot down. They need to know what I'm like in advance: that I'm not lying and that I'm caring for mankind just like you are.

Why are we having yet another fight over what I've said? I'm so tired of this.
XO

I sensed that I had to capitulate at this point to restore peace and promote further healing. Therefore, I wrote to her, "NO FIGHT!!! PEACE!!!" And here came the truce. I could practically hear Sherrie's giggling and childish voice in her words.

Sent: November 04, 2005
From: Sherrie Lea Laird
To: Adrian Finkelstein, M.D.

Okay, goodie!
Hey, did you know there is a Marilyn movie on tonight? It's with Mira Sorvino and just now she opened pills and put them in a drink. I'm so proud of myself 'cause all that knowledge came from me. When I was Sher going under regression, I just

assumed she popped pills. I haven't seen all of this movie. Just by coincidence only [saw] this bit of it. And I was right, the pics that Bert Stern took a few weeks before she died were in her house 'cause I recognized the brown furniture. Did it really have all that stuff in it? Do you think they recreated it? And have you ever seen this movie? It was very weird.

Prior to this round of exchanges, I had e-mailed her the itinerary for regressions.

Sent: October 25, 2005
From: Adrian Finkelstein, M.D.
To: Sherrie Lea Laird
Subject: Travel Plans

Hi dear Sher,
How are you? I hope you're feeling better and more rested. I've just purchased the plane tickets for Toronto and made the hotel reservation . . . Shulah will accompany me to visit with one of my cousins, Anca, who lives in Toronto. However, we will have plenty of time to perform about 20 hours of regression, which are needed. I'm looking forward to them. I know you are not looking forward to the regressions. But, like M, when it came to that reluctance to do something she was very thorough on the movie set, and we must do the same with the regressions as they will constitute the essence of our entire work, per Bob and John, and I fully concur with them. This is because I see how difficult it is to get an Iris Recognition Test done. It seems it is a government-sensitive issue, as this test is performed now on a limited scale by select government employees in different airports in order to catch terrorists. Therefore . . . we need more proof for skeptics and disbelievers, as far as that goes, to back it [biometric proof] up with regressions. I'll still do my best to find the right connection to have the Iris Recognition Test done. But until then, regressions are extremely important. Bob told me yesterday that the final manuscript should be finished by the end of January, which is the deadline. Otherwise, it will not be published in the spring

of next year 2006. As you can see, time is of the essence. I know you are not looking forward to the regressions, but what can we do? I promise I'll make it very easy on you. I'm putting together now a regression questionnaire for about 20 hours of regressions, with nondirective questions for emotional abreactions as much as possible . . . But it would be most important that you make a list of what you think you should be regressed on, like unfinished business, and e-mail it to me prior to my arrival in Toronto. Thank you!

God's blessings,
Adrian

Shulah and I boarded the plane at LAX for Toronto for the next round of regressions on November 10, 2005, unsure of what awaited me there, unsure if Sherrie was willing to do the work or if under further questioning inconsistent responses would mar our previous results. Given the complexity of the situation, I wondered if I was skilled enough to deal with this intense dynamic.

Part III

Ten
THE KENNEDYS AND
THE FINAL DAYS

It was the evening of November 10, 2005. I could see the lights along the runway at Pearson International Airport in Toronto. My view stopped at a blue light flickering from a distance as the plane was landing. And in that fraction of a second, I had a premonition. I could see Sherrie and Kezia in my mind's eye smiling and ready for the hard work ahead of us. I had the feeling that the three of us were determined to do our best. This allayed some of my fears about a hostile reception and a grudging commitment on Sherrie's part.

We made reservations at the same hotel we stayed at during the May regressions, though in a different wing. We were assigned a spacious, very decent non-smoking room on the tenth floor. Shulah and I had dinner and then went to bed early, as we were tired out by our long flight from Los Angeles. I slept well, knowing that the final leg of a long journey was at hand.

Just before 9:00 the following morning, as the elevator descended to the lobby, I wondered, given the rocky patch in our recent communications, if Sherrie and Kezia would meet me on time. I was punctual and a little surprised that they were waiting for me in the hotel lobby. They were casually dressed and wearing big, happy smiles on their faces, very glad to see me. It was reciprocal. Shulah headed out to take a city tour with Anca.

We stopped to take a picture of a Christmas tree in the front lobby and then headed for the restaurant. After we ordered from the menu, I began explaining to them the goals of these regressions. "This time is different because we'll focus more on the feeling and thus the healing aspect of Sher's memories during the regressions. I'll also ask some memory questions, as much to reinforce your acceptance of your Marilyn identity as to prove anything to the skeptics. And remember, whatever the results, whether you remember certain names, events, and other details clearly, doesn't diminish the indisputable results of your May˜ regressions."

"This will be more compelling proof?" Sherrie asked.

"The average reader will probably be more impressed with memory questions, my colleagues with the 'emotional' truth of your responses. But remember, we're not here to prove you're the reincarnation of Marilyn Monroe, but to heal you of this past-life trauma—although proving it to you is also part of that healing. You won't heal if you don't believe or use that disbelief as an excuse."

"This time I am afraid of what may happen. I never liked these regressions. There is so much pain," complained Sher.

"I promise that I'll do my best to be gentle on you," I reassured her. "But, releasing the poisonous energy is a big part of the healing, what we're here to do this time."

"I want to know if you'll regress me. Do you think I can slip into it like Mom?" asked Kezia.

"Be positive and release and it'll happen."

After breakfast, we got into the elevator and went up to my room on the tenth floor. The décor was more or less similar to the previous room, which I had asked about when making the reservations in order to provide a reassuringly familiar environment. That morning I had made some preparations, mounting my digital video camera on the round table by the window. Sherrie had brought her own recording equipment used for her musical recordings. We wanted to have two parallel recordings, one audio and one audiovisual, so we wouldn't miss any part of the upcoming regression sessions and so we would have a backup if either system failed.

Kezia placed Sherrie's recording equipment on the same table and we tested both systems, which were ready for action. And so were we. Close to the table was one of the twin beds. Sunlight coming through the window, plus the light from two nearby lamps, provided enough illumination. Sherrie lay down on the bed and Kezia attached the microphone from her equipment to her mother's blouse, close to her mouth.

I reiterated that our task was to draw out through certain lines of questioning some of the deepest wounds Marilyn had suffered so Sherrie could release the poisonous venom from her system. Thus, this would be a more emotionally cathartic experience and appear more traumatic than her responses to the purely memory questions of the last round. I wanted to make sure that this was fully understood by both Sherrie and especially Kezia, who would have to witness her mother's trauma. They fully understood my explanations and agreed to proceed with the regressions. I began with Sherrie.

Past-Life Regression Conducted by Dr. Adrian Finkelstein on Sherrie Lea Laird; November 11, 2005; Toronto, Ontario

I began to place Sherrie under a somnambulistic state of hypnosis. As with our previous round of regressions, I gave her the hypnotic suggestion to erase all information about Marilyn Monroe that she had derived from books, movies, and any other outside sources. If she is the reincarnation of Marilyn Monroe, I told her to answer my questions from her unadulterated memories, feelings, and experiences. I checked to make sure that Sherrie was in a somnambulistic state, as evidenced by her very deep relaxation and waxy facial appearance. I now gave my final instructions:

Finkelstein: And now I'm going to count backward from

three to one. At the count of one there will be action, you will be there. Number three, number two, pay attention to details. Number one, be there! And now, you're there and I want you to tell me as you take a look at yourself, just a glimpse, are you or are you not Marilyn Monroe? The first impression you get.

Laird: [Whispering unintelligibly]

Finkelstein: You say yes? Can you speak louder?

Laird: Yes.

Finkelstein: Good. Now, if you are Marilyn Monroe, I'm going to ask a few questions that are very important. I want you to go backward or forward in time, from wherever you are now, to when you first met John F. Kennedy. When did you first meet John F. Kennedy? Also, before you answer, were the two of you ever lovers, and if so, when did you first have sex with him? Describe how your relationship progressed over the years. Did you ever have a tryst with him in the White House? Where was the last time you saw John F. Kennedy? Take your time, all the time you need.

Laird: It seems some . . . people are there. Some kind of . . . he's not a president . . . People are being annoying to me now. Some are just meeting and talking. I see him sitting at a table, a long table, and we start talking . . . about my family. That's all.

Finkelstein: When did you first meet John F. Kennedy? Do you know the date or how long it was before he became president?

Laird: It feels like 1954.

Finkelstein: 1954.

Laird: Just to see him . . . coming there . . .

Finkelstein: Were the two of you ever lovers, and if so, when did you first have sex with him?

Laird: In a car.

Finkelstein: Whose car?

Laird: It's a car. Someone's driving. It's just playing around. Touching.

Finkelstein: Does it happen in 1954 or later?

Laird: Later. 1957, '58, '57.

Finkelstein: 1957, and can you describe how your relationship progressed over the years?

Laird: Friends and lovers, a genuine friendship and concern and admiration and laughter and we . . . and we believe in the same things.

Finkelstein: Such as?

Laird: We . . . we feel for everybody coming . . . poor people. He's very anti-racial, but he knows those around him will not take this too well. He loves people and he loves hard working men, families. We talk about making things better, but he has to hide his true feelings.

Finkelstein: Why is it he has to hide his true feelings?

Laird: There's people around him that are prejudiced, that are controlling. They make it hard for him.

Finkelstein: Where do you meet with him?

Laird: Many places and we meet around friends. We meet at Peter's house. We meet at hotels at night; sometimes restaurants and later in the car.

Finkelstein: Did you ever have a tryst with him in the White House?

Laird: I think I go to the White House but I don't have . . . Yes . . . Yes.

Finkelstein: When was the last time you saw John F. Kennedy?

Laird: In the first week of June. June.

Finkelstein: What year?

Laird: 1962.

Finkelstein: And can you describe what's happening between you two in the first week in June of '62?

Laird: June 3rd. He doesn't want me to go.

Finkelstein: Doesn't want you to go? June 3rd.

At this point a very dramatic emotional experience began.

Laird: [Crying and screaming loudly] Oh . . . No, no!

Sherrie has an unexpected and extremely violent emotional fit. Her face is contorting and all her body is trembling. The tears are pouring from her eyes and are rolling down her beautiful face. She screams nonstop.

Finkelstein: [I dared to ask] What's happening?

Laird: [Her cries and screams become louder and louder.] No, no!

Sherrie is distressed, crying and screaming like a mortally wounded animal. It is profoundly affecting.

Finkelstein: Why are you upset?

Laird: I don't want him (JFK) to leave me . . . My arms are numb. Help me, help me, help me! [Crying loudly] Help me, help me!

Finkelstein: [I try to comfort her, tightly squeezing her right hand. She squeezes even harder, trembling all over, as her face is washed with tears. I'm shocked. I'm hardly able to utter words. Then, finally regaining my composure, I say] Calm down! It's okay!

Laird: [Screaming nonstop] Help me!

Finkelstein: I'm with you right now. Nothing will happen to you. Okay. I want you to get away from this emotional experience for a moment, okay? I'm gonna count to three. At the count of three you will be away from this experience. Just one, two, three! You're now away from your experience. You're just watching it as a spectator. Nothing bothers you. Okay. Okay. Okay. All right. Okay.

Laird: [The screaming stops. She is just crying.]

Finkelstein: It's all right. It's okay. It's all right. All right. Relax now. You're out of that situation. You're just watching everything as a spectator. Right now you're not involved in it. You're just out of it. You're just a spectator. It's okay. It's okay. Now, I'll let you relax.

Sherrie relaxes for a few minutes, regaining her composure. After a while, she indicates that she is ready to proceed.

Finkelstein: I'll ask you this. Did you ever have an affair with Robert Kennedy? Did he ever promise to marry you? And, when was the last time you saw Robert Kennedy? Take your time, all the time in the world.

Laird: Yes. Robert . . .

Finkelstein: Are you saying yes? In other words, you did have an affair with him?

Laird: Yes. Yes.

Finkelstein: Was it at a time you were also with his brother, with John, or afterwards?

Laird: After. Before. There was a time before. Before, yes.

Finkelstein: Did he ever promise to marry you?

Laird: Momentarily.

Finkelstein: Did he?

Laird: Not really. He told me he wished he could.

Finkelstein: Did he promise to marry you?

Laird: Maybe one day.

Finkelstein: And when was the last time you saw Robert Kennedy?

Laird: August 1st.

Finkelstein: The 1st of August?

Laird: Maybe it's August, the 1st or the 2nd, the 2nd, it's the 1st and 2nd.

Finkelstein: 1st and 2nd of what month?

Laird: August.

Finkelstein: August. What year?

Laird: 1962.

Finkelstein: Do you ever record any conversations between you and him or between you and Jack?

Laird: No. I think there is some, they believe, on my tape recorder, but it's erased.

Finkelstein: Do you believe your tape recorder is erased?

Laird: Yes.

Finkelstein: Who erased it?

Laird: Me.

Finkelstein: And what is the reason you erased it?

Laird: I never planned to keep it. Just playing. Showing him how it works, what I do with it.

Finkelstein: So your purpose of recording was just to show him?

Laird: Yes. Just showing him how my voice sounds on it.

Finkelstein: Did John or Robert Kennedy ever tell you state secrets? If so, what were they? Did either of them ever discuss the existence of extraterrestrial beings?

Laird: The . . . John would tell me his . . . He would fire someone and Bobby, Robert, was to call them and inform them. [Robert] told me of his cases he's fighting, sometimes just things.

Finkelstein: Anything specific he told you?

Laird: [John's] telling me that things get very drastic for Fidel and Cuba. It's going to be possibly a lot of resistance, a big fight.

Finkelstein: I see.

Laird: But he's going to get him.

Finkelstein: Fidel? Fidel Castro?

Laird: Yes.

Finkelstein: And I see. Anything he's telling you about extraterrestrials on earth? Or his brother, Bobby?

Laird: No. No. From other people I hear about extraterrestrials, other people talk about it. We talk about it. Peter talks about it.

Finkelstein: Peter Lawford?

Laird: Yes. He's making jokes.

Finkelstein: I see. Did you conceive a child with John F. Kennedy? If so, did you have an abortion? When and where?

Laird: I think I'm pregnant.

Finkelstein: You are pregnant?

Laird: I think so. I feel like I am. But somehow I think I am.

Finkelstein: What are you doing? Do you have an abortion?

Laird: No.

Finkelstein: So . . . ?

Laird: I still think that I am.

Finkelstein: Were you checked by a doctor?

Laird: No.

Finkelstein: So, what's happening? Are you going to have an abortion or give birth to a baby?

Laird: No. I think it's not lasting. It doesn't last.

Finkelstein: You mean it's a spontaneous abortion?

Laird: Yes. My period is late, but then I have a period.

Finkelstein: Then you have a period?

Laird: Yes.

Finkelstein: How long are you waiting for that?

Laird: Seven . . . three weeks, seven weeks.

Finkelstein: Three weeks or seven weeks?

Laird: All together seven weeks.

Finkelstein: I see. Now, in the in-between state, after Marilyn, but before you're reincarnated as Sherrie, look back at your death. Was the overdose of narcotics, of barbiturates, that killed you an accident? Were you murdered? And if so, by whom? Allow impressions to freely flow in.

Laird: I'm not murdered.

Finkelstein: You're not murdered?

Laird: No.

Finkelstein: Did [you or] anyone give you an enema or yourself of barbiturates? Yes or no? Just the impression.

Laird: I think I try. I try to. I was wanting to. I was planning to. I don't think I do. I was going to, maybe. No, no, no, don't do that.

Finkelstein: Does anyone, one of your doctors or anyone that you know, or anyone else, give you an enema that kills you? First impression.

Laird: [No answer]

Finkelstein: Take all the time in the world.

Laird: I think my doctor. I don't know.

Finkelstein: You don't know?

Laird: I don't think so.

Finkelstein: Now . . .

Laird: I can't see anybody.

Finkelstein: Nobody's around?

Laird: No.

Finkelstein: Is anyone in your house? Yes or no, during this time that you're in the last moments of your life, is anyone in the house that day?

Laird: Yes.

Finkelstein: Or the day before?

Laird: Yes. Somebody is there at night.

Finkelstein: Who is there at night?

Laird: There's people coming and going. My housekeeper is there. She's not close. She's ironing.

Finkelstein: What's her name?

Laird: Mrs. Murray. She's ironing. She's sewing. She's listening to the radio or television or TV, something. Noise. It's noise. It's August 3rd.

Finkelstein: Can you just rest for a minute? Rest a minute. Okay. What do you remember? So, coming back to that question— was it an accident or were you murdered in this life as Marilyn? If so, by whom?

Laird: By me.

Finkelstein: By yourself?

Laird: Yes.

Finkelstein: Did you do it intentionally? You wanted to die?

Laird: I don't care.

Finkelstein: You didn't care or you don't care? What makes you say that you don't care?

Laird: Everyone.

Finkelstein: Everyone?

Laird: Uh-huh. And I'm angry. I feel very angry.

Finkelstein: Angry at everyone?

Laird: And I feel very angry.

Finkelstein: What makes you so angry now?

Laird: Seeing everything.

Finkelstein: Such as?

Laird: August 3rd. I'm coming home. It's evening. I feel like its 9:00 o'clock and Mrs. Murray is ironing and cleaning. She's ironing and . . .

Finkelstein: What date is that?

Laird: August 3rd. I am drinking. I don't want to be here. I want to go away.

Finkelstein: Why?

Laird: [Whispering] I don't . . .

Finkelstein: Speak louder!

Laird: I don't want to see. I want to . . . I want to go away. Go away. Away.

Finkelstein: Just to be able to see all this or what do you see?

Laird: Yes, yes.

Finkelstein: All right. Well, why don't you stop at this point and we'll resume on this a little bit later. I wonder, from this state looking back at your life, can you summarize the spiritual lessons you are here to master? What are the lessons you need to master in your next life as Sherrie?

Laird: I'm doing it as Sherrie. She wants to take care of others. She wants to help others. Trying to . . . I am doing it. I am doing it.

Finkelstein: In what way are you doing it? You are Sherrie now; I want you to be Sherrie this moment. In which way do you want to help others?

Laird: I'm helping others because I don't think of myself and . . . and others came and I am doing it. It's just that nobody can see it, [crying] even now with this. Nobody cares. I can't do it. I'm tired again of it all. [Crying]

Finkelstein: All right. Just relax. It's all right. It's okay.

Laird: Suffering the same again. Suffering again. [Crying]

Finkelstein: What does she have to learn not to suffer? What does she have to do?

Laird: To not care about others. [Crying]

Finkelstein: How may you not care? You said this is what you want to do, help others.

Laird: She'll die again. I'll die and . . . [Crying]

Finkelstein: You won't die this time. Now you understand. You won't die because you want to learn the lesson. That's why you're here. You want to learn.

Laird: [Crying]

Finkelstein: It's all right. I want you to distance yourself from this experience and just watch it from a distance.

Laird: No.

Finkelstein: No. It's all right. Nothing happens. You are safe. You are safe now.

Laird: I need to go to the bathroom. I can't do it.

Finkelstein: Just relax now. It's okay.

Laird: No. No . . .

Finkelstein: I'll bring you out, okay? All right. Just relax. We're finished. You don't have to go into more stuff right now. Okay? That's it. It's enough for now. It's enough for now. All right. And you're coming out at the count of ten. As I count, you're gradually emerging. Ten, you'll be back with only positive, healthy, and constructive effects from this experience. And you will be able when you enter a trance again to go in again and revisit your life as Marilyn Monroe . . . I want you now to come back as I count to ten with only positive, healthy, and constructive effects from this experience. And one, coming back; two, more and more; three, feeling great; four, five. Next time you'll go deeper quicker and achieve more and feel more at ease. Six, seven, feeling okay, wonderful, you're really satisfied that you've done a wonderful job. Eight, nine, in full control of your body and mind. Ten, gently open your eyes and feel good!

Laird: Yeah. You didn't say ten. [It seems that Sherrie wants to be sure she is completely alert, due to having such an emotional ordeal. Thus she blocked my first count of ten.]

Finkelstein: Ten. You're with it.

Laird: My hands are very numb.

Finkelstein: It's all right. That's normal. They're numb, but it's okay. They will be all right in no time.

Laird: I can't get out.

Finkelstein: I'll count to ten again and I'll clap my hands and you'll be completely with it. One, two, three, four, five, six, seven, eight, nine, ten. [Clap] That's it.

Laird: Whoops.

I began explaining a few things, talking about Sherrie as the third person.

Finkelstein: What we have been discussing is that Sherrie was down to a very trying emotional experience and we're leaving her life, pain, and suffering as Marilyn Monroe that she would not want to revisit because it's too painful for her. So, she was afraid that she would die during the process. That's why she e-mailed me before . . . she was afraid of that and I assured her that nothing [would] happen and I was explaining that this was a corrective experience for her because now she sees, she's alive . . . She would like to help, and nobody can be in that situation and imagine it—how it feels—and only she does, but at that point I reassured her that the rest of the regressions would be milder. We're going to just approach the essential part of the regressions now, in the beginning, and the proof is in the pudding that she's alive and well.

Laird: [Listening]

Finkelstein: Sherrie's fear was baseless. Okay. So, that's part of the healing and we just call it catharsis or emotional abreaction and this is what you've done. We don't intend to repeat this over and over.

Laird: Right.

Finkelstein: At least not with that intensity.

Laird: Right.

Finkelstein: But with a lower intensity and it will take more time.

Laird: Right.

Finkelstein: But that's the process. It's not just a snapping of fingers. It's a process and you are on the right track.

Laird: Okay, okay.

Finkelstein: That's what we're trying to establish, so that's the reaction. What do you have to add to that or to say or to elaborate about?

Laird: Well, what just came to me right now was how letting somebody else's love for you not have such an impact on you, like what happened to me when, you know, I'm realizing that Jack, you know, doesn't care about me, to feel that much pain, no. That's not right, to feel that much pain because someone doesn't want you or doesn't love you. That's not right. That's bothering me right now. I'm thinking to myself that might have a lot to do with my healing also.

Finkelstein: Right. So, what makes you feel that pain? I mean . . .

Laird: Whatever that was, what I felt, that feeling of such chest pain and such hysterical reaction.

Finkelstein: So nothing was actually happening at that moment? It was just you felt that.

Laird: He told me . . . What I'm saying is, you know, don't call me and stuff like that. Then I'm feeling that kind of pain. Whatever happened to me, that crying, I felt like I was going to go into a seizure.

Finkelstein: Yes, because you'd been together for several years and all of a sudden he's telling you . . .

Laird: I guess so, but I don't know if I feel that kind of love in this life except for like family, Kezia, and I want to love like that, but if that . . . I think . . . I think if it means to love like that, means to feel like that, then I can't. Then I'm not capable of that kind of love in this life.

Finkelstein: You're talking about Jack or about Bobby?

Laird: Well, the time that I had the almost seizure it was Jack.

Finkelstein: I see. So, if you want to tell me, I would ask you who was the greatest love you had as Marilyn Monroe. Jack or Bobby?

Laird: I can't tell. It sure seemed like it was Jack right then. I would rather it be Bobby. Bobby made me happy. What I saw was Bobby made me happy, like more floaty and light and fluffy, and not so heavy and feel that . . . because some times, even when I was hysterical, how much of it was love and how much of it was rejection, like I feel. It has to be from her upbringing; that kind of rejection was much harder on her that it would ever be on me because I have family. Like that kind of rejection was so intense. I've never experienced something that painful, what I felt under hypnosis.

That's the first time I've ever felt such rejection and pain. I imagine I was saying help me, help me. That's what it felt like I was saying. Like help me, help me. I felt like I was falling and drowning and dying. I was just, like, dying. I don't know. I'm surprised she didn't drop dead right there, June 3rd or whatever date I said.

Finkelstein: But what you were saying is that you didn't use an enema, did you?

Laird: I didn't see an enema. I just . . . I don't know.

Finkelstein: How can an enema kill somebody?

Laird: I don't know if it's something she did or does on a regular basis, so it wasn't really even something I thought of. Like you have to forget, like it's not fair to me and I say this to the camera and the public. This is not fair because there're all these books and stories and stuff and even though you regress me and take it out of me, that doesn't stop the fact that some of it's true. Maybe she takes enemas. I don't know. And the thing is, while I'm under there, she looks like she could've easily taken enemas on a regular basis. That didn't happen. That's not something Sherrie knows, but when I was back there, yeah, it sounds like she was contemplating an enema, but I didn't see one.

Finkelstein: Now that you're thinking in retrospect, do you feel that you gave yourself an enema with barbiturates?

Laird: I didn't feel an enema.

Finkelstein: Is she capable?

Laird: Yes, she's capable of taking an enema.

Finkelstein: Did she do it?

Laird: I don't think so. No. I thought I would see it for sure.

Finkelstein: Okay.

Laird: No. I'm saying definitely no, from my perspective, no. You know, she was drunk and blurry and staggering to start with.

Finkelstein: Could it be because of that, that she didn't pay attention if somebody would've entered, let's say, the room and administered an enema to her?

Laird: That crossed my mind, because you said to see if "anybody is there with you," and I was looking and I felt no presence, no psychological presence, nothing.

Finkelstein: Okay. Fair enough.

Laird: And I even was aware that people were coming and going. It seems like somebody visited with the housekeeper. I do feel the presence of somebody coming in and maybe even leaving again, but the thing is that the rest is just a blank. It's just not there. It just seems all me. I feel that if I was murdered I would have much more fear of other people and much more fear of politics and much more fear of being an outspoken person.

Finkelstein: But you see it's good that we carry on without you being in a hypnotic trance right now, because it's intense and we don't want to push it too much; you know you can now maybe just discuss it.

Laird: Right.

Finkelstein: Without going in a trance and just revisiting the days before the death of Marilyn Monroe and what happened in her life, I mean, not from books and all this but from your own unadulterated experience. In a kind of experience that you just got from your hypnotic trance. So, what are your first reactions, gut reactions? What did you plan? What did you experience? Forget about the books and magazines and that stuff.

Laird: Right, right.

Finkelstein: At a gut level, what did you plan?

Laird: On which? Healing or in job, jobs or what?

Finkelstein: No, no. What did you plan to do in your life, and then you'll come up with some specifics.

Laird: Okay. Well, this is my feeling what I think from there. From you know, when you hypnotized me before, and told me to keep remembering, so things keep coming to me, thoughts and feelings and ideas and things. I definitely feel that she didn't want to be fired [from the movie *Something's Got to Give*], and that even though she's not caring about those people so much, she does want to make herself step up to the plate and behave more, so she was asking more of herself. Finish the movie, don't cop out. Don't use drugs and then always phone in sick. So, she had actually made a conscious effort to say, you know what? Maybe it is me. I'll try harder, so that was one. Joe . . . I feel the Joe marriage was true and he was telling her, "Finish the movie, we'll take a little break. Come back to me."

Finkelstein: Was he more understanding?

Laird: Joe or . . . ?

Finkelstein: Joe.

Laird: Very.

Finkelstein: So he changed?

Laird: Yes. Yes, he did. I think very much so.

Finkelstein: What do you think made him change?

Laird: Loss. Not having her, not being with her. Other losses, too, I feel. Family losses, maybe. That's what comes to my mind and I don't know this. Age, maybe. Like, just maturing. Like, just realizing that being a jealous and a controlling man for a woman doesn't really get you anything really.

Finkelstein: Do you really see that you plan to remarry him?

Laird: I believe that firmly, that that was going to happen. Maybe not with a big wedding. Maybe more like just on an island in front of someone. The thing that keeps coming to my mind is that to go with him . . . But I remember I told you last time, in the last regression, that they go to Hawaii. And the thing is that I feel like they're going to Hawaii and they're going to get married by one of those spiritual [kahunas], like the Hawaii people that marry. Like, someone is there and maybe they do it on island. Maybe surprise everybody and possibly have a party. I think maybe if they planned a wedding, they were going to trick people, because I think Joe didn't want people to know. I'm thinking Joe's plan is to go to Hawaii and elope, come back married, and then have a party. That's what I'm thinking. I don't know if it's true. He didn't say or I don't know. We could find out.

Finkelstein: Tell me something about Peter, Peter Lawford. You said that you met with him on the 3rd of August.

Laird: I feel like yes, the 3rd of August. I'm coming home from a restaurant. Now, the first regression was a lot deeper on the Peter thing. It really was much deeper. I could see Peter and then I regressed by myself.

Finkelstein: Yeah!

Laird: But just this time, all I see was me coming home. Before I see me in a restaurant. This time I see him coming home, only I didn't see who I was with. I just assume it was Peter. I felt strongly that I had seen Peter.

Finkelstein: I see.

Laird: But I don't understand why it feels so early in the night, like 9-ish. I would've thought . . . because I thought I would've been crawling home at 3:00 or 4:00 in the morning, but I get the feeling I was home early, and then the drinking and the pills and things start throughout the night.

Finkelstein: When do you telephone Jack, or when did you try to talk with John F. Kennedy?

Laird: If anything, that had to be the 3rd, through the night. Has to be through the 3rd and going into the 4th, like all that night. Has to be that, because the 4th, there just seems to be nothing. Nothing. Just nothing like Jack and I. After the last regression, when you said when I was found, we said it's hours before they find me, and I started counting one, two, three, four, five, six, seven, eight, nine hours, like . . . It seemed endless, so when I counted backward, if they're finding her in the morning of the 5th, you know, I'm putting the death between 4:00 and 7:00 of the respiratory thing, like say 4:00 and 8:00 [on the 4th]. There's definitely a coma. I think there's obviously a coma, and then the respiratory thing in between. Then, because she's quite dead, quite gone, like all the way from the eight, nine zone all the way to the morning.

Finkelstein: Okay. So, what is your overall feeling right now after you've had this experience and we've discussed all these things? Do you feel a little bit more at ease with it or, let me rephrase it, do you feel we can continue with the regressions if they're milder and you won't get too upset?

Laird: Milder, yeah . . . I think we can have it more like you putting me in a trance so that you can make me reenact . . . think or feel Marilyn Monroe and answer you, direct answers, or you can make me try to give the spontaneous first answer or something like that. The deeper I'm having to [go to], the deeper I have to go, you know, [the more painful it is], already when I went right under I start crying. I could feel it.

K. Laird: Your nose was getting redder.

Finkelstein: Yeah.

K. Laird: Because I always wonder, like, what . . .

Laird: I think I was going right back to the death experience.

K. Laird: I always wonder what you see because automatically, as soon as you start to go under, your nose gets red and you get upset.

Finkelstein: And this is very characteristic. It's very typical that the subconscious remembers beforehand.

Laird: Right.

Finkelstein: It anticipates because, you know, it has the psychic.

Laird: Right.

Finkelstein: So it knows what's going to happen.

Laird: So it knew I was going to start crying.

Finkelstein: It has the premonition, so it can foresee.

Laird: It's like, uh oh! Here comes the flood.

Finkelstein: All right. So, we're done with this— [End of tape]

While we changed tapes we talked about Margaret, Sherrie's mother, and her mother's pregnancy when she carried Sherrie. We pick it up at that point.

Laird: Yes. She lost it two months later, which puts her at the exact time and to be pregnant right away from August. And so the thing is, if you calculate in math, she got pregnant right away and then what happened is she had a miscarriage and then she got pregnant right away again with me [October 1962]. And then I was born right away [July 1963]. [Sherrie is noticing the synchronicity of her birth with the North Moon Node, like Marilyn's, in the astrological sign of Cancer—the North Node moved into this sign in January 1963 thru August 1964—in order to continue the prematurely interrupted life experience and lessons of Marilyn Monroe.] That's the part I don't want people to know. I don't want anybody to know my age or my birthday. [She later agreed to release this information.] Are you going to be able to put my face back to normal? [It was numb following the hypnotic trance.]

Finkelstein: Yeah.

K. Laird: Without making her go under again, though?

Finkelstein: It's okay.

Laird: Yeah, without going under?

Finkelstein: Yeah, it's all right. You are under right now [when] your face is like that. Just take your time. Breathe deeply in and out. Not fast. Slowly. When you feel better you let me know. Good. It'll come. How do you feel?

Although I haven't put Sherrie back under with the standard regression technique at this point, she's in a semi-trance state, like in self-hypnosis. In my experience over the years, the mere request by the hypnotist to a susceptible subject to be trustworthy and to reveal only her authentic memories and not be adulterated by beforehand information is sufficient and may be as reliable as somnambulistic hypnosis—in which erasure of acquired memories from public record is obtained. It is not as sure as inducing somnambulism with selective or partial amnesia, but it is close. This is especially reliable when a formal induction was recently used on the subject. This way the subject is more susceptible and likely to carry into her semi-hypnotic state the same suggestions as in the somnambulistic state (i.e., partial amnesia of acquired memories). This cooperation with the hypnotist by the subject on a voluntary basis is substantiated in a scientific article (Lynn, Steven J., Judith W. Rhue, and John R. Weekes. "Hypnotic Involuntariness: A Social Cognitive Analysis." *Psychological Review,* Vol. 97, No. 2 [1990]: 169–185.) The fact is that during most of this seeming semi-trance, Sherrie slipped into the deepest level, somnambulistic, as evidenced by her clinical signs (numbness in the face). This spontaneous slippage into a somnambulistic trance at short notice is not uncommon, especially for individuals such as Sherrie who have already reached and are trained to obtain such a hypnotic depth.

Laird: Better.

Finkelstein: You were in a very deep trance. How do you feel?

Laird: Better.

Finkelstein: You had a very dramatic experience and it's hard to describe it to these people, you know. They want to read something sensational.

Laird: Maybe we should tape our conversation now.

Finkelstein: Yeah. It's taping now. So, it's hard for people to understand what you're going through.

Laird: We have to go earlier. I don't like the later [part of Marilyn's life]. I can't live it. It's too close.

Finkelstein: Well, I'll be gentle on you.

Laird: Because lately I've been living it. I can't. I don't want those chest pains to come back.

Finkelstein: Right, right.

Laird: And if we do it, I feel that if we keep going to the death, I could only see me. It's the same as the last time, the story that I told you. It's going to be the exact same story. I don't want to relive it . . .

Finkelstein: No, I know. I know it's very hard. It's very hard.

Laird: Even just reliving the Jack and the John thing—that hurt my chest.

Finkelstein: Yeah.

Laird: I probably could've died right then on that day, on June 3rd maybe [her last contact with JFK]. I could've died then. Maybe she tried to kill herself then.

K. Laird: Was that why you were freaking out, because of that? [Marilyn's late calls and absences on the set for *Something's Got to Give*]

Laird: They feel I had hysteria. I don't like it. Take me to happy times. I do want to see Tony and all those people. I can't relive this bad stuff.

Finkelstein: Well, the rest of the stuff is not so emotionally wrought as this.

Laird: Obviously, the bottom line is this: Because of the Kennedys she has killed herself.

Finkelstein: Yes.

Laird: And if I keep having to relive them [the memories], then I'm reliving why she killed herself. It's all the emotional stuff.

Finkelstein: And did she do it intentionally or not?

Laird: I think so. She's definitely angry inside and mad.

Finkelstein: So she's going to get revenge on them and kill herself that way?

Laird: Very angry. I have that same thing in Sherrie. I get so angry that I implode. That's why in this life I try to explode. I try to smash things. I try to get it out. Kezia sees. I'll smash things against the wall. I'll break things. It's better. But people should calm me down instead of make me like I implode. It's like I'm shrinking.

K. Laird: So, now it's very, very heavy and very, very difficult, and nobody can understand that you're being true, and we listen to this radio show or read that book. I mean, I cannot go do this because we cannot really imagine the cost and I am overwhelmed.

Laird: She must carry . . . I must carry so much of the behavior patterns still, because I obviously am not over it, and I think because we have so many Marilyn Monroe things to do that probably we need to go way back further before that life. Obviously, she has issues left over from before, but I can't do this anymore. Like, I don't want to go further. Like, unless I'm healed I can't keep going to that. I like to, maybe, be in the lifetime with you and be there. [Sherrie is referring to our common French life in the seventeenth century, when she was Louise de la Valliere and I was her doctor, Antoine Daquin.] I don't want to go to so many Marilyn things.

Finkelstein: Yeah. You know, the healing occurs as a result of your being able to abreact, to get out of your system all this emotional poison.

Laird: To get it out.

Finkelstein: To get it out of your system. Just running away from it, I understand, temporarily it is warranted because we don't want to push you too hard; but, on the other hand, the healing comes through catharsis, through getting it out of your system.

Laird: Maybe even just getting this out, I'll be healing.

K. Laird: I was just going to say that.

Laird: I do feel like . . . I feel like it's possible. I could be feeling better after this.

K. Laird: It's just such a shock because you realize you're really the person and living it like you did.

Laird: She killed herself.

K. Laird: Yeah, or the fact that you could do it again. Like that's probably more of a shock.

Finkelstein: Yeah. [More used to the idea.]

K. Laird: Did you have, like, a psychic flash or did you have a feeling?

Laird: Yeah, I feel like how I almost died recently with the other problems.

K. Laird: Yeah.

Laird: Because Kezia, you know, it's sad. It's sad for Kezia that she has to live through that. I could do this, like I almost died again in this life with pills and alcohol and . . .

Finkelstein: And when this happened were any people home?

Laird: People were home. My mother and father were home just like [in Marilyn's case]. Mrs. Murray was home and other people were in and out of the house. Before I'm taking pills and nothing is that . . . so close when you said I'm also Sherrie now [she had the same experience as Marilyn]. You felt how close it was to happening again, you know, it's so, still right now. I think I must be going through something where I'm very upset. Like, I think because of my [Internet blog] you see with the [blog], I'm still. . . It's still there. I'm still there. It's still so upsetting. Not suicidal because you cured me last time. I won't kill myself, but those feelings of, like, anger. I feel like it's about God. It's like rage.

Finkelstein: Rage at God? Yeah, because God didn't help you?

Laird: He must be trying to help me, but I just feel such rage at the world. Everything. As Sherrie I feel rage for the world, but as Marilyn, she must've had so much of an inner world rage because she had nobody and nothing. So she not only had an inner world rage, but she probably hated the industry. I hate the music industry, and I've started to withdraw from it. I really love my inner world, but I hate the outer world so. . . . But I still have that [sensation] in my chest, like I'm scared for that to come back because you cured me of that, right?

Finkelstein: Yeah.

Laird: Maybe, you know, [with the] regressions we can just make it light and fluffy.

Finkelstein: Yeah, we will. Don't worry. You know, this was something I forewarned you about before we started today. I told you that this hour is the most, how do you say it, contains the most trying questions.

K. Laird: Do you want water?

Laird: Yeah.

Finkelstein: Did you want some more water to drink?

Laird: Yeah, have more water.

Finkelstein: Water generally helps you a lot.

Laird: I didn't even know about my face. I was thinking I might not even be able to sing. I had a frozen face. [Obviously reformed by now]

K. Laird: Yeah.

Laird: It was so frozen. I had my hands and arms numb. They didn't even work . . . I just can't go back to those chest-crushing things and that's what I have at the moment. You already saved me from that. I don't want to have those chest-crushing things. You know, I get a fright and then ohhh . . .

Finkelstein: You don't want to have them, but you see . . .

Laird: I don't want to have those again.

Finkelstein: Yeah, yeah.

Laird: Maybe if I know I can't die, then maybe it's okay.

Finkelstein: You will not die. You didn't die now. We proved it to you. So, what's happening is every time you are releasing this emotional poisonous energy.

Laird: Yeah, poisonous.

Finkelstein: You're freeing yourself and I know it's hard, and you would rather not and I'm with you and I don't want you to push yourself. But, you know, Kezia made a sign also to bring you out, so I felt that she became sort of anxious so I said, well, let's . . .

Laird: Yeah, she knew.

Finkelstein: Yeah.

Laird: She knows. [To Kezia] I said if you see me going into that thing, if you see me panicking or any kind of thing, tell Dr. Finkelstein to take me out.

Finkelstein: Yeah, which is fine. I would've noticed that myself and I would've stopped it anyway, but the thing is, you know, catharsis or emotional abreaction is curing by itself. And the fact that you could get it out of your system, what you did today, what you did the last time, is healing by itself.

Laird: That's true.

Finkelstein: And in between.

Laird: That's true.

Finkelstein: It's helping. I think that we may do the same but not so concentrated.

Laird: Uh-huh.

Finkelstein: Like without being in a trance.

Laird: Yeah.

Finkelstein: Like we talk now.

Laird: Uh-huh, okay.

Finkelstein: We can talk about it without you being in trance because you're getting too close to the feeling.

Laird: Yeah.

Finkelstein: So we can do that.

Laird: Because I feel like if I was there, I could see the very last night of my living, because August 3rd, coming home, the shutting of the door . . . Well, first, getting the drinks and stuff and shutting the door, I think the drinks . . . I already had drinks while I was out, and then I had more drinks already in my bedroom, but I see that it's really the last . . . It's the last night. August 3rd.

There is no more. August 4th there's nothing. There really is nothing. It's just pills and coma all day.

Finkelstein: I was planning to ask you a few questions like what happened on August 1st, 2nd, 3rd, so you told me about the 3rd, which is very important, probably the most important. What I needed to ask you is what happened before.

Laird: I definitely was out for dinner, for sure, just like I thought. I'm accurate in that. Out for dinner.

Finkelstein: With whom?

Laird: This time I think it's very much Peter. I didn't get to see them, where we were, because you didn't ask me.

Finkelstein: Because you're very close to the experience now.

Laird: I came home.

Finkelstein: You can tell me.

Laird: Yeah.

Finkelstein: Peter, you think?

Laird: Yes.

Finkelstein: Was his wife Pat with him or not?

Laird: Ummm . . .

Finkelstein: Was she?

Laird: I would say yes, but not at the table. The table that I'm seeing, it seems like somebody has left the table, when I'm hearing the conversation that I'm hearing. But it seems like people have come later. There could be something that comes later.

Finkelstein: What people?

Laird: I don't know.

Finkelstein: No, but people . . .

Laird: The only thing I'm seeing is that I . . . Well, all I see in this particular time was me coming home, and home being warm and light and not really over.

K. Laird: Do you see everything, like, real?

Laird: I just felt like coming home.

K. Laird: Or do you just feel the . . .

Laird: I felt the hallway and I could hear her in the hallway, the sound, music or something, or I don't know if there were even TVs. I guess so. Some music or some kind of sound and then I heard, I could see that, I felt . . . everything felt warm, and I obviously must've been very intoxicated or drugged even then, because everything felt very warm, but my mind wasn't at rest. It was . . . I was . . . I don't know if it was Sherrie that was angry just now, or both of us, or her, but I felt very angry. I felt very, very angry, and the anger came so hard to my chest that . . . that's what makes me think it's intentional. It's not intentional, but just not caring.

Finkelstein: You didn't care?

Laird: Angry. I felt anger.

Finkelstein: Anger, but towards yourself?

Laird: More the sadness.

Finkelstein: Or what?

Laird: Anger more than sadness.

Finkelstein: But did you plan to kill yourself?

Laird: I just planned to take a very large amount of drugs. A lot. I just . . . I guess I must've known of the consequences, but I just felt like there was no amount enough that I could take.

Finkelstein: So what do you think about this report of John Miner that you didn't intend to kill yourself? You had some plans.

Laird: Yes, but that seems the days before. The days before, you know, I see that in July and the beginning of August, you know, being up is easy. You're up, you have plans. Those plans, and if I had . . . If she had only lived through that night, those plans would've come to something. She would've done the thing with marrying Joe. She would've made a really terrific movie and, like, even almost a very artistic movie that would be a classic even today, like something great. I think she would've loved that.

Finkelstein: To talk about something great she did.

Laird: Yeah. I think that. I can't remember the Russian movie that I feel very strongly, though, on. It starts with a C, Crrr. I don't know the name. It's on the tip of my tongue.

Finkelstein: That's all right.

Laird: Chrr. Something like that, but things would . . . Good things would've happened if she had only not taken all those pills and things like that. Like good things would've happened, the movie and really being a very different kind of actress. She would've got to really do her work for the first time.

K. Laird: Because that last movie was kind of serious and more like it.

Laird: Which one was that?

K. Laird: The very last movie. The one that didn't get finished.

Laird: Yeah. Even though she was moving away from that fluffy stuff . . .

K. Laird: Yeah, I know but that was . . . That was more of a serious role. It wasn't so much singing and dancing.

Laird: Yeah, exactly. That's what I mean. That was going to be . . . that was going to be a really good comedy. That would've been a hit. But then she was going to go into this dark thing, maybe changing hair color, maybe changing clothes, looking very ragged. I feel that she was going to look ragged and totally get away from the beauty thing. She for sure wanted to do that. Then she would've . . . they would've seen her acting and not [just] her looks, so . . . But something happens between August 1st and 2nd. Obviously it's the Bobby Kennedy thing and obviously he's now breaking it off . . . This is what it must be, because it makes sense, you know, he says he'll still see her. He would still see her, but not as often and now the hopes of him being with her are completely gone . . . August 3rd [she] is talking to Peter. How come Peter has not come forward and said he was there or anything? Has he not said a word? He's not talked about it, maybe.

Finkelstein: What?

Laird: Peter talked about August 3rd. Does he not talk about August 3rd?

Finkelstein: Where?

Laird: In any of these things that are out there.

Finkelstein: Publications? No.

Laird: He's not said a word.

Finkelstein: No.

Laird: And then he died.

Finkelstein: He died?

Laird: Isn't he dead?

Finkelstein: Well, anyway, see, what we're going to proceed with . . .

Laird: My throat feels better but my chest hurts [laughs]. [I facilitated a healing of her throat through magnetic passes, while she appeared to be under a somnambulistic trance.]

Finkelstein: Your chest hurts because it'll come out slowly, but, you know, it's good what you did, you know, it sounds like . . . You know, it sounds cruel or something, and I don't want to be cruel towards you. I want to help you to get it out of your system, and this is what I did. Now, I had to ask very important questions to start with, because I felt it's better in the beginning to have it done with, and then we will go into the easy stuff.

Laird: Okay.

Finkelstein: So, you've done tremendously. You've done a wonderful job.

Laird: I did?

Finkelstein: Just fantastic. I mean, forget about the critics and disbelievers. That's their problem.

Laird: Yeah. I don't care about them actually even right now. I just don't want to go through so much of this for them.

Finkelstein: No. You're right.

Laird: I don't mind going through it for people who want to heal themselves . . . I'm trying to help people. I try to give back, you know. I guess with killing yourself, you have to give back. I'm trying to give back. If you can give back, save lives or whatever, or change the course of someone's life, isn't that re . . . whatever the word is, repentance? Isn't that penitence for killing yourself, if you save lives?

Finkelstein: Penitence?

Laird: Yeah.

Finkelstein: Yes, it is.

Laird: Then I've done it and I don't have to live with the guilt. I've done it then. I'm healthy. I'm trying to do something, and if the skeptics don't believe, okay. This is the way I view it. If the skeptics don't believe, then they obviously don't have enough drama and pain in their lives, [or] that they're close to suicide, so they don't need me and I don't care about those people.

Finkelstein: All right.

Laird: But someone who's hanging on by a thread, like I usually am, those are the people I'm trying to help, because then those are the people who should believe. Those are the people who can come for help. Those are the people who don't have to kill themselves and then live like this. That's why I am going through this. That's the only way I can help. It's obviously a spiritual thing like that. I'm putting it into words that I know.

Finkelstein: Right. But you see this was also a corrective experience which you've gone through today because in a way you suffered a lot, but at the same time, you see the result is that you're alive.

Laird: Uh-huh, right. [Small laugh]

Finkelstein: You didn't die.

Laird: No. If I die . . .

Finkelstein: I sent you an e-mail before all this reassuring you that you would not die, that I'd do my best to be gentle on you, as you were afraid of dying during the regressions.

Laird: I know. I got very deep under.

Finkelstein: You were afraid of the astrological unfavorable position during the time of regressions.

Laird: Right. Just like the day she died. [Bad astrological positions]

Finkelstein: But, you see, that's a corrective experience. You're alive and well.

Laird: I just don't want to scare Gladys from going under. [Sherrie, now addressing Kezia, seems to have emerged from her hypnotic trance.] Will you try?

K. Laird: I don't know. I want to try. I'm just really terrified.

Finkelstein: Yeah.

Laird: Please try it.

K. Laird: No.

Laird: Did you feel like you were going under? [Referring to Kezia's test regression performed earlier]

K. Laird: No. I felt like I was just kind of like whatever . . .

At this point we had some technical snafus with the equipment.

Finkelstein: I'm going to stop it right now. You want to stop your thing and then we'll restart it [tomorrow].

After the regression were further, unrecorded conversations with Sherrie and Kezia. They lasted for a few minutes and were mainly reassurances on my part that the emotional pain Sherrie experienced during the regression would not be in vain. It wasn't meant to hurt her but, on the contrary, to facilitate the elimination of the remaining Marilyn "demons." The result, of course, was to promote the therapeutic effects of our research—to free Sherrie from the emotional poison accumulated in her past life as Marilyn Monroe and the trauma of dealing with it in this life. In other words, the more emotional outpouring, the more she released the emotional poison from her system, resulting in her healing herself, our main goal. I explained to Sherrie that the current process is comparable to a surgical procedure. The first step is painful. It is like cutting an abscess. Only that in Sherrie's case it is opening an emotional wound. The pain is emotional, which at times can be far worse than physical pain. But there is no other way to mobilize and drain out the pus from the abscess, and likewise the emotional poison from the soul. The second step, as in a surgical procedure, is the cleansing, whether pus or emotional poison. Surgically one uses gauze to wipe up the pus. Spiritually, one uses forgiveness for those who hurt us, including ourselves. The third step is to apply medicine on the wound to speed healing. Spiritually this medicine is LOVE and SELF-LOVE. In conclusion, I conveyed to both Sherrie and Kezia that it's necessary to ask a lot of factual questions, not only to prove our case but also to draw out the emotional abreaction, which is my main concern—their health and welfare.

Eleven

FORGIVING AND RELEASING

After the regression, where so much emotional poison was released, we all had a healthy appetite. We descended to the hotel lobby and headed for the restaurant. Sitting at the table, Sherrie was on my right and facing me while Kezia sat across from us. We felt a great sense of relief, joking with each other. Though tired from the emotional ordeal of the regression, Sherrie appeared considerably lighter, even playful. A huge heaviness seemed to have been lifted from her shoulders. She sighed with relief when I reassured her that most of the intense emotional abreactions were behind her. The next regressions would be milder. But this release would accelerate the integration process in Sherrie's life, which was the next step.

After lunch, when the three of us returned to the room, Sherrie didn't want to review at this time the tape of her dramatic morning regression. And I didn't blame her. She naturally needed more time to integrate an extremely powerful emotional experience. However, the consensus opinion was that, although we hadn't planned for such a painful ordeal, the result was that we had successfully purged Sherrie of some of the darkest of her Marilyn "demons," as she called them. It appears that many of the abuse and self-esteem issues in Marilyn's life, including her exploitation by powerful men in film and politics, came to a head in the break with John F. Kennedy in early June. This left her with an overwhelming sense of rejection and put her life in a tailspin that ended with a drug overdose and subsequent death on the night of August 4, 1962.

Here I must reemphasize the complexity of Sherrie's processing, and what normally transpires with patients dealing with pastlife trauma and how it complicates the normal psychological integration we go through with everyday adjustment problems. For the sake of simplicity and clarity, the general process of psychological healing consists of experiencing the traumatic events as a first step, followed by a cleansing period that leads to the final stage of adjustment aided by more therapy and, in some cases, medicine. As with patients dealing with childhood trauma, those experiencing past-life traumas have their energies or vital force trapped or fixated by the disturbing past events to the point that little energy remains to deal with current life challenges.

During this process, as in Sherrie's case, the vital force is finally released, But that energy must be reinvested in positive and constructive pursuits, in personal growth. And it's not a smooth, steady climb from the depths to the heights. Daily or even hourly, one is faced with the same pattern of behavior derived from the past trauma, and the task is to be aware of it and release the compulsion—and not allow the behavior or the trauma to control you any longer. Releasing this negativity divests its energy, prevents it from having a life of its own, and, in time, ends its existence. We may call this period "no-time," and it varies in length and intensity according to the individual's coping skills and overall personality. It usually entails developing a capacity to forgive yourself and others for past transgressions. When you forgive and release through divine love past tormentors, you have more energy to deal effectively with current problems.

Another capacity is also cultivated as you learn to place things in perspective, to compare the past with the present, or to learn from past experiences and not repeat the same mistakes. The greatest medicine, the highest in its healing vibration after God, one that enhances the healing of body and soul, is love and self-love. The adages "Charity starts at home" and "Love thy neighbor as thyself" are keys to the restoration of one's harmony and perfection. This is the essence of healing. It is not the absence of disease and the presence of health, as both are relative. It is bringing us back to a constant awareness of our being one with perfection, and this isn't relative but absolute. Hillel, a famous Jewish master of the first century, when asked by his pupils how he would summarize the Bible in a sentence, replied, "Love thy neighbor as thyself! The rest is repetition." He's also quoted as saying, while referring to love and self-love, "If I'm not for myself, who is? And if I'm only for myself, who am I? And if not now, when?" In her research Sherrie found a very profound quote attributed to the famed Greek philosopher Plato that emphasizes love, which indirectly reveals her own integration progress, "Be kind, for everyone you meet is fighting a hard battle."

As Sherrie sat in an armchair close to the window, Kezia and I repositioned our recording equipment. For this session, I would concentrate on Sherrie's current life and the integration of her Marilyn memories, starting with her early years and first recall. I would then ease her into the more traumatic teenage and early adult years as she struggled with the Marilyn patterns. Finally, we would explore the traumatic events that led her to contact me in 1998, and later break that contact with its therapeutic promise to live years of more depression, struggle, and further suicide attempts.

Past-Life Regression Conducted by Dr. Adrian Finkelstein on Sherrie Lea Laird; November 11, 2005; Toronto, Ontario

I re-induced Sherrie into a somnambulistic level of deep hypnosis with the same hypnotic suggestion used previously to erase all information about Marilyn Monroe that she derived from books, movies, and any other outside sources. When she had reached this state as evidenced by her very deep relaxation and waxy facial appearance, I gave my final instructions:

Finkelstein: . . . So I'm going now to ask you to go back to your earliest recollections, memories, dreams, or flashbacks of being somebody else or feeling that you are somebody else during your life as Sherrie Lea Laird. You will be able to answer my questions by speaking as loud and as fast as I instruct and, by doing so, you will reinforce your beautiful level even more. I'm going to count now backwards from five to one. As I do, with every count back, you'll go back in time. At number one you will be at a time when you experience your earliest recollections, memories, dreams, or flashbacks of being somebody else and feeling that you're somebody else. Number five, going back in time, back in time, back in time in this life. Number four, your body is growing smaller and smaller and smaller. Number three, people around you appear younger. Number two, pay attention to details. Number one, be there and experience! And now tell me what's happening.

Laird: [Coughing]

Finkelstein: Can you say how old are you approximately?

Laird: Two or three.

Finkelstein: Two or three . . . Sherrie, you know, I'm a person you trust and I like you very much. I like to be with you so that you can play whatever you like to play. Are you playing with something right now?

Laird: I'm on the floor.

Finkelstein: What are you doing there? Do you trust me enough to play with me? What would you like to play?

Laird: [With the very soft voice of a little girl] I'm playing with spoons and cups.

Finkelstein: Oh, I see. Well, that's wonderful. Are you cooking something or preparing something?

Laird: I'm just banging.

Finkelstein: Can you give me a cup so I can drink from it?

Laird: Uh-huh.

Finkelstein: Wow. Delicious. Did you make it?

Laird: No . . . It's just water.

Finkelstein: It's just water. I see. So it's good because I am thirsty. Thank you. Now, I want you to tell me, your name is Sherrie, isn't it?

Laird: Uh-huh.

Finkelstein: Sherrie, I was asking before to go back and to remember something about you being somebody else and that you're somebody else and you feel that way. You remember?

Laird: I just know I'm little, but I'm smart and you're older.

Finkelstein: What do you know, Sherrie?

Laird: I feel like I know everything. I feel like I'm kind of like special or psychic and a little like I'm big but I'm little.

Finkelstein: Like you're a big person in a little body?

Laird: Yeah.

Finkelstein: I see. That's what you feel?

Laird: Um-huh. Like I am smart.

Finkelstein: Smart like a big person?

Laird: Um-huh.

Finkelstein: I see.

Laird: I know what everybody's thinking and doing.

Finkelstein: Can you tell me what you know about others? What are you thinking or doing?

Laird: I see my dad and my mom is there and my grandmother and they're talking about . . . They're planning for the future and they're talking about my dad coming here.

Finkelstein: Coming to Canada?

Laird: Yes.

Finkelstein: So where are you now?

Laird: In the kitchen.

Finkelstein: You want to tell me are you coming to Canada from Scotland?

Laird: Scotland.

Finkelstein: I see. How do you feel about moving from Scotland to Canada?

Laird: My dad is leaving. [Crying]

Finkelstein: Your dad is leaving? Is he leaving first?

Laird: Yes. [Crying]

Finkelstein: Wow, well, but you will be with him. Don't

worry. He loves you and you'll be with him, okay? Please don't worry, okay?

Laird: Okay.

Finkelstein: Now, I want you to go forward in time unless there's something else you want to tell me about Scotland, leaving Scotland. Is there anything else that you know about what's going on besides the move to Canada?

Laird: My favorite. I love it.

Finkelstein: You love what?

Laird: Scotland. We live by the sea.

Finkelstein: So it's like you're going to miss Scotland, isn't that what you said?

Laird: That too, yes. But I miss my dad.

Finkelstein: Well, as I said, your dad will be with you soon, so you have nothing to worry about. He loves you and will be with you soon. So I want you now to move forward in time and I want you to tell me something else. Now, you told me that you felt different than other people. You feel like a big person in a small body.

Laird: Yes.

Finkelstein: Tell me now, when do you become aware for the first time of Marilyn Monroe in this life as Sherrie? How did you begin to associate your memories, dreams, and flashbacks with Marilyn Monroe? When did you first think that you may be the reincarnation of Marilyn Monroe? And I want you to go forward in time as I count to three and at three, you will be at that point in time and you will speak as loudly as possible. If you could also elevate your face a little bit so we can see you. Okay. Number one, number two, number three. [Sherrie was seated in her armchair and her head was bent forward, her face down. She straightened her head in my direction to show her face.] Very good!

Laird: [Sighing, nose running]

Finkelstein: And I'll help you clean your nose. [I wipe her nose with a tissue.]

Laird: Yes, thank you . . . I forgot what you said.

Finkelstein: Then I'll ask you again. No problem. Tell me your first awareness of Marilyn Monroe in this life and how you began to associate your memories, dreams, and flashbacks as Marilyn Monroe. When did you first think that you may be the reincarnation of Marilyn Monroe . . . take your time, all the time in the world you need. Whatever comes first, trust it! The first impressions are on point.

Laird: [Talking about her age] Well, you said three. When you first said three, then I forget and then I remember at five. Then I forget and then I remember at seven. Then I still keep forgetting.

Finkelstein: When you say you remember every time like at three, at five, at seven, you mean you remember being Marilyn Monroe?

Laird: Yes. And then I don't want to, so I try to be me. Then I don't like it.

Finkelstein: You don't like being you?

Laird: No. I like to be me.

Finkelstein: So what don't you like?

Laird: She's feeling to me rude.

Finkelstein: Who is rude to you?

Laird: No. To me, she's not . . . I don't like it. She's older and she's rude. It's my body.

Finkelstein: That's Marilyn?

Laird: No.

Finkelstein: Who is it?

Laird: That's my body.

Finkelstein: Yes.

Laird: I don't want to be that older girl. It's my body. I don't want to remember.

Finkelstein: All right. Okay. So don't remember now. Just rest a moment, rest and feel good. I want you to . . .

Laird: To tell you still, then at 14. Then I feel everything is going to be the same again after. At 14, everything's taking the same life.

Finkelstein: Do you feel it is taking the same life of Marilyn Monroe?

Laird: Yes. It's repeating exactly.

Finkelstein: In what way?

Laird: Everything.

Finkelstein: Like give me an example.

Laird: The modeling, the acting classes, the neighbors, the boyfriends, the behavior, everything is again exact.

Finkelstein: Exactly the same.

Laird: Yes.

Finkelstein: I would like you to take . . .

Laird: Can you help me?

Finkelstein: What are you saying?

Laird: Can you wipe my face? It's tickling me. [I wipe her face with a tissue.] Harder!

Finkelstein: Okay. Good. All right . . . So I want you now to continue. You're 14 . . . Give examples of things that are repeating. Could you?

Laird: All is the same because we moved there, and now I will marry my neighbor and he's in the Army and all the boys like me and they think I'm older. They think at school, I'll be an actress. They think I will be a Playboy bunny.

Finkelstein: Do you want to be an actress or do you want to be a singer?

Laird: I want to be a singer, but I can act. I could . . . I've got a higher grade in acting. Everybody thought I was a star, but I'm too isolated and I don't like to be around people so much. The girls make fun of me when I'm walking, just like Marilyn. They made fun of my walk.

Finkelstein: What's about your walk that they would make fun?

Laird: They said that I walked like I had a pickle up my ass.

Finkelstein: Oh.

Laird: I don't know what it means, and like a penguin. But they're following me home and trying to beat me up because they said I'm stealing their boyfriends and I didn't even know who their boyfriends were. Everything's repeating like before.

Finkelstein: I see. I see. So, are other girls jealous of you?

Laird: Yes. And I don't even care about that kind of thing because I just want to see my dog.

Finkelstein: What's the name of your dog?

Laird: Patches. And I just want to be with my family. I don't like to be so . . . Can you make me do my nose, please?

Finkelstein: Yeah, I will. [I again wipe her nose.] . . . You're talking about those girls [who] are envious and you didn't do anything purposefully to stir them up against you.

Laird: No.

Finkelstein: Did you steal their boyfriends?

Laird: I don't know their boyfriends. They lied to say they went out with me. They liked me, but I didn't even know who they were.

Finkelstein: I see. So, are you still 14 now?

Laird: Yes.

Finkelstein: So how . . . How would you . . . Besides the boyfriends and the way you walk, is there anything else that reminds you that you are like Marilyn Monroe? . . . What I was asking before, is . . . were there any of the events or happenings at this age of 14 in school, [or] elsewhere, that remind you vividly about being Marilyn Monroe reincarnated?

Laird: I just know. When I walk to school, I know I am an actress and I know that I am a star and I'm walking to school and I wonder where is my life, where am I? How come I'm here?

Finkelstein: Do you know that you're Marilyn Monroe at this time?

Laird: I say, yes, I know this. I know this inside. I don't even know who she is.

Finkelstein: Have you read any books or magazines or [seen] movies about Marilyn Monroe?

Laird: No. Not yet. One time . . . there's one time I hear her name. I'm sitting on my Auntie Mae's knee in her kitchen and she's bouncing me up and down, but I'm younger.

Finkelstein: How old are you?

Laird: I'm 12.

Finkelstein: And what is she telling you about Marilyn Monroe?

Laird: She's singing a song.

Finkelstein: What song?

Laird: "A kiss on the hand is quite continental . . ."

Finkelstein: Does it strike a chord with you?

Laird: Yes.

Finkelstein: How do you feel?

Laird: That's mine, like that's very much mine and I feel happy and angry because that's mine and why does she have it.

Finkelstein: I see. Do you tell her that?

Laird: I look at her very funny and I say what are you doing?

Finkelstein: And what does she say?

Laird: She said it's a famous lady's song.

Finkelstein: Do you react to that in any way?

Laird: I just feel kind of proud and kind of like I don't care, too. I feel that I'm powerful, that, that's how powerful I am now.

Finkelstein: Do you let your aunt know that?

Laird: Maybe. I don't know.

Finkelstein: What occurs to you to tell her about it?

Laird: We're eating breakfast so we don't care . . .

Finkelstein: Tell me this. When you go to sleep, you're 14 or 12 or any age during your childhood. Do you have any dreams about Marilyn Monroe?

Laird: Yes.

Finkelstein: Do you have dreams about being Marilyn Monroe? I'm going to count to three and you'll have one of those dreams or revisit it. Number one, number two, number three. It's happening right now and here.

Laird: I'm walking in a park. I'm walking towards the water and I'm seeing some man. He's looking at me and I'm just feeling . . .

Finkelstein: Approximately how old are you?

Laird: In the dream?

Finkelstein: Yes.

Laird: Ummm, 17 or 18 or 19. It's a sailor and he's coming there. He's talking to me.

Finkelstein: You know he's a sailor?

Laird: Yes. I don't know him.

Finkelstein: Do you like him?

Laird: He says . . . I think he says Jim. I kind of like him.

Finkelstein: I see.

Laird: It's looking like an outfit with the stripes.

Finkelstein: Yes. He calls you by name, or what's the name that you hear?

Laird: I don't know if he calls me by name.

Finkelstein: Okay.

Laird: He's touching a dog. I think so.

Finkelstein: Let me ask you this. What is your name?

Laird: A beige dog. In the dream?

Finkelstein: Yes. Are you Marilyn?

Laird: I think so, but I don't want to say it.

Finkelstein: What stops you from saying it?

Laird: Because I don't know: Is it a dream or is it real?

Finkelstein: Oh, I see. Okay. Why don't we stop the dream. Now, I'm going to ask you something else. When did you first read about Marilyn Monroe in books and magazines? Tell me what books and when you read them.

Laird: I told you already before the book, when I had [Kezia] well, then she was little and I had to find out why I feel this way and I said to the guy [in the bookstore], "Do you have any books on someone called Marilyn Monroe," and he said, "Someone called Marilyn Monroe, what do you mean?" And I said, "She's an actress," and he said, "Well, she's . . ."

Finkelstein: What?

Laird: "She's an actress," and he said, "She's famous, but I don't have a book on Marilyn. I have a book on Norma Jean." I said who's that and he said, "That's her," and I said, "Oh, that's yucky."

Finkelstein: The name?

Laird: Yes.

Finkelstein: You like better Marilyn Monroe?

Laird: Well, right now I like them both, but that's what I said to him. Then he gave me a book. It didn't have a cover and it was old and then I'm reading about this girl and even though I don't like her, I can see that it's me and I don't like her. She's like trying to be someone but she's like a hillbilly. She's getting on my nerves when I'm reading it, but I still recognize.

Finkelstein: What do you recognize?

Laird: Me. That's my life.

Finkelstein: I see. So, that's the first time then?

Laird: Yes, and I'm . . . my age is 22, 23, maybe even 24.

Finkelstein: And how old is Kezia?

Laird: She's three or four. I think she's four. She knows. She remembers. She said she does know. She knows. The little girl knows that it's me.

Finkelstein: Oh, she does?

Laird: She's psychic, too, little. She told me.

Finkelstein: Told you what?

Laird: She says: "Mommy," she's telling me, "is that book about you?"

Finkelstein: Who?

Laird: And she knows and I feel a little bit shy, but also surprised that she knows.

Finkelstein: Wow. That's very interesting.

Laird: It's, ummm . . .

Finkelstein: Wow. I wonder . . . We will revisit this period of your life . . . I'd like to ask you something else. I want you to go forward in time as Sherrie Lea Laird . . . I'll ask you to go to the year 1999. As I count backward, going back now, I'm going to count. I'm going to count from three to one. At one you will be there in year 1999 as Sherrie Lea Laird. Number three, moving backward. Number two. Number one. You're there. After you broke contact with me in 1999, tell me what transpired in your emotional life in connection with Marilyn Monroe. I want you to feel not unduly uncomfortable and to be able at the same time to relate what happened. I don't want you to experience pain; I want you just to feel well, but be genuine and tell me what happened. You have the option not to experience too intense negative feelings. Whatever happened, happened. Tell me, when you broke contact with me in 1999, what transpired in your emotional life?

Laird: 1999 . . . I don't know that year. Is that now?

Finkelstein: You contacted me in the end of 1998 and you lost that e-mail. Most of our communication took place in1999. We corresponded for a few months, and then you broke connection with me because you were concerned about your career.

Laird: Is this . . . how do you make . . . how far back is 1999?

Finkelstein: I would say it's about close to seven years back.

Laird: I got confused because I was so in the '80s and then how did 19 years go by? It doesn't make sense to me.

Finkelstein: Yeah, we'll come back to the '80s.

Laird: 1999 is just . . . I was going to tell you but you made me forget now.

Finkelstein: Okay. Well, why don't you go ahead and remember everything you want to tell me, not what I'm asking. So, I'm going to count backward now from three to one and you're going to go to the '80s as you wish.

Laird: No, no, no, no, '92, 1992.

Finkelstein: Whatever you choose. 1992, okay.

Laird: That's why.

Finkelstein: What's happening?

Laird: It's my kitchen. That's why. I had to tell you.

Finkelstein: Yes.

Laird: My floor.

Finkelstein: What about it?

Laird: It's black and white and my walls are turquoise and it's frightening. That's why I call you. I thought I tried to call you then.

Finkelstein: In '92?

Laird: Yes. I thought so, but you don't say so. I must've needed to call you, but I didn't know how.

Finkelstein: Could it be that you called me and don't remember?

Laird: My head calls for you. I don't know. I'm calling for you then.

Finkelstein: How did you find me?

Laird: I find you later.

Finkelstein: But how did you know?

Laird: I don't know. I'm calling for you because I need help right then.

Finkelstein: You didn't look me up anywhere?

Laird: I don't know. I feel like I'm calling to you somehow then. I don't know why. It's my frightening experiences.

Finkelstein: I don't want you to experience it the way you experienced at that time. Right now just tell me what happened.

Laird: I'll tell you 1999. It seems to be for drugs and alcohol and going out and being in the nighttime.

Finkelstein: Now, let me go back to 1992. You said that this black and white floor or the turquoise color of your wall frightened you. What was the connection, without getting unduly disturbed?

Laird: It's something. I have to say something happens. It seems that I keep feeling the need to say Joe slaps me, but M slaps me. [M was Sherrie's abusive boyfriend from 1992.]

Finkelstein: M slaps you?

Laird: Yes.

Finkelstein: And who is M?

Laird: No. It's hard to tell to you because you don't understand.

Finkelstein: How would you make me understand?

Laird: The kitchen reminds me of something.

Finkelstein: Something about M?

Laird: Yes.

Finkelstein: It reminds you probably of the last days of M?

Laird: No. It reminds me of Joe . . .

Finkelstein: Joe DiMaggio?

Laird: He slaps me. I didn't know 'til now.

Finkelstein: Why does he slap you?

Laird: I don't know. Because of the . . .

Finkelstein: Because of the movie? Yes, okay. So he didn't like what you did in the movie or something or . . . ?

Laird: That's why I have . . . that time in '92, but I only just found out now.

Finkelstein: I see.

Laird: And then M slaps me in the same kitchen.

Finkelstein: What is the reason he does [that] to you? . . .

Laird: Can you take me out of the kitchen?

Finkelstein: Yeah, please. When I count to three, you'll be out of that kitchen. One, two, three: out. Now you can clean your nose if you wish.

Laird: [Blows her nose]

Finkelstein: So, I understand then. You had a bad relationship with somebody by the name of M. That's correct?

Laird: I told you so many times I hate him. He reminds me of somebody.

Finkelstein: I know you told me. It's not just for me . . .

Laird: I'm sorry.

Finkelstein: It's okay. And that . . . is that man into drugs and so forth?

Laird: Yes. He's bad.

Finkelstein: Do you break up with him?

Laird: Yes, but I cry and cry first. He hurts me. I should've hurt him. How I could let him hurt me, [and] that reminds me of the past. That's why I'm calling for you to help me, to save me because I can't do it again.

Finkelstein: So what happened that you didn't get in touch with me? Let's go back to 1992. It's 1992 and you want to call me but you don't, so for some reason we don't connect. What's the reason?

Laird: I go to people near my house, doctors. They try to help me. I want them to help me.

Finkelstein: And what's happening?

Laird: Nothing. Just hospitals, in and out. I try to get help. They treat me fine.

Finkelstein: I mean, but what treatment do they give you?

Laird: They give me . . . they're thinking of giving me something like . . . they think of giving me something strong, like Prozac, but they give me needles.

Finkelstein: Needles?

Laird: And they give me Citropen? [Citalopram] So that's a Celexa, Ativan. Citropen. I don't know. Something. It's new, brand new.

Finkelstein: Zoloft?

Laird: I don't know. Something like that, yes.

Finkelstein: Zoloft?

Laird: Yes.

Finkelstein: So, now, let me understand this. So they treat you well and everything and probably you are better. Are you?

Laird: For a while.

Finkelstein: So, you don't feel the need to call me here then obviously, or you do?

Laird: After '92 I call for you again. I fail to call you in '96 and I fail to call you in '98.

Finkelstein: So what happens?

Laird: I type to you. I type a letter to you.

Finkelstein: In '96?

Laird: Hmmm, no.

Finkelstein: '98?

Laird: Yes.

Finkelstein: So, how did you find my name?

Laird: In a screen. On the screen.

Finkelstein: The Internet?

Laird: Yes.

Finkelstein: Okay. Didn't you find others, too?

Laird: I don't think so. Right away I came to you.

Finkelstein: You're sure about that?

Laird: Yes. And I liked your face on the picture.

Finkelstein: What?

Laird: I felt you are my doctor; that you needed to be my doctor.

Finkelstein: I remember that you found me and connected with me and we had some intense correspondence . . . over a period of several months through e-mails and telephone conversations after you first e-mailed to me in the end of 1998. You continued in 1999, in January, and what happened during that period of time that . . . what's happened right then? What are your thoughts, feelings, experiences? What's going on?

Laird: Then? Right then?

Finkelstein: In 1999. The first time you . . .

Laird: Oh, yeah. I'm trying to be a singer and I kind of am starting to be well known and people like it. I'm having a singing life, but I'm having a terrible life with the person who's in my band.

Finkelstein: Is it M?

Laird: No.

Finkelstein: Are you finished with him?

Laird: Yes. It's my friend B. He sings and writes songs with me . . . We're making good music, but he's not very fair.

Finkelstein: Can you elaborate on that?

Laird: He's . . . telling me things that aren't true, and he's controlling and he's mean, and he makes Kezia feel bad.

Finkelstein: I don't want you to feel unduly upset by this. I understand your feelings. Do you feel angry? Or how do you feel?

Laird: Empty.

Finkelstein: You feel empty.

Laird: But I feel somehow higher in my mind, but more empty in my stomach.

Finkelstein: Now, we continue to correspond and at one point I connect you with Ted Jordan and you seem to recognize him.

Laird: Yes. I look forward to it.

Finkelstein: Now, I want you to elaborate some more about your telephone conversations with him. What did you tell each other precisely that made you feel that you are old pals, or that you were friends before, or whatever relationship you have had?

Laird: Our voices right away. The voices we recognize instantly and we laughed and he tried to explain because he has to . . . I tell him, "You have to realize I'm Sherrie and I can only remember how I think, I feel. I can't remember because I don't have you."

Finkelstein: And what does he say?

Laird: He's enjoying me and we're talking about the weather and places and California and talking about people from movies and talking about books and people we know.

Finkelstein: So, let me understand this, please. Does he recognize you as Marilyn Monroe?

Laird: Yes. He's seeing me very strongly connected. He said that he met other people who thought they were her and said they were, and he instantly knew, no; but he said when he talked to you . . . or seen your letter [first e-mail from Sherrie addressed to me] something he got, a stomach feeling. He said he knew immediately it's true. He said in his stomach it felt like someone punched him.

Finkelstein: That's what he said?

Laird: Yes . . . He got a call from you saying maybe, and that you read the letter and described [me] and he knew before you were even finished.

Finkelstein: So, when he talked with you on the phone, did he confirm this kind of intuition he had?

Laird: Yes.

Finkelstein: That you are Marilyn Monroe?

Laird: Yes. And then he heard my voice. He said that "I knew for sure," because my voice is older now and it's deeper [in 2005]. It wasn't so deep. I worked on my voice now. It's stronger and richer.

Finkelstein: I see. So, is there any particular detail that you shared together that's not in his book about you and it's not anywhere, that only you and him would know, you shared in your conversations?

Laird: Hmmm . . .

Finkelstein: Think!

Laird: I don't know because we talked about stuff. He's trying . . . I feel the need to remind him that all my memories are not as vivid as his memories, and so I feel bad for him because he feels he can talk to me like before and I have to tell him, "But Ted, I can't remember like you can because it's different for me."

Finkelstein: But had you remembered that you used to be lovers at one time?

Laird: Yes. I felt that was true and he told me how we were very much in love at one time and I agreed. We felt very, very,

very close. But at this moment, I feel like we were like brother and sister sometime.

Finkelstein: So, you continued to remain friends after your love affair ended?

Laird: I feel like the lovemaking it's just sometimes; it's not lots of times.

Finkelstein: And for how long did you continued to remain friends after your romantic relationship?

Laird: Somehow I remember . . . 1945 comes to me, and maybe I don't see him after then. Maybe 1947 or something, '45 stays in my face.

Finkelstein: So, when you met him, how old were you?

Laird: Eighteen or maybe even 17. Eighteen. I'm going to be 18.

Finkelstein: Were you in the modeling school at the time or not?

Laird: Yes.

Finkelstein: How old are you when you enter the modeling school?

Laird: Seventeen, 18.

Finkelstein: Seventeen, 18?

Laird: Yes.

Finkelstein: All right. You're sure about that?

Laird: Yes. But I'm lying about my age sometimes, so, because I want to be older.

Finkelstein: Are you lying about your age now when you say that you're entering the modeling school at 17, 18?

Laird: No, no, no.

Finkelstein: Okay. And your meeting? When are you meeting Ted Jordan then? Before or after the modeling school or during modeling school?

Laird: Near the end.

Finkelstein: I see. So, about 17, 18 when you meet him?

Laird: Yeah.

Finkelstein: Okay. Is he younger than you?

Laird: I think he's older than me.

Finkelstein: How much older?

Laird: Like one or two, 19 or something.

Finkelstein: How do you meet him, and where will you meet him?

Laird: I see him walking by. I think he's in his bathing shorts.

Finkelstein: You like him?

Laird: I think he's looking good, but he seems different than me.

Finkelstein: Okay. Well, now, I want you to continue and go forward in time. You finished your conversations with Ted Jordan, and there comes a time when you're telling me that you would rather not endanger your career, when I asked you to come to Los Angeles for past-life regressions. That was sometime in March 1999, and you said that you are afraid for your career or something. Do you recall that?

Laird: I'm sorry. I forgot to listen. I was thinking about that day.

Finkelstein: About what day?

Laird: By the pool [with Ted Jordan].

Finkelstein: By the pool, oh. All right. Do you want to pursue that?

Laird: No. Can you . . .

Finkelstein: All right. If not, then let's go move forward to the time in 1999. It's sometime in March, probably the end, toward the end of March and you are sort of concluding all our communications through e-mails and phone conversations. You didn't feel comfortable coming to Los Angeles because of your career. You were busy and did not want to endanger your career. Do you recall that or not?

Laird: Yes.

Finkelstein: And then you dropped out of touch and now my next question is after you broke contact with me then . . .

Laird: I regretted it.

Finkelstein: Did you regret it?

Laird: I missed Ted and I wanted to see him. I felt horrible, very, very, very, very horrible. It wasn't fair.

Finkelstein: So what stopped you from connecting with Ted?

Laird: My career and money and B and too many people to know about it. It was a secret.

Finkelstein: What was the reason that it had to be kept secretive? What was so threatening in that?

Laird: Because people will think I'm crazy.

Finkelstein: Oh, people will think you're crazy, so you're afraid of that.

Laird: I'm not afraid, but I don't like it. I don't want to have it happen to me.

Finkelstein: So, after you broke contact with me, then tell me what transpired in your emotional life in connection with Marilyn Monroe? And did the patterns of her life begin to drive you harder?

Laird: Can you say the first part again? The first part of the question?

Finkelstein: All right. I'll do it slower then. After you broke contact with me in 1999, some time in the end of March, tell me what transpired in your emotional life in connection with Marilyn Monroe.

Laird: I told you, the drugs and alcohol and the emptiness.

Finkelstein: I see.

Laird: And thinking instead of feeling.

Finkelstein: Did these Marilyn patterns from your life begin to drive you even harder?

Laird: Driving me? . . .

Finkelstein: Harder. I mean, did you feel more intense[ly] that problem of Marilyn Monroe with drugs and alcohol?

Laird: Yes, but I blocked it away very much into a little box. "Leave me alone," I said to myself. "Leave me alone" and I just tried to use the . . . the thing to . . . with men to my benefit, but I don't want to feel like her and I don't want to feel that. I just want to get away from it. I try not to think about it, but it keeps popping up.

Finkelstein: Can you give me a detailed sketch of your emotional life during the years prior to 2005 after you broke contact with me?

Laird: I'm sorry. I don't understand.

Finkelstein: After you broke contact with me in 1999, which was the end of March, there were several years that passed [before you contacted me again] in 2005. I'm asking what happened during this period in your emotional life and what made you come back to me and so forth to research your past life as Marilyn Monroe?

Laird: I'm falling and I'm getting back up and I'm falling and getting back up, but each time I'm weaker. Each time I'm closer to dying. People around me don't understand anything about me whatsoever and I feel like dying . . .

Finkelstein: Why doesn't anyone understand? Sherrie, maybe explain.

Laird: I'm so different from everybody around me.

Finkelstein: Right. It's hard to explain exactly, but just to give a hint of how you feel.

Laird: The way I think. The way I behave. The things I do. What I say. What I believe in. The way I walk. What I want. What I dream of. Everything is different from anyone around me.

Finkelstein: If you'd have to write a novel . . . so that other people would be able to understand you, at least enough to have an idea of how you feel, or how you've been feeling, how would you phrase it?

Laird: How hard it is to be a woman. How hard it is to be in tune. How hard it is to be a singer. How hard it is to be a daughter, a single mom, how hard it is to have flashbacks when no one believes you.

Finkelstein: Yes. So that's pretty hard for you.

Laird: To be always struggling to have money, when you want to be with your child instead. To be evicted, to take pills, to hurt my baby, to almost die, to be in the car, to be a singer and the musicians don't understand you.

Finkelstein: Was your attempted suicide as Sherrie connected to these patterns of Marilyn Monroe?

Laird: I told you everything was exact from 14 upwards, exact.

Finkelstein: I will not bother to ask you again.

Laird: Exactly the same.

Finkelstein: Right.

Laird: Exactly the same suicidal thing. Exactly the same pills. Exactly the same alcohol pills, because everything is hitting me again, to repeat.

Finkelstein: I want you to have it clear for . . . other people to understand and thus help others by sharing your experience. That's what we're doing now. Is it clear?

Laird: Yes.

Finkelstein: We'll go to something else then. Can you tell me more about your relationship with Gladys?

Laird: My Gladys?

Finkelstein: I would like to go back in time now and you are Marilyn Monroe. I'm going to make it more . . .

At this point the recording ended. Since Sherrie felt exhausted, we decided it would be to her benefit to stop for the day.

Twelve
LEAVING MARILYN BEHIND

Since Sherrie was to appear in concert the following night, we decided to conduct our next regression at 10:00 in the morning, thus giving her a break in the afternoon. On Saturday, November 12, Sherrie could not make our scheduled appointment and arrived with Kezia at about 12:30 P.M. We all were very hungry by this time and moved straight to the hotel restaurant and ordered lunch.

At lunch we decided, given the lateness of the hour, that we would regress Kezia in today's session and wait until tomorrow to continue with Sherrie's next regression. We needed to explore whether Kezia was indeed Gladys Monroe Baker in her last life and see if she was open to regression therapy to heal some of her own past-life wounds. While Kezia excused herself to make a telephone call, I explained to Sherrie that this kind of regression may be more difficult for Kezia, given the fact that Gladys was mentally ill and institutionalized for 50 years. We both agreed to proceed tentatively and cut the session short if it proved too painful for Kezia at this time.

Regarding Sherrie's next regression, we needed to continue with the process of reconciling Sherrie's Marilyn persona, as we had in the last regression by focusing on her memories of Marilyn in this life. This time we would go back and conduct another question-and-answer session, similar to our May 4, 2005, regression, to help create more distance between her and Marilyn by recalling people, places, and situations and not so much Marilyn's emotional experiences. This would also help our "case" in proving Sherrie's claim, not only to skeptical readers but to herself as well. I also warned her that after the emotional abreaction of our recent session that she would find herself more in Marilyn's body and psyche and may be less tolerant of our probing.

After lunch we went up to my room, and with Sherrie seated nearby, I attempted to regress Kezia as she sat in an armchair near the window. Inducing Kezia to revisit her former life as Gladys was unsuccessful, as I feared it might be. Though she reached at times a somnambulistic level of hypnosis, Kezia resisted any attempt at being regressed by simply losing the hypnotic level or outright snapping out of her trance once we started. Obviously, the stress of recalling and reliving Gladys Baker's life of schizophrenic torture was unbearable. This was a form of proof in itself that she was really Marilyn Monroe's tormented mother in her last life. In psychoanalytic jargon, we call this opposition to unravel very traumatic emotional events resistance erected to defend the individual against overwhelming emotions that threaten to break lose and may result in a destructive or self-destructive event. At the subconscious level, it is safer to resist than to open the gates of hell, so to speak. In psychoanalysis the resistance indirectly implies the nature of the emotional conflict by the specifics of the resistance itself. The fact that the subconscious would allow us no entry at any point indicated that we weren't faced with horrifying specific traumatic events but an unrelenting life of torment and misery. We all decided to attempt another regression the following morning.

That evening, just an hour prior to Sherrie's performance, I received a phone call from her boyfriend Chris who said that Sherrie had spontaneously entered a trance state in spite of my suggestion to the contrary. I could understand how the circumstances of our marathon hypnosis sessions could induce under stress just such a lapse. On the phone I dehypnotized Sherrie and gave her positive suggestions for success in her concert. As a result she felt her usual self again and was able to continue. I learned the following day that her concert was a great success.

The next morning, Sunday, November 13, 2005, Sherrie and Kezia appeared in the hotel lobby at about 10:00 A.M. We had a quick breakfast that lasted about 30 minutes. We talked about Sherrie's spontaneous lapse, and I told her how unusual it was but assured her that once these sessions ended there would be no further incidents. I also talked with Kezia about her upcoming regression and told her that I wouldn't press her if we encountered more resistance. We proceeded to my room, and this time Kezia lay down on the bed in order to further enhance her relaxation. She lay on her back and propped her head on two pillows for comfort. It was daylight and the curtains were open, and two lamps were turned on as well. There was sufficient lighting for videotaping. My video camera was positioned on the table as was customary during these sessions.

I attempted a rapid hypnosis induction. But again, after reaching a somnambulistic level, Kezia slipped out of it. It was quite obvious that a profound sense of fear was behind her resistance, a fear of losing conscious control and being overwhelmed by the subconscious content. At this point I explained to both Sherrie and Kezia, "Marilyn was maladjusted with her share of emotional problems, but basically sane, so there's a healthy side of her able to look at the unhealthy side. Gladys was apparently insane for most of her later life, with no access point. And, as it turns out, it's probably healthy for Kezia, who's well adjusted and not troubled (as Sherrie was) by her past-life trauma to resist revisiting it."

I decided that in order to at least establish, which Sherrie and Kezia most definitely wanted, that Kezia was Gladys Baker, I had to adopt a method other than regressive hypnosis. I thought we had already accumulated sufficient evidence to prove that Kezia is indeed the reincarnation of Gladys. We had discovered the nine-month lapse between Gladys's death (March 11, 1984) and Kezia's birth (December 11, 1984), the behavioral pattern of Kezia "mothering" Sherrie from an early age, the astrological Taurus North Moon Node of Kezia and the 180 degrees opposite Scorpio North Moon Node of Gladys (moving from Scorpio's warlike focus to Taurus's garden of peace), and the uncanny resemblance of the facial bone structure in the two females—particularly in the eyes and ears. These were enough clues to infer with high probability that Kezia Laird is the reincarnation of Gladys Monroe Baker.

I was hoping that an emotional confirmation could come by using the psychoanalytic technique of spontaneous associations in order to indirectly derive the truth of what's hiding behind Kezia's resistance. Therefore, addressing Kezia I inquired, "Let me ask you a question straight up, right now. Can you spontaneously associate, continuously associate, and consciously—let's say you forgot the numbers and together with them you forgot that you're Gladys Baker and Gladys Monroe and Gladys Mortensen, and that your mom used to be Norma Jean Baker. Say, it's gone and you go with it. Are you going to cooperate now consciously?" I had previously explained that even a conscious level of cooperation with the therapist, by promising to be trustworthy during questioning, has a specific partial amnesia effect and would suffice in the process of unlocking the subconscious secrets. Freud pioneered the use of this "free association" technique when hypnosis was not an option. Following is an excerpt of what followed in the session:

Kezia: Um-huh.

Finkelstein: Okay. You do.

Kezia: Yeah.

Finkelstein: So what is the first feeling you get when I inquire of you: "Were you Gladys in your previous life? Were you Norma Jean's mother?" Yes or no? First impression.

Kezia: Yes, I think, yes.

Finkelstein: Yes. You think? Do you feel it? Yes or no? The first impression.

Kezia: Yes, yes, yes, yes. [Kezia bursts into tears, sobbing and becoming convulsed, crying nonstop.]

Laird: See, that's what it is. Just saying that, Kezia, frees you so much because when I had to admit I was Marilyn, when he first asked me if I was, I wanted to scream NO, but my body wouldn't let me lie. I felt like exploding.

Kezia: But mine is not much like I feel like I need to lie or I don't know. I just feel like I hear so much stuff that I get confused.

Laird: You're wondering if you should be saying it because you heard it before.

Kezia: Yeah.

Laird: But the bottom line is, can you lie? Okay, say no. Does that feel like a lie? Hurry and say no.

Kezia: Yeah. No is like a lie.

Laird: It feels like a lie. Exactly, that's what I was trying to tell you.

Finkelstein: Good, excellent. Excellent. [Addressing Sherrie] You should take my place.

Laird: No, you're so amazing. I watch you in action; it's incredible.

Kezia: My head is pounding.

Finkelstein: So, very good. Well, thank you, Kezia. You'll be all right in no time.

Kezia: Thank you!

After Kezia came out of her relaxed state and calmed down sufficiently, I asked her again to reconfirm if she was Gladys Baker in her past life, and she resolutely said, "Yes." I now proceeded with Sherrie's regression. This regression lasted more than six hours, and the transcript was almost 90 pages long. I've subsequently edited out repetitive responses and inquiries, bathroom breaks, and some irrelevant material. I added an explanation for many of the inconclusive responses where Sherrie/Marilyn did not have a ready answer or couldn't remember a factual detail, unlike the May 4th question-and-answer session. (As I mentioned, after the emotional abreaction of our November 11th sessions, Sherrie was more into Marilyn's self and not as interested in questions and answers, repeatedly saying, "I don't care"—or was this Sherrie tired of being Marilyn? Either way, the psychological explanation is simple. In my view, Sherrie was totally immersed during her regressions into Marilyn's psyche; she was Marilyn. Therefore, I would mostly attribute her "I don't care" attitude not to Sherrie being tired of being Marilyn, but to Marilyn/Sherrie, one and the same person, being herself.)

Past-Life Regression Conducted by Dr. Adrian Finkelstein on Sherrie Lea Laird; November 13, 2005; Toronto, Ontario

Finkelstein: [I proceeded with the hypnotic induction until she entered a deep level. Then I began questioning her, after I induced, on her amnesia, a somnambulistic state. I wanted to eliminate any possible influence George Barris's book had on her.] Forget everything you've read in the book of George Barris, *Marilyn: Her Own Life in Her Own Words*! You'll forget it together with the numbers that I'll ask you to forget in a moment. All the information from that book and for that matter from any other book, magazine, publication, film of Marilyn Monroe and Norma Jean and from your previous sessions that you are the reincarnation of Norma Jean/Marilyn Monroe that we already know . . . I want you to go ahead and answer my questions that pertain to your life as Norma Jean and Marilyn Monroe, and be able to forget all this stuff that we mentioned and just start now counting backward from 100. With every count back you will notice that the rest of the numbers grow dimmer and distant and eventually relax completely out of your mind after two or three counts. At that point, all the memories I mentioned about the previous life as Norma Jean and Marilyn Monroe that you acquired from public records will be gone, together with the numbers. Clear? Say yes or no!

Laird: Yes.

Finkelstein: Okay. So, I want you now to go back in time, to the time you were Norma Jean and you were a young girl. Do you want to say something?

Laird: [Coughing]

Finkelstein: It's all right. I want you to feel protected and well.

Laird: [Coughing]

Finkelstein: What do you feel? It's okay.

Laird: Hard to breathe. Hard to breathe.

Finkelstein: According to your birth certificate, you are Norma Jean. What is the name on your birth certificate, and when and where were you born? You're old enough to know that.

Laird: Norma Jean Mortensen, June 1st, 1926.

Finkelstein: 1926?

Laird: Yes.

Finkelstein: Now, I want you to tell me: How do you feel about the beginning years of your life? Can you describe your childhood experience as Norma Jean, like up to age ten? And you realize that before, you already mentioned a few things. Whatever you haven't mentioned. Can you pick up anything?

Laird: No. I'm just playing. I'm a girl.

Finkelstein: Approximately how old are you?

Laird: Ten.

Finkelstein: Where are you playing?

Laird: In the street.

Finkelstein: What are you playing?

Laird: Scotch . . . hopscotch with a little boy.

Finkelstein: Hopscotch with a little boy; I see. Do you enjoy the game?

Laird: Yes.

Finkelstein: I want you now to go ahead and describe to me what's going on in your life. You're ten, before that or after that. Who are the people that take care of you? How do you feel toward them? Allow the impressions to freely flow in.

Laird: Hmmm . . . I see the people but I don't want to be here.

Finkelstein: You don't want to be where?

Laird: I don't like it. Why? Why?

Finkelstein: All right. We'll just go over it.

Laird: [Crying in a young girl's voice] Why I do I have to stay here? I want my mommy . . . [Crying] I want my mommy.

Finkelstein: You want your mommy?

Laird: [Crying]

Finkelstein: Where is she? Norma Jean, where is she? Tell me.

Laird: She's away.

Finkelstein: She's away where?

Laird: I think she's at work. Somewhere away. She's gone. [Crying] She went to go somewhere.

Finkelstein: How old are you?

Laird: I'm nine.

Finkelstein: Where are you?

Laird: I'm standing there in the street.

Finkelstein: In the street. I see. I see. I'm now with you, so you're not alone. You're just fine.

Laird: [Crying]

Finkelstein: She'll come back. She'll come back from work. I want her to come back now and you meet with her. You see her right now?

Laird: Uh-huh.

Finkelstein: She's back, right?

Laird: Yes.

Finkelstein: Do you feel better?

Laird: Yes.

Finkelstein: Good. Why don't you hug each other? Or hold each other tight. Feeling better?

Laird: Yeah.

Finkelstein: That's good. I realize that this is hard to talk about at times when your mother is away. Norma Jean, Gladys is with you and you're with her.

Laird: My chest hurts.

Finkelstein: You want to be with her and now you are.

Laird: Yes, I have family.

Finkelstein: I see. Your brothers or sisters, what can you tell me about them? Do you have brothers and sisters?

Laird: Yes.

Finkelstein: Brothers?

Laird: A brother somewhere.

Finkelstein: Do you have sisters, too?

Laird: I have a sister somewhere.

Finkelstein: I see. How many sisters do you have?

Laird: One.

Finkelstein: One?

Laird: Or two. I don't know.

Finkelstein: Two?

Laird: Maybe.

Finkelstein: Your sisters, are they older or younger than you?

Laird: I see someone older.

Finkelstein: Do you have any pets? Do you have any pets you live with?

Laird: Noooooo! [Crying and screaming] No.

Finkelstein: Don't you have pets?

Laird: [Screaming, obviously extremely frightened] Noooooo. No. No. No.

Finkelstein: Norma Jean, nothing bad happens . . .

Laird: No, no, nooooo, no. You can't make me. Don't talk to me about that. Don't. Don't talk to me about that. Don't.

Finkelstein: I won't talk with you about that. [As a child, Norma Jean once witnessed a dog being run over by a car.]

Laird: Can you help me right now?

Finkelstein: You are away from this situation now. You step aside from this situation. You step aside from it. You're out of that. You're out of that . . .

Laird: Help me. Help me. Help me. My head is going to explode. [Crying]

Finkelstein: You're fine. You're fine.

Laird: No. I don't feel better.

Finkelstein: I'm going to count to three, and at the count of three you'll be awake and feel well. One, two, three.

Laird: [Sighing] No.

Finkelstein: [Re-inducing much quicker Sherrie's somnambulistic trance] You feel all right. Okay. Just relax. You're far away from this situation and you are in a pleasant place, a nice place, now it is a nice time in your life as Norma Jean. You're doing something that you are fond of doing and you're pursuing that right now. What's happening right now? [Long silence; Sherrie doesn't respond.] Can I ask you something that's completely different right now? You're going forward in time as Norma Jean and I want you to tell me how you acquire this slight British overtone in your diction? Did anyone teach it to you?

Laird: [Coughing] Sort of, but I hear it before in others. And I hear it in acting and TV things. Not TV, it's things, it's black and white [movies circa 1930s]. I see things. I hear it, but it's just me. It's not my fault.

Finkelstein: Then, tell me this, Norma Jean, did you ever learn to play a musical instrument and do people know you play it?

Laird: I used to be able to make the piano sound nice. I can play a little bit.

Finkelstein: Are you going to play piano later on or not?

Laird: I plan to . . .

Finkelstein: Or another instrument?

Laird: I want to.

Finkelstein: Is there any movie in the future that you can recall in which you will play piano? First impressions.

Laird: There are two, but I see one. I'm just not really playing it. It's fake [playing].

Finkelstein: Is it fake?

Laird: Yes. And I want to play piano in a movie later.

Finkelstein: Are you really playing in a movie?

Laird: Just with my fingers.

Finkelstein: Right. Okay. You happen to meet someone, a very nice lady, an older lady who was good to you somewhere in Van Nuys [California]. Can you recall her name or the nature of your relationship with her?

Laird: There is a teacher. There is a lady.

Finkelstein: An older lady. An older lady that you stayed with when your mother is away, and she's very good to you.

Laird: How old are you talking? How old am I are you talking about?

Finkelstein: Oh, probably about just before you got married the first time.

Laird: Because I love a lady, I love two ladies.

Finkelstein: Who are they?

Laird: Anna.

Finkelstein: Anna, yes. That's the one that I was referring to. And who is the other one? What's the name?

Laird: Grace, Auntie Grace.

Finkelstein: Very good. What can you tell me about your relationship with them?

Laird: They're nice. They're loving. They're caring. She's caring for me. She's making nice stew and things. She's cuddly and she's jumping around.

Finkelstein: Do you learn something from them that's memorable in your mind, that helps you very much?

Laird: Hmmm. How to dress and be on time and be polite and just . . . [Sighs] But I don't turn out like that anyway.

Finkelstein: Do they tell you that, anything about that? You say you didn't turn out this way. Did they believe in you?

Laird: Uh-huh.

Finkelstein: You believe in yourself as they do?

Laird: Um-huh.

Finkelstein: What did they tell you that makes you believe in yourself?

Laird: God, and they talk to me about being successful and being in modeling . . .

Finkelstein: Let's talk about Aunt Grace. In which way is she encouraging you to succeed?

Laird: They said I'm beautiful.

Finkelstein: Do you believe her?

Laird: Hmmm, yes, sort of. Uh-huh. I guess so. Everybody says so.

Finkelstein: So in which way does Aunt Anna encourage you? What does she tell you?

Laird: I don't know. She's telling me I'm beautiful. She's telling me everything about life. We talk about everything.

Finkelstein: I just wanted you to elaborate on your relationship with Aunt Anna, Aunt Grace. You've done it to some extent. I don't have specific questions for you. I just want you to elaborate.

Laird: I love them. She's taking care of me. I'm older. I'm mature now and I'm going to get married soon and become a lady and I don't know what you want me to tell you.

Finkelstein: Go ahead. That's very good. I want to ask you this. You are with your mother now. Well, what's her view about young girls using cosmetics? How does she feel about that?

Laird: She's not so saying yes, but she's not saying always no. She knows I'm going to.

Finkelstein: Like what are you going to use?

Laird: Lipstick. Red. It might be too thick, but so what?

Finkelstein: Are you applying makeup, too?

Laird: Powder.

Finkelstein: Powder. I see. So your opinion about your looks and . . . How did your mother advise you use your looks?

Laird: She wants me to use my looks, but she's worried about men because she doesn't feel they're safe. She's worried about older men.

Finkelstein: All of this talking about men, about boys being in school, would boys ever laugh at you in school? How would they relate to you?

Laird: Well, they laughed before at my clothes. I didn't look so very clean and . . . But that was when I was little.

Finkelstein: How about now that you're bigger?

Laird: They like me. I think I'm tall or something. They think that's fascinating.

Finkelstein: How does it make you feel?

Laird: Hmmm . . . Sometimes I don't care and sometimes I care. They're not who I want to be with, so I don't care.

Finkelstein: What does the phrase "two melons up front and two in the rear" bring to your mind?

Laird: It's a joke.

Finkelstein: About?

Laird: Me. Seems like it's about me.

Finkelstein: How does it make you feel?

Laird: Ah, I don't care.

Finkelstein: You don't care?

Laird: I don't . . . I think it's stupid. Sometimes it's funny, but I don't really care.

Finkelstein: I see. How old are you when you start dating, Norma Jean? What is your relation with girls?

Laird: Well, we're sneaking to have dates, but we're just mostly sitting around.

Finkelstein: How old are you?

Laird: Fourteen.

Finkelstein: So, tell me, when did you have your first boyfriend that you went really steady with him?

Laird: Hmmm. It's a guy there. He's maybe starting with P . . . Pau . . . Paul.

Finkelstein: Paul?

Laird: Something. It's Pa . . . something.

Finkelstein: How old are you at this time? Fourteen?

Laird: Um-huh. But it's not lasting a long time. It's like we say we're boyfriend and girlfriend, but we don't see each other at all. It's just in our heads. He's too shy.

Finkelstein: Are you fond of each other?

Laird: We're liking each other's looks.

Finkelstein: I see. And, also can you tell me, Norma Jean, please, did you want to get married at age 16? Did anyone encourage you to get married?

Laird: It's kind of exciting at the time. Yeah. I don't, but I do.

Finkelstein: So, you did get married. Whom did you marry and can you describe the wedding, your husband, the people who attended, who designed your wedding gown, things of that nature?

Laird: Hmmm. Somebody is sewing it for me. It's 30 people, around 30 people. It's in . . . it's a little church but it's the house or something. We're going to the house and I see my shoes and my dress. It's exciting. There're little kids there running around my feet. Always in my way. Screaming, squealing, and he's there smiling. He's scared. He's scared, but he's excited. It's fun, but it's kind of like it's not really happening to me.

Finkelstein: Is it like that? Do you see anyone there that is designing your wedding gown?

Laird: There's a lady but I can't see her well. She's there. I can see her. She's so proud of it. She keeps looking at it. She's touching it and she's more excited about the dress than me.

Finkelstein: Who is she?

Laird: I don't know. She's got whitish hair.

Finkelstein: Is she, by any chance, Aunt Anna?

Laird: Yes, but her hair is so white, so very white. Her hair is so silver. I thought her hair was darker. She has a veil on her . . . She has a hat with a thing on her face. She's touching the dress. She's excited. She's always adjusting my dress.

Finkelstein: Okay. Continue to experience!

Laird: I'm having wine. I'm having some wine.

Finkelstein: Okay. And you have some wine, right? At your wedding to Jim Dougherty. Tell me, have you ever dated or been engaged to Jim Dougherty before marrying him?

Laird: Hmmm, yeah.

Finkelstein: For how long?

Laird: A couple of months, three or four months. Three months.

Finkelstein: How does it go?

Laird: It was fun when we were out. We were having fun, dancing and driving. Just walking around, talking, going for snacks, French fries. I think there's a stand there. You can get things. It's nice.

Finkelstein: Do you feel attracted to each other?

Laird: Uh-huh. Inside I know, but I don't feel things. But I like it somehow. I feel something, but I feel like it's not happening to me.

Finkelstein: I see. Is your marriage to Jim Dougherty bringing any benefit to you?

Laird: Uh-huh.

Finkelstein: In what way? Can you explain?

Laird: Well, it makes me feel older. I can make choices. I feel like I'm getting older. I feel protected. I feel like I am a big shot.

Finkelstein: When do you find out that you are an illegitimate child?

Laird: I always knew.

Finkelstein: Did you?

Laird: I know when I'm older, but I somehow know when I'm nine.

Finkelstein: When do you find for the first time the facts of life and the truth about sex, Norma Jean?

Laird: In school.

Finkelstein: And how old are you?

Laird: We talk about it. Hmmm, 12 or 13. We're making jokes. We don't understand.

Finkelstein: Well, you don't care about sex.

Laird: We know what it is.

Finkelstein: I see. How about when you marry Jim?

Laird: It was exciting.

Finkelstein: Exciting?

Laird: And scary.

Finkelstein: Scary. In what way scary?

Laird: Well, do you think it's exciting and scary for a girl?

Finkelstein: What can happen that's scary, what scares you?

Laird: It could hurt.

Finkelstein: Oh, I see. Were your scary feelings proven to be true?

Laird: Somewhat . . . But it's exciting and you feel more loved.

Finkelstein: Do you feel that you're frigid with Jim or with anybody else later on?

Laird: Sometimes, because I don't love him then, because I'm not attracted. That's why. Because I don't like it if I don't like them.

Finkelstein: I see. What does Jim think of you as a wife? Does he find any deficiency in you as a wife? Is he complaining about anything?

Laird: [Small laugh] My cooking.

Finkelstein: What's about your cooking?

Laird: He says that I'm making things wrong. He's laughing. He's not mad.

Finkelstein: I see . . . Is Jim encouraging you to become a model or an actress? What is his opinion about Hollywood?

Laird: Hmmm . . . He thinks they're faking and scammers. He thinks they're just not good. He doesn't like that kind of people.

Finkelstein: I see. Do you think the same?

Laird: Sometimes he makes me think it. Sometimes he has a point.

Finkelstein: I see. And is Jim jealous? If yes, what makes him jealous? Do you think you really give him a reason to be jealous?

Laird: Well, I'm not giving him enough attention. If I gave him more attention, he wouldn't be jealous at all. He would trust me, but I don't give him the attention because I don't feel the same. I don't want to stay here. This is not enough for me. If I were to have a job and love him, even if I were to have a modeling job, but I can't focus on him. I have to focus on me. I feel sorry but I just don't care.

Finkelstein: I see.

Laird: I can't. If I care, I'll stop. If I don't care, I can keep going.

Finkelstein: I see. Tell me this . . . do you recall what you worked at during World War II after Jim Dougherty was stationed out of town?

Laird: It's a big place. It's place for parachutes.

Finkelstein: Parachutes, I see. What do you do there?

Laird: Just things. Just things, folding things.

Finkelstein: Folding.

Laird: They're big. It's very big. It's exciting because it's war, G.I.s.

Finkelstein: It's exciting because you're helping G.I.s?

Laird: Yes.

Finkelstein: So, would you call it like a defense plant?

Laird: Yes.

Finkelstein: Where was it?

Laird: It's a jump thing. Like a jumper. I don't know.

Finkelstein: It doesn't matter the name. But tell me this. Where is Jim stationed at first?

Laird: That's hard. It's an island or something. He's far away.

Finkelstein: Europe? Africa? Asia?

Laird: It's . . . it's not an island. It's something S.

Finkelstein: Something S. I'll give you another letter. Sh . . .

Laird: Sh . . .

Finkelstein: The second letter is H and the third is A.

Laird: Sha . . .

Finkelstein: Shanghai?

Laird: Yeah.

Finkelstein: And while working there . . . in this defense plant and, you know, [with] these parachutes. While working there, you encounter an Army photographer. He feels your picture will do what to the troops?

Laird: [Laughs] You know, just to make them like "wow wee" and things like that.

Finkelstein: Oh. Be like a morale booster?

Laird: Uh-huh.

Finkelstein: And what's the name of this photographer, do you recall?

Laird: Uh-huh. It's right on the tip of my tongue. His name is Da . . . it's a short name.

Finkelstein: All right. You don't have to remember necessarily. I can give you a clue. His first name starts with Da. Correct.

Laird: Yes, yes.

Finkelstein: What is it?

Laird: I don't know.

Finkelstein: All right. David Conover.

Laird: Yes.

Finkelstein: All right. Well, this is not the most important name, but I think . . .

Laird: That's the name.

Finkelstein: I can get it for you, yeah. Are these pictures of you not the first that appear in a publication?

Laird: Huh? Is it the first?

Finkelstein: Yeah, you're right. It's the first. It never appeared before?

Laird: Uh-huh. It's very exciting for me. Of course, I know I want to be a star.

Finkelstein: There's a publication in which your pictures appeared for the Army camp, and they had a very interesting name. It has to do with the flag of the United States maybe.

Laird: I see some things, a W.

Finkelstein: What is the flag? I mean, what is the design on the flag?

Laird: Stars and stripes.

Finkelstein: Exactly. That's the name of the publication, *Stars and Stripes*. Who first helps you to do modeling in Los Angeles? What does it do for you?

Laird: He takes me to a lady.

Finkelstein: Do you recall precisely who's instrumental in getting you the first modeling job? What is his name?

Laird: A photographer.

Finkelstein: What is his name?

Laird: It's a photographer. He's there taking a picture.

Finkelstein: Do you recall his name or not?

Laird: I don't know.

Finkelstein: Okay. Tell me this, are you . . .?

Laird: The camera, the kind that is big.

Finkelstein: Are you paid for modeling in the beginning?

Laird: Early. I'm paid for modeling before I'm at the modeling school. They give me some money.

Finkelstein: Tell me this: What does the first commercial photographer like about you?

Laird: He likes my posture. He likes my shape. He thinks there's just something about me. It's girly, but womanly. Sexy.

Finkelstein: Sexy?

Laird: He says I'm sexy.

Finkelstein: Is it something, like, that you work hard at . . . or it comes to you without much effort?

Laird: It seems I'm trying.

Finkelstein: Okay. Does he . . . does he like the fact that you have this natural look?

Laird: Uh-huh. I actually work hard.

Finkelstein: I see. You're 19 years old. Who runs the largest model agency in Los Angeles and what is its name? Do you recall anything about it?

Laird: [No answer]

Finkelstein: Who?

Laird: Mrs. . . .

Finkelstein: What is her name?

Laird: Miss Emmeline Snively.

Finkelstein: Snively, right. At this time, do you have a romantic affair with a young man? If so, what is his name?

Laird: He's a guy. I think I told you.

Finkelstein: You told me? Eddie?

Laird: Yes.

Finkelstein: Okay. Eddie Friedman.

Laird: Yes.

Finkelstein: All right.

Laird: We're friends, too.

Finkelstein: This is the one that later on would be known as Ted Jordan, right?

Laird: Yes.

Finkelstein: What is your payment arrangement with Miss Snively for modeling school tuition?

Laird: I'll do some jobs first and she'll take it off of there.

Finkelstein: Right. Okay. Very good. Now, what is your first modeling job? What do you do? What do you model?

Laird: I stand there on the blocks. My first modeling job with a guy and that big camera. I'm on the blocks . . .

Finkelstein: What are these blocks made of? What material, in the first modeling job? Is it metal or not?

Laird: Hmmm . . . I don't know.

Finkelstein: All right. Could it be that you're a hostess at an aluminum exhibit? Do you recall that?

Laird: No.

Finkelstein: Okay. And what are you modeling for in your second job?

Laird: I need to go down, down, down.

Finkelstein: Deeper?

Laird: Yes.

Finkelstein: Okay. All right. Well, I'm going to ask you to count backward from 100 and as you do, after two or three numbers, the rest of the numbers will just relax completely out of your mind. At that point, you'll be as far down as you need to be able to give me your information. And I want you to start now. You count backward from 100.

Laird: One hundred, 90 . . .

Finkelstein: Are all the numbers gone?

Laird: Hmmm . . .

Finkelstein: When all the numbers are gone, you let me know. Are they gone?

Laird: Ninety . . . They're still there.

Finkelstein: You need to count until they disappear, so they relax out of your mind. Don't worry. Usually two, three, four numbers and then the rest go away.

Laird: Ninety-nine, 98, 97, 96. No, they're still there.

Finkelstein: Don't watch them. Just count until they disappear by themselves. Let them go. I can't do it for you. You have to let go of them. You did it before.

Laird: One hundred, deeper, deeper . . . I don't let them go.

Finkelstein: Okay. Then, let's forget about the numbers for the time being and I want you to open your eyes. Close your eyes. Deeper, deeper, deeper. Open, close. Deeper, deeper, deeper. Open, open, open, close. Deeper, deeper, deeper. Open, open, open, open, close. Deeper, deeper, deeper. All the way. Open, open, open, open, close. Much deeper, much sounder. Open, open, open, open, open, close. So deeply and soundly. Enjoy it! It is so beautiful, enjoyable. Now, open them, close them, open them, close them, open them, close them, open, open, open, close. Very deeply. You're just sinking, limp, loose, completely relaxed, in your mind and body to your satisfaction. Just enjoy it! You don't try hard, you don't try to resist. Just let go and let God. I'll talk with you in a minute . . . I want you to count backward as you feel very deeply relaxed in mind and body, count backward, saying after each number deeper relaxed, like you say 100 and then deeper relaxed. Say 99, deeper relaxed, and so forth and so on and you'll see after a few numbers the rest of them will just relax completely out of your mind. At that point, your mind will be completely relaxed. You will be as deep as you can go, as all the memories of Marilyn Monroe, Norma Jean, and everything connected to outside public record will be gone together with the numbers. Start now.

Laird: One hundred, deeper relaxed. Ninety-nine . . .

Finkelstein: Are the numbers gone?

Laird: Yes.

Finkelstein: Okay. Now, I want you to listen to my questions and answer them to the best of your ability. How do you fare in your second modeling job as Norma Jean?

Laird: [No answer]

Finkelstein: Do you do well?

Laird: No.

Finkelstein: You don't? What's happening?

Laird: I don't know. Something that I do is wrong.

Finkelstein: What do they tell you? Probably Ms. Snively is telling you what was wrong.

Laird: I mean, somebody's telling me finally, "Too sexual." [Apparently, Miss Snively explained to Norma Jean that being "too sexy" would distract people buying the swimming suits being advertised.]

Finkelstein: Too sexual? I see. Well, that's not good for the modeling, is it?

Laird: I don't know.

Finkelstein: Okay. So, I see. What did you model, basically, that you were too sexual?

Laird: Clothing.

Finkelstein: What kind of clothing?

Laird: Sweaters and skirts and bathing suits.

Finkelstein: I see. How do you feel about the modeling school and how do you improve yourself as a model? What do you do to improve yourself?

Laird: I practice and I look at my pictures and other people's pictures. I look and practice in the mirror.

Finkelstein: What kind of clothes do you model that makes you very popular?

Laird: Hmmm . . . Sweaters and shorts and bathing suits.

Finkelstein: And what is your hair color at this time, Norma Jean?

Laird: It's light.

Finkelstein: This is your natural color?

Laird: Kind of.

Finkelstein: Do you model as a blonde or as a brunette, Norma Jean?

Laird: Both. Not dark. It's not black.

Finkelstein: But when is this that you become blonde and for what reason?

Laird: A couple of people later. Miss Snively tells me.

Finkelstein: What would be the reason, why should you be blonde and not brunette?

Laird: Because it looks better in the pictures.

Finkelstein: Oh, I see. Okay. And do you recall any person in particular that firstly advised you that you would look better blonde for the pictures?

Laird: A photographer.

Finkelstein: Do you change your hairstyle and length when you bleach your hair blonde?

Laird: Not 'til later.

Finkelstein: In what way?

Laird: It's coming up past my shoulders. Then it's up and up up up.

Finkelstein: Up? Like an upsweep?

Laird: No, just up, shorter, shorter, shorter.

Finkelstein: Oh, I see. Do you like how your hair looks like now after all these changes?

Laird: Hmmm, uh-huh.

Finkelstein: How does it help your modeling career now that you are a golden blonde? What kind of pose and pictures are you assigned to make?

Laird: I'm trying to make pictures that are exceptional.

Finkelstein: I see. Like glamour poses?

Laird: Uh-huh.

Finkelstein: How about "cheesecake" pictures?

Laird: Uh-huh.

Finkelstein: All right. Who describes you being built like a sex machine that you could turn on and off?

Laird: Eddie says that. Says it's my thing I turn on and off [meaning extraordinary sex appeal]. Everybody says it.

Finkelstein: How about photographers?

Laird: Everybody knows it.

Finkelstein: I see. Do you completely believe that you are built like a sex machine?

Laird: I guess so now.

Finkelstein: Yeah, but at that time?

Laird: I don't completely believe it, but I want to.

Finkelstein: Does it surprise you that you appear like in many magazines by now, especially men's magazines?

Laird: Hmmm . . . I like the pictures, but I don't care.

Finkelstein: A great industrialist and inventor related to Fox Studios introduces you to an agent who, together with a cameraman, do something for you. They help you. Who is that great industrialist that took an interest in you?

Laird: Are you talking about Ben?

Finkelstein: No. This is a great industrialist.

Laird: What's an industrialist?

Finkelstein: Well, a big multi, multimillionaire.

Laird: Hmmm . . .

Finkelstein: And let me make it more specific. He's building planes.

Laird: Oh, him. Yes. Hughes.

Finkelstein: Hughes, right. So, Howard Hughes. And Ben is correct, what you said. Ben Lyon.

Laird: I don't see Hughes so much.

Finkelstein: But you see Ben?

Laird: Yes.

Finkelstein: And who is the cameraman who works together with Ben to do something good for you, to help you?

Laird: Leon.

Finkelstein: Leon Shamroy?

Laird: Yes.

Finkelstein: Are you doing something together with them that, apparently, is not something that was allowed by the studio?

Laird: Yes. We're taking the footage from the camera.

Finkelstein: All right. Good. During the screen test, you are asked about your acting experience, aren't you?

Laird: I think they know I don't.

Finkelstein: Okay. What is Ben Lyon's relation to Jean Harlow?

Laird: He's been around her for sure. He helped her somehow. He has been in her pictures.

Finkelstein: Oh, I see. What picture? Do you recall the name of it?

Laird: He helped her. Oh, something funny. Some funny name.

Finkelstein: Yeah, like "Hell's" something?

Laird: *Hell's Angels.*

Finkelstein: Right. And who is Darryl Zanuck? Does he know about your screen test at this time?

Laird: He finds out. He's asked to come to see it.

Finkelstein: But did he know about it, like at the time when it was done by Leon and Ben?

Laird: It was done at nighttime.

Finkelstein: So I assume then he didn't know or he did?

Laird: No.

Finkelstein: No. What dress are you wearing for the screen test and who gives it to you?

Laird: They give it to me. It's looking like it's an actress dress. It's black.

Finkelstein: Is it a day dress or an evening?

Laird: Evening.

Finkelstein: Okay.

Laird: It's exciting.

Finkelstein: I see. What do you do for the screen test? Are you confident going on or do you pray for success?

Laird: Uh-huh. I'm nervous but I just stay numb. It's just luck. I just got lucky.

Finkelstein: Yeah.

Laird: Because sometimes I'm shaking.

Finkelstein: What does Leon Shamroy tell you once he's watched the screen test?

Laird: He whistles.

Finkelstein: Why?

Laird: He just says it's very smoking, it's very like hot. Like he doesn't say that, but like fiery or something.

Finkelstein: Does he compare you to another actress that did the same?

Laird: I don't know. He says whew . . . He just says there's something, something really good. He's hoping so.

Finkelstein: Right. So, Shamroy said something about you that made you feel uplifted? What did he say?

Laird: Yes. He said, "You should be in movies."

Finkelstein: What kind of movies?

Laird: He just said Hollywood movies. "You should be in movies."

Finkelstein: Did he make any remark or imply that your emotions and the sex appeal in the pictures [would] appeal to the public?

Laird: Everybody's talking about my sex appeal in pictures, so he doesn't have to say it again. He just says there's something magical that pops out of that.

Finkelstein: I see. Now, what is Darryl Zanuck's reaction when he first sees the test? Does he hire you?

Laird: Uh-huh.

Finkelstein: Who is suggesting you change your name to Marilyn?

Laird: Ben.

Finkelstein: Ben, right. And who signed the contract with Fox on your behalf and suggested using your mother's maiden name, Monroe, as your last name?

Laird: Someone . . . Someone in my family. I think it's Auntie Grace.

Finkelstein: Yes. Do you like your name, Marilyn Monroe?

Laird: Yes.

Finkelstein: And what is the reason that you accepted it? Is it to make your mother proud?

Laird: Yes.

Finkelstein: Now, you're divorcing Jim Dougherty. Under what circumstances?

Laird: I don't love him. I can't wait to get away, but I know I have to be polite.

Finkelstein: What's your whole experience?

Laird: He's angry. He's feeling very betrayed. Used. He feels used and he doesn't see me the same way. He thinks I've changed, but he doesn't realize that's who I was to begin with. He just ignored it.

Finkelstein: So, in other words, what you're saying is, you didn't change. It's just that he didn't realize who you were.

Laird: That's right.

Finkelstein: Now it's over, your relationship with Jim. Tell me, do you attend free classes in acting, dancing, pantomime, and singing? If so, who provided them for you?

Laird: Hmmm . . . Darryl.

Finkelstein: Darryl, and Fox Studios?

Laird: Yes.

Finkelstein: After the first six months of the seven-year contract with Fox, was your second six-month option picked up?

Laird: Yes.

Finkelstein: Do you remember whether or not you were advanced and what was your weekly salary at the time? Do you remember?

Laird: One hundred and fifty dollars.

Finkelstein: Okay. In August 1947, was the third six-month option with Fox picked up?

Laird: No.

Finkelstein: How do you manage financially now that Fox didn't renew you?

Laird: I just get some friends. Sometimes they help me. They try to find me a job.

Finkelstein: Uh-huh. Have you ever been, especially when you didn't have the money because you were unemployed, have you ever been a kept woman by a married or older man, you know, to fulfill your ambition to become an actress?

Laird: Yes.

Finkelstein: Can you tell me something about how you did that? Can you tell me the feelings attached to that or anything that you experienced?

Laird: It's kind of harder than acting, but still I want to be famous.

Finkelstein: How do you feel about being used by others, especially men?

Laird: I don't like it, but they have to realize I'm using them.

Finkelstein: Right. What studio hires you after Fox?

Laird: Metro-Goldwyn-Mayer.

Finkelstein: Mayer obviously comes after but there's another one before.

Laird: Universal. I don't know.

Finkelstein: How about Columbia?

Laird: I can't remember.

Finkelstein: How do you get acquainted with Natasha Lytess?

Laird: Somebody hires her for me.

Finkelstein: What is Natasha teaching you, Marilyn?

Laird: She's teaching me to go very inside, the acting is in me, the talent is in me, that it's all within my own . . .

Finkelstein: What is your relationship with her over the years?

Laird: She's looking over me.

Finkelstein: On October 23, 1948, the publication *Motion Picture*, referring to your role in the film *Ladies of the Chorus*, remarked, "One of the brightest parts is Miss Monroe singing." In other words, they felt that your singing is one of the brightest spots in the movie.

Laird: Yes.

Finkelstein: After this publicity, does Columbia studio keep or drop you?

Laird: They drop me.

Finkelstein: They drop you, right.

Laird: And I was devastated because I was broke.

Finkelstein: What is the reason they dropped you?

Laird: I don't understand why. They think I'm just a regular that they already have so many.

Finkelstein: I see. In 1948, when Columbia Pictures does not pick up your contract option, what do you do?

Laird: I cry.

Finkelstein: You're pushed to do something extraordinary. What is that?

Laird: I start to mingle with many people. Something extraordinary, what does that mean?

Finkelstein: Well, maybe you did something that is not very acceptable in the film business.

Laird: Yes. So what? I'm not accepted.

Finkelstein: By posing . . .

Laird: Yes, and I didn't get pushed. I do it because I say why not.

Finkelstein: Do you get well paid for this posing?

Laird: No.

Finkelstein: How much, do you remember?

Laird: It's 50 dollars.

Finkelstein: Right. And who is the photographer?

Laird: Tom.

Finkelstein: Tom Kelly.

Laird: That's right.

Finkelstein: So, since your career got in gear after your nude picture publicity, you got a role in a movie. What is this movie? Can you name it?

Laird: *Love Happy*.

Finkelstein: Right, *Love Happy*. And with what actor?

Laird: Groucho.

Finkelstein: Yes. And what is your famous line in the movie that Groucho himself composed for you?

Laird: "Some men are following me."

Finkelstein: "Men keep following me all the time." Do you recall, how long does the scene last?

Laird: Two minutes.

Finkelstein: How do you describe the five-week tour of some of the larger U.S. cities following your success in *Love Happy*?

Laird: There were people everywhere. There were men everywhere.

Finkelstein: How did it make you feel?

Laird: Happy.

Finkelstein: It is 1948. And now who is Lucille Ryman?

Laird: Lucille Ryman, she's a stylist or a teacher; a teacher of some kind. She's yelling at me.

Finkelstein: She's yelling at you?

Laird: Yes.

Finkelstein: Hmmm. But is she doing any good for you or on the contrary?

Laird: Yes, yes. I think she's writing or something.

Finkelstein: Right, but for what big film company?

Laird: She's . . . I think. I don't know. It's . . . MGM.

Finkelstein: Right, MGM. Anyway, she's a casting agent at MGM and a teacher of yours, yes?

Laird: Yes. She's a teacher of mine.

Finkelstein: *The Asphalt Jungle* is an MGM movie that Lucille Ryman thinks can skyrocket your career.

Laird: Maybe . . .

Finkelstein: What is your impression of *The Asphalt Jungle*?

Laird: I think it's okay. I think I might be drinking alcohol then.

Finkelstein: You're drinking?

Laird: I think so. I think I'm taking pills.

Finkelstein: Some people say that this is one of your best, the movie that skyrocketed your career, especially Lucille Ryman: *The Asphalt Jungle*.

Laird: I never remember that one.

Finkelstein: Lucille is telling you about a wonderful guy who can help you. He's a vice president of a big Hollywood talent agency. What is the agency and who is the man?

Laird: Morris . . . William . . .

Finkelstein: William Morris and who is the agent?

Laird: Johnny Hyde.

Finkelstein: Right. Johnny Hyde, your agent, is taking you to see the producer and the director of *The Asphalt Jungle*. What is the name of the girl you play in the story?

Laird: She's a criminal. The name is Angela.

Finkelstein: How do you feel about the director, John Huston?

Laird: I know he's letting me do it my way. He's great.

Finkelstein: Good. Who is the writer who signed you on for the movie *All about Eve* as a result of your success in *The Asphalt Jungle*?

Laird: What do you mean writer?

Finkelstein: There's a writer who signed you on for the movie *All about Eve*. If you don't remember, it's fine. We're not here for a memory test. We're just to free you of burdening, past, bottled-up emotions, which we've already done successfully.

Laird: [Sherrie seems to remember] I can see. It's got to do with a W, but I don't know.

Finkelstein: W, yeah. How about Mankiewicz, with a W.

Laird: Joe.

Finkelstein: Yes, Joseph.

Laird: Yes, that's the name.

Finkelstein: What is your character's name in *All about Eve*? If you remember, fine. If not, fine, too. It's a "Miss" somebody.

Laird: Yes, it's a Miss, that's right. I'm going to tell you Miss Cas . . .

Finkelstein: Caswell, yes. Who now puts you under contract with Fox? Who is the big shot that is doing that? Who now puts you under contract with Fox?

Laird: Sidney Skouras.

Finkelstein: Spyros Skouras, yeah. And do you or Betty Grable get the most requests for photos at Fox Studio at this time?

Laird: Me.

Finkelstein: Very good. Let's see, in 1951, Fox signed a seven-year contract with you at a weekly salary of how much?

Laird: For 100 dollars, 150 dollars, more.

Finkelstein: And how much raise, like every six months?

Laird: Seventy-five dollars, 150 dollars.

Finkelstein: Right. What movies were you in following contract with Fox through the intervention of Spyros Skouras on your behalf?

Laird: What movies was I in?

Finkelstein: There're a few movies he made.

Laird: Something L— Love—

Finkelstein: *Love Nest?*

Laird: Yes.

Finkelstein: And something funny was . . . something legal, what is that?

Laird: Yes. That's the one.

Finkelstein: *Let's Make It Legal?*

Laird: Yes.

Finkelstein: And anything with being young or feeling that way?

Laird: *Young as You Feel.*

Finkelstein: All right. Now, do you take it easy with your work?

Laird: Somehow I do. I'm feeling more confident, so I'm probably not giving my best. I think something's the matter with me now.

Finkelstein: What is it?

Laird: I don't know. Something's not right about my behavior.

Finkelstein: Is it as a result of your drinking and drugs or what?

Laird: Yes, I think so.

Finkelstein: What made Fox take you off suspension for your refusal to do a remake of a movie of Betty Grable?

Laird: My fans or friends helped me do that.

Finkelstein: There is somebody that you marry who has an influence on them.

Laird: Are you talking about Joe?

Finkelstein: Right.

Laird: Yes, because Walter Winchell helps me.

Finkelstein: He's friends with Joe, right.

Laird: Yes.

Finkelstein: Okay. After marrying Joe, what comes next in your career?

Laird: My better movie.

Finkelstein: What is that movie? Obviously, Joe has a connection to Winchell with Fox and so forth. What is the movie?

Laird: *The Seven Year Itch.*

Finkelstein: How does Joe relate to your full-time work and schedule?

Laird: He's trying to adjust. He's trying to understand it. He likes it at first, but he's just concerned. It's taking up my studying time, my nighttime, my attention.

Finkelstein: Is there anything that's going on between you and Joe at this time that is so private that nobody knows about and will never know in relation to him?

Laird: We secretly want to have a baby.

Finkelstein: And what's your position?

Laird: I want to have a baby.

Finkelstein: You do?

Laird: Yes. We want to in our hearts.

Finkelstein: And what is it that stops you?

Laird: Hmmm, I'm having my career.

Finkelstein: Is there an incident on the movie *The Seven Year Itch* that makes Joe mad?

Laird: Yes.

Finkelstein: What is it?

Laird: Everybody knows. They're standing and people looking at me from down upside. He's mad because of the people down below, not because of the street people.

Finkelstein: This is when he slaps you?

Laird: Yes. He knows that some of the men want me or that's what he heard.

Finkelstein: So it seems like your marriage to Joe is on the rocks now. Is it?

Laird: Not quite all the time, but by then later it's near the end.

Finkelstein: What is the cause of your breakup with Joe? What was the last straw? The conversation about getting a divorce?

Laird: I want to say that it's my baby in my stomach.

Finkelstein: Are you pregnant?

Laird: Yes.

Finkelstein: So, if you're pregnant, what's the reason you have to have a divorce? I mean, this is what you said before you both wanted.

Laird: Abortion.

Finkelstein: Abortion? You go for an abortion?

Laird: Yes.

Finkelstein: Does he know about that?

Laird: Yes.

Finkelstein: So, it's with his consent that you do it?

Laird: No.

Finkelstein: I see. Who's suggested the idea of the scene where your dress was flying waist high in *The Seven Year Itch*?

Laird: My producer Charles. [Charles Feldman]

Finkelstein: You recall the name of the photographer and the director?

Laird: Josh . . . Josh Logan. I don't know.

Finkelstein: It's all right.

Laird: A funny guy. I love him. Wilder . . .

Finkelstein: Wilder. Billy Wilder.

Laird: Yes.

Finkelstein: Correct. This is the director.

Laird: We love him.

Finkelstein: And the producer is Charles.

Laird: He said it.

Finkelstein: Well, yeah, they all agreed.

Laird: We said it's going to be huge.

Finkelstein: But you agreed to that scene, that scene that was pretty outrageous?

Laird: Yes, because we knew. We had a feeling in our stomachs. We knew it would be . . . great for the movie.

Finkelstein: So was anyone with you in that scene?

Laird: Yes. Tom.

Finkelstein: Tom. Tom Ewell.

Laird: That's why I was able to do it, because I liked him and he made me feel very safe and he said it's okay, never mind. I'm sure he was scared. He was a little nervous for me.

Finkelstein: Right. Can you describe the scene? When was it filmed and who was in attendance? What time during the day or night was that?

Laird: It was the nighttime. It was hot and it was in the night-time in the early morning. We were there a long time.

Finkelstein: But there were some people in the crowd, do you know who were they?

Laird: Joe was there.

Finkelstein: Who was the friend with him?

Laird: Walter.

Finkelstein: Walter Winchell, right.

Laird: But there's another guy there, too. Maybe some kind of friend.

Finkelstein: What part of your body on which the director was focusing the camera upset Joe the most?

Laird: Underneath. He doesn't like it so underneath.

Finkelstein: You mean on your crotch?

Laird: Yes. Underneath my dress. He thought I looked like I was a whore.

Finkelstein: You think that Joe doesn't have a reason to be a jealous?

Laird: Well, I think he has a reason to be jealous, but he could've loved me differently. It's work. It's art. It's . . . I don't feel so great about it, but I still go with my work. I don't want to hurt him. I don't want to upset him. I do love him and I feel like he's my friend. He's my best friend in many ways, but he's also my worst enemy.

Finkelstein: Because he doesn't understand you or what?

Laird: He doesn't understand my work. Why does he take it out on me when this is the man's world? He's the man. He understands what I . . . He knows I'm just trying to get by.

Finkelstein: If he would have his way, in what role would he want you?

Laird: He wants me to be an actress but he wants me to be a serious actress. And not do these kinds of things.

Finkelstein: How does that scene help you in your career? What happens?

Laird: Well, then I'm her from then on. She's just always the same now. She's the blonde.

Finkelstein: You are her now.

Laird: A sexpot. Yes. But I'm saying it like that. That's she and there's me.

Finkelstein: Uh-huh. Who literally said, "No one wants to be known as Mr. Marilyn Monroe." What do you feel about this remark?

Laird: I think Billy says that.

Finkelstein: Billy Wilder?

Laird: Yes. And I try to understand and I think Tom said it, too. He said it's hard on him. Walter said it and people are saying it's hard for him to be Mr. Monroe.

Finkelstein: Can you elaborate on the Marilyn Monroe Productions and Milton Greene?

Laird: Yes, I love it.

Finkelstein: Why?

Laird: Because it's going to be my decision and they have to go through my people before they can get to me.

Finkelstein: Uh-huh. What movie do you produce in your company with Laurence Olivier?

Laird: It's not my own film, but it's *The Prince and the Showgirl*.

Finkelstein: Do you want Laurence, Larry as you call him, Larry Olivier, to play in the movie as an actor and also direct it?

Laird: Not really.

Finkelstein: But it's your production. I mean, can't you decide on that?

Laird: I don't want the actor to direct it.

Finkelstein: Uh-huh. But you let it be, so how is that?

Laird: I think Arthur is with me. He's telling me to let him do it.

Finkelstein: I see, but it's not necessarily your choice, is it?

Laird: No, it's not exactly.

Finkelstein: Do you sell this movie to television?

Laird: I think somebody else does.

Finkelstein: You are now 36 years old. On the film *Something's Got to Give* you agree to do the nude swimming pool scene for director George Cukor.

Laird: Yes. I'm a little worried about my body but, still, they encourage me.

Finkelstein: What made you agree to the nude scene?

Laird: Because I want to steal the thunder from somebody.

Finkelstein: From whom?

Laird: You know who.

Finkelstein: Elizabeth? [Elizabeth Taylor]

Laird: Yes.

Finkelstein: So what happened during the filming of the scene?

Laird: I'm just splashing around and coming out and sitting there and having fun and the guys are there and I get a cold from it actually.

Finkelstein: So you get sick?

Laird: Yes.

Finkelstein: I see. So what do you do for entertainment?

Laird: I'm very alone.

Finkelstein: You don't have any friends?

Laird: Yes, I have friends. Peter and Pat, Patricia. And my group, too. Sammy . . .

Finkelstein: Sammy Davis?

Laird: Joe . . . There's more.

Finkelstein: What do you think is the best performance you ever gave and why?

Laird: I love *The Prince and the Showgirl* and I love *Bus Stop* and I love *Gentlemen Prefer Blondes*.

Finkelstein: I see.

Laird: I like *Something's Got to Give*. I like it a lot, but I don't like that lady. Cyd Charisse. She's there with her coat.

Finkelstein: What is it that you don't like about her?

Laird: She's not . . . It's not her. She's okay. I don't like the attitude of the people around me; they're pushing me away. They're being snobby. They don't trust me. They think I'm a drug addict. They think I'm bad.

Finkelstein: When you say they, you mean who?

Laird: Everybody. They're talking about me.

Finkelstein: I see. One of the movies that you did at the time, you felt that it is good and you have fun with [it]: *Some Like It Hot*.

Laird: Uh-huh.

Finkelstein: What is your relationship with Tony Curtis before, during, and after the production of this movie?

Laird: I tried to tell you before. We admire each other's work. During, we're getting a little tired and after, we're admiring each other's work.

Finkelstein: Is there anything that's going on between you and him that nobody would know, that's not public record or that you can tell me about right now?

Laird: I love kissing with him and he knows that and I told him. That's why they say . . . And he pretends to say that [Hitler line], but he doesn't say it because he knows that we have a thing. I think he's protecting his girlfriend or wife. He's pretending because we feel very excited. We could've been together at some point as lovers but I'm not feeling so great.

Finkelstein: I see.

Laird: I'm very excited by his handsome face, but I have problems. Even now I feel very, very affectionate towards . . . Jackie. We call him Jackie.

Finkelstein: So he tries to downplay it by saying he kissed Hitler during the kissing scene in *Some Like It Hot*?

Laird: He didn't say that exactly. Someone's saying it in the background and he said yes, but joking . . . There're people around him when this happens. They're trying to make it look like he said it because they just want a big thing.

Finkelstein: So what is the reason that he said yes?

Laird: He's just trying to be funny and also to protect his girlfriend or wife.

Finkelstein: So, that is being funny then?

Laird: Well, he's not going to say it's fabulous.

Finkelstein: Right. Okay.

Laird: I think he's got a famous girl.

Finkelstein: Is he going out with the mother of Jamie Curtis?

Laird: Yes. I think so. Yes. Janet, is it right?

Finkelstein: Janet [Leigh], uh-huh.

Laird: . . . It's Janet. I think it's something like this. Yes. He's protecting her.

Finkelstein: I see. Is there anything in your relationship with Tony Curtis that only you and he might know that no person, no other record exists about?

Laird: We were kissing still. We were feeling to be near each other. We're making love . . . I can see he is very well endowed as a man and has a dark birthmark in his private area. [Days after the regression, while reflecting on the dark mole or birthmark, Sherrie wasn't sure whether she saw it on Tony Curtis, or one of her husbands, Joe or Arthur.]

Finkelstein: So, this was off the movie set?

Laird: Yes. We had some drinks together, maybe by the beach, and we took drugs together. [Tony Curtis, without prior knowledge of this regression, acknowledged in the January 2006 issue of *Esquire* magazine that he had a romantic affair with Marilyn Monroe in 1949–1950.]

Finkelstein: Uh-huh. You said that you were drinking, but you also took drugs with him?

Laird: Yes, I think we take drugs. I think it might be cocaine. It's some kind of powder. It's beige.

Finkelstein: Yes.

Laird: Maybe it's worse. Heroin. Yes, I think so.

Finkelstein: I see. And do you, or does he, get hooked on those drugs?

Laird: Hmmm, maybe, I think so. It's possible.

Finkelstein: Who introduced you or him or both of you to these drugs?

Laird: Somebody on the movie. No, he brings something.

Finkelstein: He does?

Laird: Yes, I think so.

Finkelstein: I see.

Laird: Do you think I'm making it up? I feel it. I see it.

Finkelstein: Uh-huh.

Laird: I don't want to say that about him if he doesn't want me to tell anybody.

Finkelstein: Oh, yes.

Laird: Drugs are everywhere, anyway.

Finkelstein: I see. I want you to tell me what your relationship with Jane Russell is. But before you go to that, do you really make love with Tony? Yes or no?

Laird: I want to say yes.

Finkelstein: Yes.

Laird: But somehow I don't believe it, but I say yes. We're doing things, but I just don't remember if I can feel anything with him. I think there's something wrong with me right then, but I want to believe, because I love him in a way . . .

Finkelstein: You haven't been feeling well because of the drugs and alcohol and all this and your state of mind, that's what you mean?

Laird: Uh-huh.

Finkelstein: And your relationship with Jane Russell before, during, and after filming *Gentlemen Prefer Blondes*. Can you relate details of this relationship that nobody would know about?

Laird: Jane . . . Before I met her, she's respected but she's new somehow.

Finkelstein: Yes.

Laird: She doesn't . . . she's not making the same [mistakes]. She's . . . How do you say it, she's . . . The business of movies is not making her [jaded]. She's innocent.

Finkelstein: Innocent, uh-huh. In other words, she doesn't care about money, movies.

Laird: Yes.

Finkelstein: Career, prestige?

Laird: Yes. She's just . . . she just is good. She's good and she does her work. And she wants everybody to be successful and happy in the movie.

Finkelstein: Well, is there anything that's just private between you and her that nobody would know?

Laird: I'm thinking she's giving me advice. She's worried about me. She's trying to tell me to believe in God more, but she's worried about my behavior and she hopes that the rumors aren't true. She likes me a lot. She always calls me "kiddo."

Finkelstein: Kiddle?

Laird: Kiddo.

Finkelstein: Kiddo?

Laird: Yes. We talk about people and we talk about directors and we talk about men and we're making fun of them. But like she says, "Isn't that awful," because she feels bad for laughing. And she covers her hand to her mouth, but we're laughing so hard.

Finkelstein: She says, "Isn't it awful"?

Laird: She's saying isn't it awful that we're laughing and she's making fun of some of the men, while I'm making fun of them and so is she, and we're laughing.

Finkelstein: Uh-huh. I see. I see.

Laird: We think they're funny.

Finkelstein: Anyone in particular?

Laird: Just the way the men are acting. But we like the little boy, the [III], the little boy, something the III. Mr. Samuel . . .

Finkelstein: Tell me this. As a result of your national film tour, which included New York, you meet George Barris, a famed photographer who is taking a lot of pictures of you. What is your relationship with him? Can you recall details of this relationship that are not found in any books, magazines, or any other source of public information?

Laird: Hmmm. He's taking many pictures and we're driving places and we are . . . Are you talking about earlier or later?

Finkelstein: Anytime. Anything that is not in public record that's just between you and him?

Laird: I'm trying, but I see only working and I see . . . he's trying to bring me a gift. He's bringing me a gift. Something he spent on his own money.

Finkelstein: Uh-huh.

Laird: And he's so wonderful and nice. But it's very wonderful what he's doing. We want to make a book together.

Finkelstein: Uh-huh.

Laird: He's taking me to lunch and describing how we want it to look. We're describing if we can get the most natural pictures of me being real, a girl, or a real lady, a woman. We're talking about the book being the book that's finally about me and we want to make it the best book for Marilyn's keepsake. It's the keepsake book and I was supposed to sign it. And I was supposed to be going around signing it for everyone.

Finkelstein: I see. Well, is there anything romantic going on between you and him?

Laird: I see him as very handsome and cute, but I can't see something sexual. Maybe. But somehow I personally don't want to because I need to concentrate. It's like I feel not attractive anymore. I'm nervous. Does he find me attractive? I don't know if he finds me attractive because I feel older now. Like an older girl who's not attractive. I'm not sexual anymore. It's because of my relationships I feel old now.

Finkelstein: Is there anything else about George Barris that would be just between you and him and nobody knows, that's very private and you can tell me?

Laird: I told you it before, but I told you many things. [At times Sherrie brings forth not only the specific memory that I instruct her to retrieve, but also the associated memories.]

Finkelstein: About some problems in his family?

Laird: There is somebody next to him. A woman is giving him trouble. I don't know if it's his mother or wife, but there's a woman giving him trouble. And he's not comfortable somehow.

Finkelstein: Because of you?

Laird: Because of a woman. No, he's trying to tell me something because of a woman and I see a young girl with him. I don't know if it's his sister or a daughter or a cousin. She's a young girl with a ponytail. She's there. Maybe she's with me.

Finkelstein: Yes.

Laird: She has a ponytail. She looks like Sandra Dee, but it's not her. She's looking like that girl.

Finkelstein: But she's not the one that gives him trouble. Is she?

Laird: No. She's at that friend's house. I think she's a teenager neighbor.

Finkelstein: A teenage neighbor, I see. And what is the relationship with you and with George?

Laird: She's watching [the photo shoot], but I don't see George. Suddenly, I see Bert. Bert Stern.

Finkelstein: Do you have something going on with Bert Stern?

Laird: I think so. I hope he's not gay.

Finkelstein: Is he nice to you?

Laird: Yes. He's handsome. Very handsome.

Finkelstein: Do you make love?

Laird: I don't know. I think so.

Finkelstein: Yeah? I see. Tell me more about somebody that you know and you had some private moments with that nobody knows about, such as June DiMaggio.

Laird: I first see her little. I think she's 18 and I don't see much, but if it's her I'm smoking pot with her.

Finkelstein: Does anyone know what you do with her?

Laird: No. And if it's her, she's talking about her boyfriend. They're going to have sex.

Finkelstein: Yeah? Do you encourage her?

Laird: Yes, but sort of I don't because I don't want her have the heartache I have. I just feel so bad for the younger. They have to go through it all over.

Finkelstein: Yeah. Does she know that you are planning to remarry her uncle?

Laird: Yes. I'm starting to be happy about Joe.

Finkelstein: Uh-huh. Besides the friends already mentioned, is there any other close friend of yours, Marilyn, who is still alive in your life as Sherrie that knows Marilyn you can name?

Laird: I would like to see Jimmy [James Haspiel]. I hope he's alive. I wish I saw him when he's young, but he must be old now. I really like him. He's a good little friend to me.

Finkelstein: I see.

Laird: And he is little Jimmy.

Finkelstein: Is there anything going on that is unique and unknown in public that only you and he would know?

Laird: He comes in the car with me sometimes. Sometimes when I'm driving somewhere, he comes with me just for the ride.

Finkelstein: I was asking if there's anything else like besides the rides in the car, is there anything, an exchange you have with him, anything that's unique between you and him that occurs to you?

Laird: He tries to tell me that they [Hollywood] don't know what they're talking about and they should put me in an action film. He likes the Godzilla movies. He likes movies like that.

Finkelstein: Uh-huh.

Laird: He likes to see me in *King Kong.* He knows that I'm going to have an orphanage and he knows that I'm going to have lots of pets on the farm.

Finkelstein: Tell me this, when he's telling you that you should be in an action movie like *King Kong*, what's your reaction?

Laird: I laugh but I think yeah, why not. I sort of laugh because it's teenage stuff.

Finkelstein: Oh. I see. Approximately how old is he?

Laird: He's like 17 or 18, like that.

Finkelstein: Uh-huh. I see. Is there anyone else besides James Haspiel that is still alive, that you think would identify you as Marilyn Monroe, because you remember something about him or her that no one else does?

Laird: Maybe. Mickey Rooney. Christopher Lawford.

Finkelstein: Uh-huh.

Laird: Where is Pat? Where are my friends? Where are they?

Finkelstein: Well, they may or may not be alive. We can check that Mickey Rooney is probably here, and Christopher . . .

Laird: Anna . . .

Finkelstein: Anna?

Laird: My friend. Is she alive?

Finkelstein: We can find out. Anna, okay.

Laird: There're some Strasbergs. They're still alive. They need to see me and talk to me, or they can talk to you.

Finkelstein: Let's go to another topic. What is . . .

Laird: Can we please stop?

Finkelstein: I'll make it go faster just because we're almost through. You are now 36 years old, and you are doing a movie in Canada. Do you recall the name of that movie?

Laird: *River of No Return.*

Finkelstein: Right. That was the Canadian Rockies, right? Do you get injured while filming in that location?

Laird: Yes. I fell. My leg is stuck.

Finkelstein: And what happened as a result?

Laird: I'm hopping. I'm laughing but crying.

Finkelstein: Do you like this movie?

Laird: Yes. I like my man to be like him.

Finkelstein: You have favorites as actors and they're Marlon Brando, Greta Garbo, Jean Harlow—the blonde bombshell, Kay Kendall, Gerard Philippe, and I'll stop at Gerard Philippe because he's been one of the actors that I was a fan of as a teenager.

Laird: Uh-huh.

Finkelstein: He wanted to make films with you.

Laird: Uh-huh. I think he wants to make something dark and kind of passionate. Something political, like a spy girl.

Finkelstein: Right. Spy girl?

Laird: Yes, like she's in espionage, something dark, rain, nighttime . . .

Finkelstein: Right.

Laird: They call it film noir.

Finkelstein: Uh-huh, film noir?

Laird: Yes.

Finkelstein: You thought to make a film with him. And when he dies, he was 36 and you thought he was too young to die.

Laird: Does he die during a car accident?

Finkelstein: Uh-huh. You know what was the cause of his death?

Laird: Is he in a car?

Finkelstein: It's like a heart attack or something.

Laird: I don't remember.

Finkelstein: Well, anyway. How do you feel about Marilyn?

Laird: Marilyn?

Finkelstein: Yeah, Marilyn Monroe?

Laird: How do I feel about myself?

Finkelstein: Right.

Laird: Do you want to hear the sad or the good?

Finkelstein: Anything that you feel like saying about you, Marilyn Monroe?

Laird: She's trying . . . She's pretty good. She's sad. She's beautiful. She's talented. She's not realizing her dreams yet. She's alone. She's generous. She's angry and she's going to die.

Finkelstein: Does she want to die? Does she plan to die?

Laird: Well, when I visit all these things from the past, no, she doesn't want to die, but if you want to talk about the other topic [the Kennedys] then, yes, she wants to die.

Finkelstein: Uh-huh.

Laird: But you said we won't go there.

Finkelstein: No, we won't. I see.

Laird: When she's acting, she doesn't want to die. When she's not acting, she wants to die.

Finkelstein: Do you recall by any chance the address of the Brentwood house? If you don't, that's fine.

Laird: Yes.

Finkelstein: What is it?

Laird: I see 1 3 5 0 9, something like that.

Finkelstein: Something like that. Okay.

Laird: 1 2 3 5.

Finkelstein: Right. In between 3 and 5 is a 0.

Laird: Yes.

Finkelstein: Good. What dog did Frank Sinatra give you as a gift? What was the name he gave it and why?

Laird: I give it a silly name, but that's not really his name.

Finkelstein: What kind of dog was it, what breed?

Laird: It's my little poodle.

Finkelstein: Right. What color?

Laird: I don't want to talk about it. [Crying]

Finkelstein: No, we won't talk about it. Now, how about your close friends, Frank Sinatra and Dean Martin: Can you say just a few words about them? Frank Sinatra and Dean Martin. Were you close to them?

Laird: Yes.

Finkelstein: Yeah. You are now 36 years old and we're finished and now I'm going to ask you one thing as to just relax and feel at ease. Everything is done and it's over. I'm going to ask you to come out of your trance and to feel good, with only positive, healthy, and constructive effects from this experience with the full memory of what you have experienced, full memory that I suggested to you before about all your regressions. The next time you will go deeper if necessary and faster and achieve whatever we left over and that would be for tomorrow. We will also have a lot of talk without hypnosis about some of these issues and you will be able to spontaneously associate about them and to bring up a lot of very important details.

Laird: Yes.

Finkelstein: Do you go along with me?

Laird: Yes.

Finkelstein: Good. And now I'm going to count: One, coming back. Two, more and more. Three, feeling great. Four, five, six, seven, feeling wonderful, eight, nine, in full control of your body and mind. Ten, gently open your eyes and feel good!

Laird: I can't move my body yet. My head can't get up.

Finkelstein: You can move your body little by little and stretch, first stretch and take a sip of water, maybe.

Laird: I can't lift my head for some reason.

Finkelstein: I'll help you.

Laird: Thank you. Ohhh, thank you.

Finkelstein: Stretch. That's good. It helps sometimes. Pockets of adrenaline in your muscles are pumped out this way.

Laird: Oh, I want to go pee-pee now. I have to go . . . I'll roll off the bed.

Finkelstein: Your feet are exactly like George Barris pictured them, like Marilyn's.

Laird: I know they are. I sent them before. [The feet pictures to compare with Marilyn's]

Finkelstein: Such a resemblance!

Laird: That's what I'm thinking the hands and the palm lines are also the same.

Finkelstein: Is that so?

K. Laird: Yeah, I saw them, too.

Laird: I know. It's crazy.

Sherrie and Kezia hurried to the bathroom, and I waited a few minutes until they returned. Sherrie sat in the chair by the window.

Finkelstein: Sherrie?

Laird: Yes.

Finkelstein: So what's been your experience today with the regressions and what do you think is the most relevant in what you presented today?

Laird: Today, it was probably more relevant for me because of . . . Gladys. That was the most important for me, when Kezia realized she was Gladys because she was fighting it. That made me very happy; what also made me happy was I don't hate Marilyn so much anymore. I've been hating her a lot lately because of the fans and the people making it look like that's somebody I want to be.

Finkelstein: Right.

Laird: And I don't want to be that person, so I developed a hatred for her. Like I think you know from my blog how I say how much I hated her, how I hate being Marilyn, but this [regression] I got to be Norma Jean and just be . . . I just got to live the life and realize that it's better I stop fighting it and just admit it. Somehow the world can learn to live with reincarnation and healing and not focus on Marilyn Monroe, but just the fact that Marilyn Monroe is one of the people that happened to reincarnate. Well, of course she did. They want her back and stuff, so . . .

Finkelstein: What do you think that you will do with this information or this confirmation that you are Marilyn Monroe rein-carnated? How will it contribute to your life and to your project?

Laird: To my project in music or my project just in the healing?

Finkelstein: Anything that you think is important that you want to pursue in your life.

Laird: Well, I think it's important for my own sense of healing so I don't feel . . . I've got to learn to stop feeling so desperately down and all the things that go with my past, but I just . . . I think I want to live with more exuberance and try to accomplish some-thing.

Finkelstein: So . . . ?

Laird: I just want to be able to speak out to the world, that if I can go through this, they can, and it exists and it's definitely [helpful]. I have to say that your upcoming book and Walter's [Semkiw] book regarding the non-racial thing and the non-religious prejudice, those are very key factors [for] why reincarna-tion exists at all, for people to realize that they've been that, they're going to be that next, this and that [race or nationality] . . . why it has to be focused on Marilyn Monroe, I still really don't know. [Sherrie is referring to one race or nationality reincarnating into the other, so people will learn not to hate each other for being different and peace in the world will triumph.]

Finkelstein: So, you as Marilyn Monroe, do you know how great a service you can offer to humanity?

Laird: Sure.

Finkelstein: You are giving the message that we shouldn't hate each other, that we are reincarnating sometimes as the oppo-site and that you attest to that. Marilyn/Sherrie gives a message of inner and outer freedom, love, healing, and peace to the entire world.

Laird: Reincarnating into what you hate.

Finkelstein: Right. So, there's no point to hatred in this world. And do you realize what a voice you would have as Marilyn Monroe that people listen to in the world more than they would listen to other people? Do you know what importance is in what you say?

Laird: I understand.

Finkelstein: You carry magic in your words.

Laird: Well, I . . . yes, I can see what you're saying, but I don't think that I . . . it's hard to believe that as Marilyn reincarnated I have such weight, but if that's what it takes to make this world understand and if that's what it takes to make people realize, then maybe she was famous back then for a reason, so they're clinging to her and there must be a reason she still has such a hold on the world. I'm sure if Elvis would be sitting in this position or his spokesperson, it would be just equally or maybe more wonderful. I think I have to try and understand her as a spokesperson, well now me, but being her, yes, it has some weight. I just hope they understand. I hope they can get it because it's very . . . today's and yesterday's regressions were so powerful but you pushed me, you know, to [do the] extra . . . You let me go to the most painful things I've ever experienced, so that there are no doubts. I can now stand before anybody and say, well, there's no one in the world that could come here and be on this bed and have the details that I have. They just won't.

Finkelstein: What would it take for the world to recognize your life as Marilyn Monroe? What would make them take your word, as if they would take it, not from Sherrie, but from Marilyn Monroe?

Laird: Marilyn Monroe doesn't speak through me. I'm not channeling her . . . But what would it take? It's going to take a lot of patience on our part. It's going to take open minds on their part, and they just need to listen to the story from the start to the finish, because I think the whole story, the whole things we have, the birth chart [Moon Node positions], the regressions, the voice [comparisons], and me knowing that Kezia was my mother, when she was a little . . . You know, how do you say to a little three-year-old that you think she's your mother. I mean, that psychic and special gifts from God, you know, and I think maybe even praying, on our behalf, but it's going to take other psychics to be around us.

Finkelstein: And how do you overcome people's prejudice

that it has to be something "scientific" in order to be believed and that the psychics are imprecise?

Laird: I believe the iris [comparisons], the handprints in terms of the physical proof, and I wish that they could find a way—and I'm sure there is a way—because the palm lines on our hands are there for a reason. I can see just by looking at them and because I'm a palm reader myself, that these lines are specifically there for a reason, so one day people will realize that they're connected and the irises being similar.

Finkelstein: But anyway, thank you very much for being so brave. I mean, not everyone who thinks they are Marilyn Monroe would go through what you went through.

Laird: Yes.

Finkelstein: And . . .

Laird: Not a lot of people who think they're Marilyn Monroe would want to go through it.

Finkelstein: And whatever we have as proofs that you are the reincarnation of Marilyn Monroe way exceed what others have that you're not, as you once put it.

Laird: And we took a long time and it's exhausting for you and costly for you, exhausting for us. This is not like going out to a nightclub and having dinner and drinks. This is exhausting work, like this is gut wrenching from my entire being.

Finkelstein: Right.

Laird: Thank you, Dr. Finkelstein.

Afterward, Sherrie and I rehashed the results of our session. I questioned her about her responses and misses, and she pretty much agreed that she was more in her Marilyn self in this regression in her "I don't care" attitude. Sherrie's feeling was that the process was over, task completed, and she's more resigned than ever to get on with her life and finally leave her Marilyn persona behind her.

Part IV

AFTERWORD

After this last round of regressions in Toronto in mid-November, my wife and I flew back to Los Angeles. I had a few rescheduled sessions with patients as part of my holistic psychiatric practice and a last stretch of teaching grad students before the 2005 holiday break. I felt pleased not only with the high level of Sherrie's regressions but also with her and Kezia's cooperation and willingness to just "bite the bullet" when it came to unearthing and dealing with the awful trauma of Marilyn's life and the legacy passed on to Sherrie in this life. I knew from years of experience with regression patients that, like childhood trauma or sexual abuse, facing the music was the first step, which I facilitated, but releasing the experience and integrating the raw emotional energy was the all-important second step that was mostly in her hands.

Immediately upon my return, an initial flurry of e-mails was exchanged between Sherrie and me. The floodgate of past-life memories and dreams, from her Marilyn life and also as Louise de la Valliere, began to open—a sure sign of the healing process, especially when they were dominated by "good" memories, not traumatic ones. It was as if she were coming to terms with Marilyn, loving her and saying goodbye. Interestingly she had a dream of Laurence Olivier, which was more like "Larry" sending his regards than an actual dream. [People who lose loved ones often have similar dreams the night of or day after their passing, which I've always classified as "direct contact" with the spirit of the deceased person.]

One troubling note was Sherrie's initial preoccupation with the Marilyn Internet sites and her ongoing battle to prove her case to a mostly doubting and derisive audience. Having to prove herself instead of accepting her Marilyn legacy could've complicated the progress of her healing. However, a positive response from several of the site members seemed to put this obsession into perspective, and Sherrie backed off and redirected her energy toward her life and career, the healthiest sign of all. She was writing new songs at this point and managing a band, and her relationship with Kezia was flourishing. Kezia was becoming less the "mom" and more the good friend, a sign of her own healing. She didn't need to be regressed to resign herself to the fact that she had been Gladys Baker, Sherrie's mother in their last life together.

The holiday season couldn't come too soon. Conducting this research project and ongoing therapy over the past nine months had taken me away for long periods of time from my wife and family. Added to the hours of research, preparation, and two rounds of regressions in a foreign city was the now daunting undertaking of rewriting the first draft of my manuscript by the end of January 2006. Having Thanksgiving dinner with my daughters and their families put my ambitions for my project into perspective: Nothing was more important than my love for my wife and my children.

As I had mentioned earlier, therapy doesn't happen in a vacuum: "Physician, heal thyself" had never been more of a pressing issue than during the course of this research, with its many issues and heartstrings being pulled at many levels. Taking on such a time-consuming research project at this stage in my life put a strain on all of my relationships, family and friends alike, but if it were not for their loving support I could never have seen my way through the difficulties it presented.

As the new year approached, full of prospects for both Sherrie and me and our book project, the constant stream of e-mails from her began to ease off. She was standing on her own two feet and dealing with her everyday problems, now less complicated without the "monkey on her back," as she would say. The process of her integration in my experience would no doubt take months and even years of work, but I felt strongly that Sherrie now had the distance and the tools to deal with her past-life trauma and get on with her life. Like those marred by childhood abuse, one never really "gets over" it; one learns to deal with chaotic emotions and not let them rule you.

I know the launch of our book in the upcoming months and the reactions to it will bring a whole new set of challenges for both of us. I can only hope the process of our mutual healing over the past year will prepare us to "put it all" in perspective and not let it run us. I am secure in the fact that with more than 30 years of past-life regression work I can say unequivocally that Sherrie Lea Laird is the reincarnation of Marilyn Monroe. I can also say that in my experience the course of our regression work together has literally saved her life, if not from certain death by her own hands or through neglect, but from years of continued torment, including drug and alcohol abuse.

I can only hope, which has always been the secondary goal of this research project—the first and foremost of course being the healing of a soul—that this sensational case and the course of its exposition in these pages will open people and especially those in the healing arts to the potential for past-life regression therapy. It may be a good first step if only those troubled by recurrent emotional problems without clear antecedents in this life, and those entrusted with their care, would consider the mere possibility of trauma carried over from a past life. This doesn't necessarily need to lead to full regression therapy; just the acknowledgment can work wonders and open up paths to healing through more conventional methods.

And in conclusion, I would be remiss in my duties as a physician and metaphysician if I were not to mention that the underlying theme of this work, as it has been in every past-life case that I've treated, is the truth of reincarnation and what it means to our troubled world. We have each of us walked in the shoes of people of every race, nationality, creed, and gender— rich and poor, the abuser and the abused—as we evolve our souls to the point that we realize that there is only one life, God's life, and that we only kill, maim, and bomb ourselves, or the God in each of us. The message that Marilyn/Sherrie brings to the world is: Love yourself and each other, and in this way heal yourself, and thus live in peace and experience God's joy.

ABOUT THE AUTHOR

Adrian Finkelstein is a board-certified psychiatrist, a First Research Award graduate of the Menninger School of Psychiatry, former chief of the outpatient department of psychiatry at Mount Sinai Medical Center, and former assistant professor of psychiatry at Chicago's Rush Medical School and University in Chicago. Now in private practice, Dr. Finkelstein also served as assistant clinical professor of psychiatry at UCLA, where he taught therapeutic hypnosis and past-life regression therapy, in which he has been a world expert and pioneer for thirty years. He is currently teaching UCLA psychiatric residents, medical students, psychologists, and social workers at Cedars-Sinai Medical Center complementary and alternative medicine; holistic therapeutic hypnosis, including orientation/introduction to past-life therapy; and spiritual healing concepts and practices.

Dr. Finkelstein lives in Malibu, California, and can be reached by phone at (310) 456-1044, or at his website: www.pastlives.com.

Sherrie Lea Laird has two websites: www.marilynmonroe returns.com and www.pandamoniaband.com.

Hampton Roads Publishing Company

. . . for the evolving human spirit

HAMPTON ROADS PUBLISHING COMPANY publishes books on a variety of subjects, including metaphysics, spirituality, health, visionary fiction, and other related topics.

For a copy of our latest trade catalog, call toll-free, 800-766-8009, or send your name and address to:

HAMPTON ROADS PUBLISHING COMPANY, INC.
1125 STONEY RIDGE ROAD • CHARLOTTESVILLE, VA 22902
e-mail: hrpc@hrpub.com • www.hrpub.com